Cooking for Occasions

FAY MASCHLER

AND

ELIZABETH JANE HOWARD

Cooking
for
Occasions

MACMILLAN

LONDON

First published 1987 as *Howard and Maschler on Food*
by Michael Joseph Limited

This revised and expanded edition published 1994 by Macmillan London
a division of Pan Macmillan Publishers Limited
Cavaye Place London SW10 9PG
and Basingstoke

Associated companies throughout the world

ISBN 0-333-60058-4

1 3 5 7 9 8 6 4 2

A CIP catalogue record for this book is available from
the British Library

Photoset by Parker Typesetting Service, Leicester
Printed and bound in Great Britain by
Mackays of Chatham plc, Chatham, Kent

for
Jane's daughter, Nicola Starks,
and
Fay's mother, Mary Coventry

Acknowledgements

Cooking is a magpie business. Inspiration, guidance and facts are gleaned from so many sources: relations, friends, chefs and cookery book writers. It will be clear from the references throughout the text with which cookery writers our sympathies lie, but we should like to thank the following, to whom we owe a great debt of gratitude: Elizabeth David, Jane Grigson, Marcella Hazan, Madhur Jaffrey, Richard Olney, Claudia Roden. As acknowledged in the text, recipes have also been inspired by Victor Gordon, Anton Mosimann, the Roux brothers, Delia Smith, Fortune Stanley and Alice Walters.

Cooking at home can be a lonely business and we should like to thank Lily Uniacke and Hazel Short, both of them loyal and marvellous collaborators in the kitchen.

Contents

Introduction

This book was originally published seven years ago, and we remarked then that a moratorium on cookery books would not be a bad idea – there were so many. Now, of course, by the nature of things, there must be even more of them, so why republish? The chief reason has been that, in a modest way, this book seems to have stood the test of time; the people who bought it are still using it, talking about it and telling their friends, who, in the more dogged instances, have been reduced to hunting for a second-hand copy. We felt that they might prefer a new book, unmarked by olive oil, egg yolk and the tiny dried flies that encrust the pages of used cookery books.

The idea of doing a book about the occasions that recur for most of us in the course of domestic life was born one dank evening in a cavernous Chinese restaurant in extremely north London, illumined by the trusty glow of the night lights under our dish warmers and the hellish but fitful glare glimpsed when the swing doors to the kitchen were pushed open by the waiter bringing our food. We were the only customers except for a lone man who had finished his meal and was drinking tea and pretending to read a newspaper. By the time we were writing a list of occasions and had reached Abandoned Man and Funeral Tea, he had stopped any pretence of reading: it occurred to us afterwards that he may have thought we were planning a murder.

Everyone who cooks has a repertoire, but inevitably life demands that he or she cooks outside it. This book is the collected experience of two people who have come to see cooking as an indispensable skill for living, a necessary aptitude if you are going to get by, or get through the occasions that life throws your way, be they the dinner when you know your guests are likely to be greedy (or dull), the meal you want to prepare for an invalid, or, on a happier note, a prospective loved one, a supper the day you or your friends move house, a picnic, or the day you are desperately short of time. It is designed to deal with the pure sociability of food – the ways in which it can be used to please, to impress, to lure; as a weapon, as a last resort, as an expression of power or love. The chapters accommodate cooks with limited resources, with pressures of time, the rich, the young, the put-upon and the eccentrics. Naturally, chapters overlap as our index will indicate; the one on vegetarian cooking, for example, would have relevance to the one on cooking when you are hard up.

Inevitably, interests and fashions in cooking change, and in this country Italian food has come much to the fore since we first produced this book.

We kept this in mind as we went through the book, and found that we wanted to make changes. We have removed some recipes that seemed either to be insufficiently rewarding, or that had simply become old hat. (There is an interesting difference here between a dish that has enjoyed a brief fashion and one that, once fashionable, is good enough to become a classic.) We have added over a dozen new recipes to cater to the two current trends – the enormous popularity of Italian cooking already mentioned that has captured the British taste at all levels, and the resurgence of enjoyment in traditional English food.

We make the following assumptions. 1: That the reader understands the fundamentals of cooking, although we do provide a certain amount of basic information – such as how to make mayonnaise, for example. Indeed it would be *possible* for an intelligent beginner to start with this book, but the book was not designed for beginners. 2: That you have, on the whole, the kitchen equipment that you need and can afford. Many books set out the most alarming array of *batterie de cuisine*, but as one of the best cooks we knew made his fantastic meals with three dented old saucepans and a cooker endearingly called 'The New Suburbia' whose oven door had a fairly large hole in it, we will simply remark that we regard a food processor as indispensable, that one of us gets frantic about knives being razor sharp and the other is set upon steamers that will take anything from a large fish or bird to a quantity of vegetables.

Neither of us cooks metric, infinitely preferring ounces and pounds. We have provided the metric equivalent, but if you have the choice, we recommend that you follow our preference, since there is never an *exact* translation of ounces to grams; but whichever you do, we assume that you will take instructions about quantities seriously. This is also the place to make the time-honoured point about reading right through a recipe before you do anything else about it.

CHAPTER ONE

Foolproof Dinner

There was a halcyon time when the even comparatively less well-off could afford to entertain friends in a restaurant. Victorians (think of Mr Pooter) ate out on occasion and food that is now in the luxury class was generally available. Oysters will never be 9d a dozen again, nor sirloin of beef 8½d a lb, or, indeed – including inflation – anything like it. If we want to entertain our friends, we have to cook at home. This is fine for many people: even if they don't like the day to day drudgery of cooking family meals, they enjoy preparing the odd – more festive – meal for friends.

But not everyone feels like that. Some people really hate cooking because they find it so anxious, unpredictable and difficult; the idea of making a three-course dinner for friends where everything is timed right fills them with terror, and they know that the evening holds no pleasure for them. The pleasure of their guests is consequently much reduced. Apart from waiting till starving while the potatoes get cooked, or chewing their way through half-raw ones, the anxiety of their hostess is contagious: the kinder guests may find themselves in the kitchen attempting to advise about a separated sauce, a sunken soufflé or burned pastry while the others sit soaking up quantities of drink – bad for them and expensive for you – and longing for something simple and immediate, like ham sandwiches.

The point of entertaining your friends is to *see* them – a spot of mutual enjoyment is what you are aiming at. So the more nervous you are of providing the food, the more necessary it is that your dinner should be foolproof: at least half an hour before your friends are due, you should have done it all, should be feeling relaxed and expectant – be looking forward to the evening.

Obviously, the main aim is for you to have done your cooking well in advance, when making mistakes won't be such a big deal. But also, your confidence will steadily increase if you concentrate upon making a few things well. For the acutely nervous, we suggest that you practise beforehand, but all the dishes below should be foolproof if you follow directions *precisely*. (Perhaps it is worth saying here, that a great many cooks who are nervous and make mistakes *don't* read a recipe carefully. Read it through and make sure that you understand it before you begin.) It doesn't matter if your repertoire is small, provided that everything you make is pleasant to eat; indeed, you could get famous for your fish pie or your treacle pudding – people may end up by flocking for miles, their mouths watering with nostalgic greed. The most noticeable characteristic of a failed dish, however, is its failure – the fact that you've explored another avenue that has turned out to be a cul-de-sac will neither comfort nor impress your guests.

Right; when you have read the recipes below, decide which ones you want to make and then do a careful shopping list without ever assuming that you have got any ingredient without checking. We suggest that you start by making your pudding before your hands become tainted by onion or garlic.

Artichoke Soup   Polish Beetroot
Kipper Fillet Salad   Glazed Carrots
Salade Niçoise   Peas French Style
Fish Pie   Puréed Vegetables
Lancashire Hot-Pot   Treacle Sponge
Oxtail Stew   Butterscotch Sauce

Artichoke Soup

Serves 6

2 lb/1 kg Jerusalem artichokes	2 pints/1.1 litres chicken stock
1 large onion	nutmeg
1 oz/30 g butter	salt and pepper
1 tablespoon oil	

Scrub and cut up the artichokes; you need not peel them, but clean them thoroughly.

Peel and chop the onion. Heat the butter and oil in a pan and fry the onion until it begins to turn colour. Add the artichokes and stir gently to get them coated in the onion mixture. Add half the stock by degrees and let it come to the boil, making sure with a wooden spoon that nothing has stuck to the bottom of the pan. Then add the rest of the stock and simmer until the artichokes are soft. Pass the mixture through a mouli (or liquidize if you prefer, but this tends to make too suave a texture), season with some grated nutmeg, pepper and salt.

Reheat for serving. If liked, this soup can be served with a dollop of soured or fresh cream.

Kipper Fillet Salad

Nowadays it should be possible to buy kipper fillets undyed with Brown FK. Seek them out for their more genuine flavour and to support the anti-additives lobby. In the heyday of kipper fillet salad, enthusiasts would remark that it was almost as good as smoked salmon. It is nothing like smoked salmon, but nevertheless excellent in its own right. Use the best olive oil you can find for the dressing.

Serves 4

8 kipper fillets	2 tablespoons lemon juice
1 large onion, peeled and sliced	4 tablespoons olive oil
into thin rings	freshly ground black pepper

Rip the silvery skin off the kipper fillets and then slice the flesh on the diagonal into strips about $\frac{1}{4}$ inch/0.6 cm wide. Place them in a shallow dish and scatter half of the larger onion rings on top. Pour on the lemon juice and turn the fillets and onion in the juice. Leave in the fridge or a cool place for a few hours, occasionally stirring the kipper around.

Drain off the juice, pour on the olive oil, scatter about the remaining onion rings – you then have differing textures of onion – and grind on black pepper lavishly.

Serve with thinly slice brown bread and butter.

Salade Niçoise

There are many variants of this and we are not sticking to the classic recipe, but suggesting ingredients we find good. This is a first course that is better in summer months as it depends upon new and small vegetables.

Serves 6

1 lb/500 g new potatoes
8 oz/250 g small French beans
1 lb/500 g young, small broad
    beans
8 oz/250 g smallest peas you can
    get
½ cucumber
1 red and 1 yellow pepper (green
    will do if you can't get the
    others)
small bunch of radishes

bunch of spring onions
1 lb/500 g tomatoes
1 fennel root
1 tin anchovy fillets or one tin tuna
    fish, whichever you prefer – or
    both
parsley
fresh basil – if you can get it
chives – easy to grow yourself
fresh French tarragon
8 oz/250 g black olives

Cook the potatoes; they will need to be scraped for this dish in order to look nice. Put them in boiling salted water and boil gently; be careful not to overcook them.

The French beans and podded broad beans should be steamed until they are *al dente* (crisp, but tender, which should take only about 5 minutes). Shell the peas, but use them raw.

The cucumber should be diced, rather than sliced. Leave the skin on; it makes cucumber more digestible as well as looking pretty. Slice the peppers into thin strips. Clean and trim the radishes and spring onions.

Skin the tomatoes by dipping them into near boiling water for half a minute and then peeling off the skins. Wash and then slice the fennel as thinly as possible.

If you are using anchovies, open the tin and drain the fillets well. Then cut them into pieces about 1 inch/2.5 cm long. With tuna, you take it out of the tin, drain and flake.

Chop the herbs and put them in the fridge in a jam jar covered with clingfilm.

Put all the ingredients except the herbs into the largest serving bowl you have, reserving some olives, radishes and some of the red and yellow peppers for garnishing.

Then make a French dressing as follows:

1 level dessertspoon salt	*a heavy screwing of black pepper*
1 level dessertspoon sugar	*3 tablespoons tarragon vinegar*
1 level dessertspoon mustard	*¼ pint/150 ml best olive oil*
* powder*	

Put all the dry ingredients into a small mixing bowl and combine with a fork. Add the vinegar and stir until everything has dissolved. Add the oil and beat thoroughly. Pour over the salad and mix gently but very thoroughly. If you don't feel that there is enough dressing (test it by tasting) make some more – it is very much a question of preference. Arrange the garnish on the salad's surface.

Just before serving, sprinkle over the fresh herbs.

Fish Pie

Serves 6

12 oz/375 g fresh haddock or cod	*1 oz/30g butter*
* (buy a middle section, not a*	*1½ oz/45 g flour*
* tail)*	*juice of ½ lemon*
12 oz/375 g smoked haddock (try	*salt and black pepper*
* to buy Finnan haddock)*	*8 oz/250 g fresh prawns*
¾ pint/475 ml milk	*2 hard-boiled eggs, sliced*
1½ lb/750 g potatoes	*1 tablespoon chopped fresh parsley*
milk and butter for the potatoes	

Turn on the oven to 190°C/375°F, Gas 5.

Put the fish in an ovenproof dish large enough to hold it in one layer. Pour over the milk, plus about ½ pint/300 ml of water. The fish should be more or less covered. Bake in the oven for about 20 minutes or until the fish flakes away easily from the skin and bones. Boil the potatoes and, when cooked, mash with plenty of butter and hot milk, and season with salt and pepper. It is not advisable to use left-over potatoes as it spoils the texture.

In a heavy-bottomed saucepan, make a roux with the butter and flour. (You put in the butter and the moment it has melted, add the flour, stirring until the mixture is smooth and comes away from the pan.) Stir in enough of the fish poaching liquid to make a consistency of double cream. Add the liquid by degrees, stirring all the time and you won't get lumps. Season with lemon juice and salt and pepper.

Carefully fold in the flaked fish, the prawns, the hard-boiled eggs and the parsley. Put into a pie dish and cover with the mashed potato. Plough the potato with a fork. Dot with butter and return to the oven for 30 minutes, or until the potato is lightly browned.

Lancashire Hot-Pot

Making this dish in a straightforward manner is not so much to contribute to its foolproof quality, but to its homeliness and correctness. Some talk of adding bacon or carrot or mushrooms to the assembly, but we like a down to earth meat-and-potatoes approach. Lambs' kidneys, however, are essential to add richness to the gravy. Another essential is a crusty brown layer of potatoes, so if necessary turn up the oven a little for the last half-hour of cooking.

Serves 4–5

2 lb/1 kg lamb chops (neck or best end)
seasoned flour
2–3 lambs' kidneys
4 onions, peeled and sliced

1½ lb/750 g potatoes, peeled and sliced
salt and freshly ground black pepper
1 bay leaf
butter or dripping

Turn on the oven to 150°C/300°F, Gas 2.

Trim the obvious fat from the chops, melt that fat in a frying pan, flour the chops and brown them gently. This step improves the colour and texture of the gravy. Put the chops into a pot – a round-bellied earthenware pot is traditionally used. Trim the kidneys of any fat or gristle and chop them into pieces. Layer the kidneys, onions and potatoes on top of the chops, seasoning as you go along, adding the bay leaf and finishing with a layer of overlapping slices of potato. Add ¾ pint/475 ml of water. Brush the top surfaces of the potatoes with butter or dripping, season with salt and pepper and cover with a lid.

Cook for 1½ hours, then remove the lid, turn up the oven a little and cook some more until the potatoes are brown and crispy.

Oxtail Stew

Serves 4–6

4 lb/2 kg oxtail (get the butcher to
  cut it in pieces for you)
2 oz/60 g flour
salt and black pepper
2 tablespoons sunflower seed oil
1 small head of celery
1½ lb/750 g carrots

2 lb/1 kg onions
2 bay leaves
3 cloves
3 pints/1.8 litres beef stock (beef cubes
  will do – but there is nothing like
  beef stock)

Turn on the oven to 160°C/325°F, Gas 3.

Cut as much fat as you can from the pieces of tail. Roll the pieces in flour that you have seasoned with pepper and salt. Fry them gently in a pan with oil until the oxtail is thoroughly browned on all sides. As they are done, put the pieces into a large pan or stewpot. Add all the vegetables, cleaned and sliced, together with the bay leaves and cloves. Scatter any remaining flour on top of the meat and vegetables. Then add the stock.

Cover the pot and stew in the oven for about 3 hours, or until, when you test the meat, it will come away easily from the bone. When it is cooked, remove the lid, allow it to cool and then put it into the fridge overnight.

The next day, you should be able to skim off any fat that has come to the surface. If the liquid seems thinner than you like, add a flat tablespoonful of flour scattered over the top of the dish before you warm it up. This is also the moment to check the seasoning. The oxtail will need about 1½ hours to complete its cooking, again in a slow oven, 160°C/325°F, Gas 3.

This stew – like many stews – is better made the day before you eat it, and the more fat that you can remove from the pan before the final cooking the better.

Polish Beetroot

Serves 6–8

2–3 lb/1–1.5 kg cooked beetroot   *black pepper*
3 oz/90 g butter   *2 tablespoons wine vinegar*

Turn on the oven to 150°C/300°F, Gas 2.

Peel and grate the beetroot. Place it in a buttered ovenproof dish with knobs of butter. Grind on a liberal quantity of black pepper (far more than you would usually put on things: beetroot has a unique capacity for absorbing pepper). Add the wine vinegar, then put it in the oven to heat. After 15 minutes or so, take it out and give it a good stir to mix the butter and vinegar well with the beetroot. Put the dish back into the oven until you are ready to serve.

Glazed Carrots

For some reason, adding sugar and butter to the cooking water for your carrots can allow you to be insouciant about timings as the carrots never seem to disintegrate finally, however wildly and lengthily you boil them. What seems like an impossibly subtle process – that of having carrot pieces cooked at the time the water has evaporated and the butter and sugar caramelized – is, in fact, easy. Cooked this way, carrots become luxurious and so partner well the frugality sometimes implicit in stews.

Cumin and carrots have great affinity, so should you stock cumin seeds or know where to buy them (any competent supermarket or oriental grocer) do use them.

Serves 6

2 lb/1 kg carrots (old ones work   *1 tablespoon brown sugar*
  very well in this recipe)   *1 heaped teaspoon cumin seeds* or
1½ oz/45 g butter   *chopped fresh coriander* or *parsley*

Peel the carrots. Cut them as follows: in half across, then stand the halves on the flat round surface and quarter them vertically. You end up with batons, nicer than fat circles reminiscent of institutional food.

Put them in a sturdy saucepan, add water to cover by about ½ inch/1.25 cm, and the butter and sugar. Set to simmer. After the carrots have simmered for about 15 minutes, turn up the heat and start to reduce the liquid. Your aim is to drive off the water and oblige the sugar and butter to form a shiny glaze; watch carefully at the end that the glaze does not burn.

Scatter the cumin seeds in a small heavy-bottomed frying pan and put on a high hat (with no fat) for a minute or two, stirring with a wooden spoon, until a spicy smell comes off them. Scatter on to the carrots and serve. Or, if you are using coriander or parsley, sprinkle that on.

Peas French Style

This recipe transforms frozen peas into a thing of delectation. Try to buy what they call *petits pois* rather than the larger garden variety. With frozen peas, the frost provides almost enough liquid.

If you use fresh peas, remember that 1 lb/500 g of fresh peas gives you probably less than ½ lb/250 g of podded peas, so buy accordingly, and buy them as young as possible or they will resemble bullets. You must add a little more water for fresh peas.

Serves 4

1 lb/500 g frozen petits pois   *a few fresh mint leaves if available*
1 small Dutch lettuce   *1 teaspoon white sugar*
4 spring onions   *salt and freshly ground black pepper*
1 oz/30 g butter

Put the peas into a heavy-bottomed saucepan. You can, and should, cook them from frozen. Trim any damaged leaves from the lettuce. Use your judgement about whether the other leaves should be washed. Often hothouse (Dutch) lettuces are disturbingly dirt-free. Slice the pristine leaves into ribbons about ¼ inch/0.6 cm wide. Clean the spring onions, trimming off the base and most of the green part, leaving about 1½ inches/3.75 cm green. Wash and slice lengthways so that you have long, thin pieces. Mix the lettuce and onions with the peas.

Add the butter cut into pieces, mint if you have it, the sugar and a pinch of salt and pepper. Put in 1 tablespoon of water just to get the thing going (more if fresh peas are being used). Cover and place over a medium heat. When the liquid that forms comes to the boil, lower the heat and simmer for about 15 minutes with the lid at an angle so that some of the liquid can evaporate.

Test the peas for tenderness and boil off any remaining liquid but leaving a thin buttery sauce to which the silkiness of the lettuce will have contributed.

Puréed Vegetables

Puréed vegetables, that once highly fashionable garnish, are ideal for a dinner which is carefully planned because they can be made in advance and either kept hot or reheated in a double saucepan. A food processor is invaluable and even the most elliptically involved cook should consider the purchase of one. The alternative is a mouli-légumes or the task of pushing the vegetables through a sieve. If the last is what you decide to do, make sure to overcook the vegetables to the point of craven malleability.

Most root vegetables respond well to this method of preparation but cooked sprouts, whizzed in a food processor, make an excellent purée and since left-over sprouts are not unknown, e.g. after Christmas lunch, it is worth keeping this in mind. Should you have garnished them with peeled chestnuts, include them too.

The recipe below will work well for parsnips, celeriac, carrots, swedes (which will need lavish buttering) and leeks.

Serves 6

2 lb/1 kg root vegetables (see above), peeled and chopped into pieces measuring about 1½ inches/4 cm square.
3 oz/90 g butter

1 tablespoon cream or top of the milk
a pinch of grated nutmeg
salt and generous amounts of freshly ground black pepper

Boil the vegetables until they are well and truly tender. Drain them in a careless way so that they are waterlogged rather than absolutely dry. Put them into the bowl of a food processor or the goblet of a liquidizer with the butter, cream and seasonings, and whizz to a purée. You may need to do this in batches. Put the purée into the top of a double saucepan over simmering water. Taste for seasoning, adding more if necessary, and keep hot until you need it.

If you are using a sieve or mouli-légumes, push the vegetables through, place the purée in a pan and, over a low heat, stir in the butter, cream (or milk) and seasonings.

Treacle Sponge

The only trick about this recipe is allowing enough time for the pudding to steam and being around to check on the water level so that it does not boil dry. The actual preparation takes only minutes, particularly if you use a food processor.

Serves 4–6

2 tablespoons Golden Syrup	*2 eggs*
grated rind and juice of 1 lemon	*5 oz/150 g self-raising flour*
1 oz/30 g fresh breadcrumbs	*a pinch of salt*
4 oz/125 g butter	*milk*
4 oz/125 g caster sugar	

Mix the syrup with the lemon juice, stir in the breadcrumbs and put this mixture over the bottom of a lightly buttered 3-pint/2-litre pudding basin. Cream the butter with the sugar and the lemon rind, add the beaten eggs, and stir in the flour which you have sifted with a pinch of salt; then add the milk, a spoonful at a time, until you have a batter that drops reluctantly from a spoon. Pour into the pudding basin, and tie on a cover of foil or greaseproof.

Place the bowl in a saucepan that will hold it comfortably. Add boiling water to about halfway up the bowl and steam, covered with a saucepan lid, for about 2 hours, checking the water level from time to time.

Remove the foil or greaseproof paper, place a large plate over the basin and turn the basin over. The pudding will come out easily. Serve with custard or more syrup heated and sharpened with more lemon juice.

Butterscotch Sauce

It is quite possible now to buy high quality ice-cream made with proper ingredients rather than whale fat and emulsifiers. New England ice-cream is one variety that we would recommend, and this recipe for a luxurious sauce, particularly suited to vanilla ice-cream, was given to us by Bill Blackburn, the founder of the company.

Serves 6–8

4 oz/125 g butter
8 fl oz/250 ml single cream
6 oz/180 g soft brown sugar

2 tablespoons brandy
4 drops pure vanilla essence (not the ersatz kind)

Melt the butter in a double saucepan or over a very low heat. Add the cream and blend together, then stir in the sugar; cook gently for about 30 minutes. Add the brandy and vanilla essence, stir and remove from the heat – the sauce will thicken as it cools.

This recipe makes a considerable amount, but any left-over sauce can be stored for a few days in a screw-top jar in the fridge.

CHAPTER TWO

Dîner à Deux

Food plays many roles in life: the fundamental one of simply fuelling, but beyond that it is also used to bribe, to honour, to placate, to harass, to slight, to cherish, to repair and – to seduce. Early on in most romances, food plays a central part. The first time someone prepares a meal for a loved one, or a prospective loved one, is often the first time that that person has spent a protracted length of time in the cook's home. Making a meal takes some of the heat out of the scenario and also lends a backdrop of touching sights – as so many movies over the years have reminded us – of the heroine with a dab of flour on her nose, the hero coming to the rescue with some invaluable tip or a bottle of wine and so forth. Men cooking can tug at the heartstrings effectively, as anyone who has seen Jack Lemmon straining spaghetti through a tennis racket in the film *The Apartment* will know.

For the purposes of this chapter devoted to a *dîner à deux*, we are supposing that it is not an impromptu meal, a merry fry-up or taking pot luck, but a planned event. Someone has come into your life, and the next canny move would seem to be to entertain them deliciously and let them glimpse a side of you of which they were perhaps not fully apprised. We are talking about concealed virtues like imagination, well-judged extravagance, simplicity, knowing how to deal with a scallop.

There are most definitely foodstuffs that are sexy and foodstuffs that are banal. This perception does not have to be taken to the point of absurdity, as so often it is, so that seductive food has to be representational, e.g. phallic leeks or the moist crevasses of oysters, but whilst a lobster does seem romantic, mince does not. That the one costs a good deal more than the other is a point but not the whole point. Food for a candlelit dinner – and however much you subscribe to fashionable up-lighting or the halogen bulb, candles cast a glow so flattering that it would be foolish not to take advantage of them – should be neat, easy to eat with grace and style. Mince might well dribble down your chin.

When a meal is deliberately designed for two, and more numbers would rob it of its aim, then items like the aforementioned lobster are particularly apt. Wild duck divides neatly. A rack of lamb has just the right amount of cutlets to feed two, one slightly more greedy than the other. True piggishness is not catered for in these recipes as lovers' minds should be slightly abstracted and certainly not whole-heartedly fixed on their stomachs. There will be time later for roistering scenes based on *Tom Jones* or naked greed when you are greedily naked.

From the dishes that follow it would be possible to assemble a meal that can be prepared entirely in advance, but from experience it is often quite useful to have something to jump up to attend to. It can fill a lull in the conversation, or give you a moment to pull your thoughts together, or check your profile. If the meal is going well and you wish to prolong it, and also bring out some other bottle, then a savoury is worth part-preparing.

Presentation is important for a *dîner à deux*. It is worthwhile having the table laid before your guest arrives and to polish glasses and silver so that they do sparkle in the candlelight. Flowers, leaves, ribbons and so forth can all do their work, but whilst you may not want to exaggerate, making it look too much like a put-up job, you also don't want to be scrabbling around looking for clean napkins at the last minute. This is the moment, by the way, for large cotton or linen napkins, not the paper variety.

A last word of warning on the tricky business of sentimental entertaining: implicit in the event is a lack of familiarity with the other party, so be original but not too outrageous with the food, generous but not reckless so that if during the cheese course you realize you have made the most frightful mistake, it is not going to take you weeks to restore your bank balance as well as your emotional one.

Quantities can usually be doubled quite safely if you want to use one of the recipes for 4 people.

Devilled Almonds	Scallops with Leeks
Gulls' Eggs or Quails' Eggs	Cold Wild Duck
Asparagus	Rack of Lamb with Herb Crust
Oyster Stew	Hot Lemon Soufflé
Œufs en Cocotte à la Crème	Instant Berry Sorbet
Gravad Lax	Scotch Woodcock

Devilled Almonds

*8 oz/250 g almonds with their
    skins on*
1 tablespoon olive oil

2 teaspoons sea salt
good pinch of cayenne pepper

Turn on oven to 120°C/250°F, Gas ½.

Put the almonds in a bowl. Pour on boiling water and after a minute or two drain into a sieve. The skins should now slip off fairly easily. Dry the nuts, then coat them in the oil. Spread on a baking tray. Sprinkle on the salt and cayenne pepper and bake for about 2 hours until they are a light golden colour. Cool and store in an airtight tin.

Gulls' Eggs or Quails' Eggs

It is now no longer possible to buy plovers' eggs, a very seductive egg, because they may no longer, by law, be gathered. However, in the early summer you can buy the eggs of black-headed gulls which are almost as good. With their greeny-blue shells freckled with brown they look very attractive piled into a china dish or rush basket. They are sold hard-boiled. Serve them with celery salt and cayenne pepper and thinly sliced brown bread and butter. To make more of a meal of them, you could also serve mayonnaise.

Quails' eggs are available fresh throughout most of the year. If you buy them raw, boil them for just 1 minute. You can also fry or poach quails' eggs which make very dainty dishes; fairy food. Make a 'nest' of lightly dressed mustard and cress and perch the quails' eggs upon it. Soft boiled, they are also good served in a manner similar to the way the Connaught Hotel treats them: in a pastry boat, on a purée of mushrooms and covered by a light hollandaise.

Asparagus

Asparagus is one of those items that is symbolically sexy, the fat white French ones presumably more so than the thin green English variety which, in its truly weedy state, is referred to as sprue. It is important not to overcook asparagus. If you don't have a tall thin pan so that the tender asparagus heads can stay above the water and just steam, try steaming the whole vegetable. However you cook it, start testing for 'doneness' after about 9 minutes as you do not want your asparagus floppy.

1 lb/500 g of asparagus is plenty for two people. As well as considering a hollandaise sauce, melted butter or a vinaigrette as an accompaniment, here are some other ideas for dipping sauces.

Browned Butter and Soft-boiled Egg

3 oz/90 g butter   *salt and freshly ground black pepper*
2 eggs

Melt the butter and cook it just beyond melted, i.e. let it start to turn brown but take it off the heat just as it reaches a nutty colour. Do not let it burn. Prepare the eggs softly boiled, that is for 3 minutes. Place each egg in an egg cup and cut off the top. Mix salt and freshly ground black pepper together. The form is: each person dips an asparagus spear by turn into the browned butter, the soft egg yolk and the heap of salt and pepper.

Parmesan and Mimosa

2 hard-boiled egg yolks   *salt and freshly ground black pepper*
2 oz/60 g freshly grated Parmesan
*   cheese (not from a packet)*

Push the egg yolks through a sieve – they now resemble mimosa blossom. Mix with the Parmesan and season with salt and pepper. Serve the asparagus with a little melted butter and this mixture in which to roll the tips.

Red Pepper Purée

The colour of this is a lovely contrast to green asparagus.

2 red peppers	*1–2 anchovies*
1 clove garlic, peeled	*a pinch of sugar*
asparagus water	*salt and pepper*

Char the peppers by turning them under the grill. Put them immediately into a polythene bag to steam for 5 minutes. The skin can now be scraped off easily. Remove all the seeds and pith and cut into squares. Boil with the garlic in water (the asparagus water if you have already cooked the asparagus and are planning to serve them cold). When the peppers are tender, liquidize together with the garlic clove and the anchovies, and with just enough of the water to make a purée. Season with sugar, salt and pepper. Don't make this sauce too far ahead as it tends to separate.

Oyster Stew

We know a man who invariably employs this dish in his seductive dinners. He has legendary success, which may be to do with the recipe, the touching sight of a man cooking, or just him. It is possible, and indeed preferable for reasons of energy and cost, to make this stew using frozen Japanese oysters which are obtained in oriental supermarkets. They have good flavour and obviate struggling to prise open shells, probably stabbing yourself and sitting through dinner with an unattractive plaster on your thumb. Take the precaution of discovering whether your guest is allergic to oysters.

Savoury crackers, for example cream crackers or saltines, are the correct accompaniment.

4 shallots, peeled and finely	*16–20 frozen oysters*
chopped	*½ teaspoon salt*
3 oz/90 g butter	*white pepper* or *paprika*
12 fl oz/375 ml milk	*chopped parsley*
4 fl oz/125 ml double cream	

To make it into a bisque: *2 egg yolks*

Use a heavy-bottomed pot that later you can surround with water in a larger pot, i.e. a double saucepan or a *bain-marie*. Sauté the shallots gently in the butter until they are softened. Bring the water for the double saucepan arrangements to a simmer. Into your sauté pan put the milk, cream, oysters, salt and pepper. Cook slowly over, or surrounded by, water until the oysters float, whereupon the stew is ready. Check the seasoning, sprinkle with parsley and serve.

To make this into an even more wickedly rich dish, it can become a bisque: beat two egg yolks in a bowl and slowly add a few spoonfuls of the oyster stew liquid. Whisk until foamy. Return this to the stew, mix gently and heat through without boiling until slightly thickened.

Œufs en Cocotte à la Crème

½ oz/15 g butter
2 tablespoons double cream

2 fresh free-range eggs
salt and black pepper

Turn on the oven to 180°C/350°F, Gas 4.

Warm 2 cocottes (small round fireproof dishes) and put them in a baking tin half full of hot water, with a small knob of butter in each one. When the butter has melted, paint it up the sides of each cocotte. Bring half the cream to the boil and then put it into the cocottes. Break the eggs and place one in each cocotte. Season and put the rest of the butter in small knobs on top. Put the tin in the oven and bake for between 5 and 7 minutes: the whites should be set, but only just, and the yolks should be creamy. Just before serving, spoon over the top the rest of the cream, which should be cold.

This is not the classic way of making this dish, but we have found the contrast between the cold cream and the hot egg particularly delicious.

Gravad Lax

This is not a dish for a sudden romance as it requires at least 24 hours' marination in the refrigerator. If, however, you are plotting a meal with someone special in mind it is an ideal first course. Large quantities of a luxurious ingredient, e.g. salmon, are always romantic and this process of pickling it in sugar and salt works equally well with the cheaper farmed salmon, so make plenty and serve it in thickish chunks rather than the skimpy thin slices favoured by restaurants.

1 tail piece of salmon weighing
   1½–2 lb/750 g–1 kg
1 heaped tablespoon sea salt
1 rounded tablespoon sugar

1 teaspoon coarsely ground pepper
1 rounded tablespoon dillweed
   (chopped if fresh)

FOR THE SAUCE:

mayonnaise (preferably home-
   made) into which you mix:
1 tablespoon German mustard

1 teaspoon sugar
1 teaspoon dillweed
dash of vinegar

Bone the fish which will give you two kite-shaped pieces. If you haven't found a tail-piece, a small salmon or salmon trout will do, in which case clean, bone and behead it.

Mix together the salt, sugar and pepper. If you wish, moisten with a little brandy. Put some of the mixture plus a third of the dillweed into a dish that holds the fish quite snugly.

Lay on it the first piece of fish, skin-side down. Spread on more pickle, more dillweed and sandwich with the other piece of fish, skin-side up. Scatter on the remaining pickle and dillweed. Cover with a double layer of aluminium foil and then a weight – tins or a brick. Leave in the fridge for at least 24 hours, but no longer than 3 days, turning the fish occasionally.

To serve, drain from the pickle, remove the skin, slice generously and accompany the fish with the sauce described above, some rye bread or hot boiled new potatoes.

Scallops with Leeks

Fresh scallops, which are becoming increasingly easy to find, are the perfect lovers' meal; nourishing, unfattening, delicate and quick to cook. Forget any idea of bedding them down in mashed potato and instead try this method adapted from a recipe of the three-star Michelin chef, Roger Vergé.

4 thin or 2 fat leeks
1 oz/30 g butter
6–8 scallops
5 tablespoonfuls of the white wine
you have chosen for the meal

a squeeze of lemon juice
3 tablespoons double cream
salt and pepper
fresh parsley

Trim the leeks and clean them really thoroughly, sacrificing outer layers until you are sure that no grit lurks. The root must be taken off and most of the green part. Cut them in half lengthways and then into narrow strips (about ½ inch/0.6 cm long). Melt ½ oz/15 g butter in 4 tablespoons water in a small saucepan and cook the leek strips until tender, about 15 minutes. Set the saucepan on one side but keep warm.

Cut each scallop in two horizontally, but leave the corals whole. Remove the thin, dark intestine and the little muscle, which would toughen. Melt the remaining butter in a pan, sauté the scallops for 30 seconds and then add the wine. Bring to the boil and simmer for 2 minutes. Remove the scallops and keep warm with the leeks.

Reduce the scallop liquor by boiling it vigorously. Add the cooking juices from the leeks, plus a squeeze of lemon juice. Boil again until you are left with about 4 tablespoonfuls of liquid. Add the cream, boil briefly and season.

Arrange the leeks and scallops prettily on a warmed plate. Pour over the sauce and scatter chopped parsley on top.

Cold Wild Duck

1 plump wild duck, dressed
2 small oranges
2 oz/60 g butter

1 small onion
salt and pepper
4 thin strips streaky bacon

Turn on the oven to 200°C/400°F, Gas 6.

Wipe the insides of the duck with a damp cloth. Grate the rind of one orange and squeeze the juice. Cut the other orange into thick rounds.

If you have a chicken-brick, we have found this ideal; if not, then a *small* earthenware dish or baking tin will do. Put half the butter into the dish and heat it until the butter melts. Put the orange slices into the dish. Rub the duck breasts with the rest of the butter, and put the onion – quartered if need be – inside the bird. Rub the grated orange rind on to the buttered breasts, season with salt and pepper and then cover with the bacon.

If you are using a chicken-brick, put on the lid: if not, cover the dish with aluminium foil. Roast in a hot oven for 30 minutes; then remove the lid or foil, baste the bird and cook for another 20 minutes. This last cooking will vary a little in time depending upon the size of the bird; your aim should be to have the bird slightly pink, but not running with blood when you prick it. After taking the duck from the oven, allow it to cook in its juices for a little while. You can then strain off the fat, and use the remaining liquid in a Cumberland-type sauce if liked, but since one eats such a bird largely with the fingers, it is very good without any sauce.

This is best cooked the morning of the day you are going to eat it, and not refrigerated. Watercress can also be eaten with the fingers and is a good accompaniment.

Rack of Lamb with Herb Crust

Rack of lamb is also called *carré d'agneau* or you could ask your butcher for best end neck trimmed for roasting. The meat should be chined, meaning the backbone is split, and 2–3 inches/5–7.5 cm of clean bone should protrude from the cutlets. Remove the skin and most of the fat before coating the meat and roasting it. One best end of lamb will give 2–3 cutlets each for two people, so it makes a perfect intimate dinner.

1 clove of garlic, peeled
salt and pepper
1 tablespoon mellow mustard
*   (Dijon or something sweeter if*
*   you prefer)*
2 tablespoons fine breadcrumbs

2 tablespoons chopped fresh herbs – try
*   to include both parsley and thyme,*
*   perhaps a few leaves of mint and*
*   finely chopped sprigs of rosemary*
lemon juice
a knob of softened butter
1 rack of lamb

Turn on the oven to 230°C/450°F, Gas 8.

Crush the garlic with the salt and mix with the mustard. Stir in the breadcrumbs and herbs, a squeeze of lemon juice and the softened butter – enough to give a spreading consistency. Spread the mixture between the cutlets, on the ends and over the trimmed fat. Place on a rack in a roasting tin and cook for 20–25 minutes which will give a crisp crust and pink meat. If you prefer your meat well done, cook for 5 minutes or so longer. Let the meat rest in a warm place for 5 minutes before serving.

If you are cooking this when broad beans are first in season, serve a dish of baby broad beans, which you have boiled, skinned and reheated in a little butter. In winter, a puréed vegetable (*see* page 10), would go well. Serve a fruit jelly, for example redcurrant or quince, either home-made or produced by a reputable firm or a Women's Institute stall.

Hot Lemon Soufflé

This recipe, taken from Elizabeth David's *French Country Cooking*, is so quick and simple that you can leave it until the end of the meal to judge whether, indeed, you want a pudding at all or find your sweet times elsewhere. Pessimists, however, could prepare it up to a point, i.e. beating the yolks of the eggs with the sugar and lemon juice beforehand and whipping the whites at the end of the meal just before you pop it into the oven.

4 eggs, separated   *juice and rind of 1 lemon*
3 tablespoons caster sugar

Turn on the oven to 200°C/400°F, Gas 6.

Beat the yolks of the eggs with the sugar and lemon rind and juice for several minutes. Butter a 1½-pint/1-litre soufflé dish. Whisk the egg whites until they stand in firm peaks. Fold the lemony mixture in with a light hand. Pour into the soufflé dish and cook for about 12 minutes.

Instant Berry Sorbet

This elegant idea was suggested by Prue Leith and exemplifies both her sympathetic approach to the home cook and the constraints of serving restaurant food. Any new, or even well-worn, partner will not fail to be impressed by the effective simplicity of this dessert and the immediacy of flavour in the fruit. Soft fruit such as raspberries and strawberries work well, but there is no reason not to use redcurrants, blackcurrants or even, more magically, whitecurrants.

Either buy frozen fruit or freeze fresh fruit, but make sure it is thoroughly frozen before you start. Add sugar to one-third the weight of the fruit, which is the proportion which makes the sorbet successful. You might also like to squeeze in a little lemon juice to tone down the sweetness.

12 oz/375 g frozen strawberries   *4 oz/125 g caster sugar*
   or raspberries   *juice of ½ lemon*

Note: this recipe is predicated on the ownership of a food processor; a liquidizer will work but you will have to do the fruit in batches.

Empty the frozen fruit into the bowl of the food processor. Sprinkle the sugar on top and leave for about 20 minutes, until the fruit is beginning to soften around the edges. Turn on the motor and whizz, either using a pulse button or switching on or off, until you have a purée the consistency and temperature of sorbet.

Add lemon juice to taste and whizz again. Serve immediately or freeze until it is wanted.

Scotch Woodcock

Some think this the best of all savouries, others might put forward the case for a roasted snipe on toast, but ingredients for this assembly are more easily available.

2 slices toast, trimmed of crust,   *salt and freshly ground black pepper*
   about 3 × 2 inches/7.5 × 5 cm   *2 egg yolks*
   in size, well buttered   *2½ tablespoons double cream*
6 anchovy fillets or if you prefer, *½ oz/15 g butter*
   use 1 heaped tablespoon finely
   chopped cooked ham

Turn on the oven to low to keep the toasts hot.

Arrange the toasts in a small ovenproof serving dish. Pound the anchovy fillets, mixing in a little pepper, and spread them on the toasts (or do the same with the ham). Keep them warm in the oven.

Beat together the egg yolks and cream and season with salt and pepper. Melt the butter in a small, thick-bottomed pan, stir in the egg and cream mixture and stir over an extremely low heat until it begins to thicken. Don't let it scramble. Pour over the toasts and serve immediately.

CHAPTER THREE

Budget Dinner Party

Two do not live as cheaply as one and six do not eat as cheaply as two, but finance need not be a deterrent to entertaining – except in the realm of drink where you must tactfully impress on your guests that they should contribute. 'Bring a bottle' may conjure up visions of tawdry parties where you spent a good deal of time sitting on the stairs, but there is no rule that the bottle of wine should not be a good one and for you, the host, there is the added pleasure of an element of surprise and the enjoyment of something you have not thought about, made decisions about and trailed out to purchase.

The 'bringing' ethic can also successfully be extended to food in the shape of one course where the considerations of novelty and the feeling of being entertained in your own home are even more relevant. Somehow, not having to make, say, a dessert or a first course or even a salad, lightens the burden of a dinner party immeasurably, and removes a little of the responsibility for its success. However, this ploy, it must be said, only works well among good friends who have the same points of view about cooking. If you have a secret horror of aspic, your evening would be off to a disastrous start should a guest arrive proudly clutching a jellied savoury tomato mould filled with Russian salad. It could happen.

Food that is cheap to buy is often expensive in terms of the time taken to prepare it. This is a truism that gets bandied about and like many truisms has little substance. Some cuts of meat may take hours to cook but you do not have to be sitting beside them while they do, and if you are wondering how much the electricity is costing to have the oven on, then probably a dinner party is too perilous an undertaking at the moment. Many seemingly drawn-out tasks, including making bread, only require brief bursts of activity from the cook. Indeed, making your own bread can, for hardly any financial outlay at all, make people feel cherished, almost spoiled. To achieve the same effect practically instantaneously, you can knock up some Oat Cakes or Water Biscuits to accompany cheese and salad.

What is and what is not expensive food changes over the years as demands fluctuate and fashions alter. Where once butchers would practically give away offal, they now sell it at a premium price to Arab restaurants and shrines of *haute cuisine*. Chicken, once a dish for special occasions, has become the bore of butchers, though the maize-fed and free-range varieties can be diverting. Vegetables always strike us as good value, particularly root vegetables whose price never seems to shoot through the roof, and one of the great bargains of all times is the potato. A positive outcome of being obliged to think in terms of a budget is that you are likely to do something interesting with, for example, potatoes. This can prove much more delicious and unusual than a hunk of meat or fillet of fish.

For a dinner party on a shoestring, it is important to avoid the obvious cheap items like the symbolic (of shoestring) spaghetti or the worthwhile Shepherd's Pie. These have their own valuable role in everyday life but are too familiar for a festive evening. Fresh pasta with an interesting sauce does not come into the Spaghetti Bolognese category. Abandoning the usual three-course formula, with the most important course being the middle one, is a wise tactic. A substantial and relatively unusual first course, e.g. Curried Parsnips served with poppadums and a cucumber raita, means that you can follow with something very simple, perhaps just some mussels – still a bargain – and your guests will feel in no way short-changed. Indeed, what must be avoided is a lot of stodge which makes everyone feel got at and apt to dwell on the fact that it is usually the rich who are also thin.

The following recipes are ideas around which you might build a meal, using salads and fresh fruit and affordable cheeses, like Ricotta, for some of the courses. In other words, it would not be our intention that you start with a Mussel and Potato salad, move on to the Breast of Lamb Stuffed with Spinach and Kasha, and end with the Marlborough Tart. That might be a fairly cheap dinner but it would not be cheerful.

Bean and Lentil Soup
Brown Rice Salad with Anchovies
and Pimento
Warm Mussel and Potato Salad
Hummus
Smoked Haddock Soufflé
Breast of Lamb Stuffed with
Spinach and Kasha
Feuilleté of Kidneys
Chicken Liver Risotto
Curried Parsnips

Rösti
Gujerati Carrot Salad
Marlborough Tart
Pierre Martin's Apple Tarts
Brandy Snaps
Oat Cakes
Water Biscuits
Fried Cheese Sandwiches
Devils on Horseback
Welsh Rabbit

Bean and Lentil Soup

This soup is, as they say, a meal in itself. You could serve it to a friend for supper, with either a pudding or savoury for afters. These quantities are generous portions for six.

Serves 6

8 oz/250 g haricot beans
1 large onion
3 large carrots
5 stalks of celery
6 oz/180 g streaky bacon
3 oz/90 g ham
3 tablespoons olive oil

5 cloves garlic
8 oz/250 g red lentils
1 tin chopped tomatoes
2 inches of tomato purée
1 flat dessertspoon brown sugar
3 pints/1.8 litres chicken stock
salt and black pepper

Soak the haricot beans in boiling water for 2 hours. Then put them into a pan with cold water and boil until soft. This will take time, and you will need to top up the water.

Chop all the vegetables quite small, and cut the bacon and ham into narrow strips. Heat the olive oil in a large pan and add the bacon. When you have fried this gently for a few minutes, add the garlic and then the onion. Continue to fry, stirring so that nothing sticks. Then add the celery and carrot. Fry for a few more minutes until the onion is translucent. Then add the lentils and stir until they are all coated with the oil. Add the tomatoes and tomato purée and the sugar. Add the stock. When the haricot beans are soft, add them, and cook gently until the lentils have thickened the soup and the other vegetables are soft. Season with pepper and salt.

Brown Rice Salad with Anchovies and Pimento

Serves 4

8 oz/250 g brown rice
2 red peppers (green or yellow
  will do, but red looks prettier)

1 tin anchovy fillets

DRESSING:

2 tablespoons olive oil
juice of 1 lemon

salt and black pepper

Wash the rice in a hand sieve with cold water. Then boil it in salted water until it is cooked; brown rice takes longer than refined rice – usually between 20 and 25 minutes. While you are cooking the rice, heat your grill – first covering the grill pan with aluminium foil. Cut the peppers into flat strips, removing all seeds and undue pith. Lay the strips skin-side up on the grill pan and grill until the skin is black and can be easily removed. Then cut the strips into small rectangles.

Make a dressing with the olive oil, a level teaspoonful of salt, the juice of a lemon and a plentiful screwing of black pepper. Put the rice into a bowl while it is still warm, but not hot, and mix in the dressing thoroughly. Add the peppers and the anchovies – drained of their oil and cut into small pieces. This dish can be garnished with either fresh chopped coriander or, if you cannot get that, fresh chopped parsley.

Warm Mussel and Potato Salad

Mussels remain one of the most reasonable forms of interesting protein and this dish, which is a felicitous combination of textures and flavours, benefits in that it not only economizes on mussels but in the time it takes to clean them, since you need fewer to serve many.

Serves 6

2 lb/1 kg waxy potatoes
3 lb/1.5 kg mussels
1 glass white wine
6 shallots or spring onions, cleaned
    and chopped

parsley – some chopped, some in sprigs
black pepper
6 fl oz/180 ml well-seasoned
    vinaigrette

Boil the potatoes in their skins. When cooked, peel and slice them. While they are cooking, scrub the mussels thoroughly, remove any barnacles with a sharp knife and pull away the 'beard' that protrudes from one side. Discard any cracked or open mussels or any that you can push sideways, which indicates that they are full of sand.

Put the cleaned mussels, wine, shallots, some parsley sprigs and some freshly ground black pepper into a large pan, put over a high heat, cover and bring the liquid to the boil: remove the mussels as soon as they open, discarding the shells.

Put the mussels in a dish to cool and strain the hot cooking liquid over the potatoes. Drain the potato slices when they are not quite cold, mix them with the mussels and trickle on enough vinaigrette to moisten well. Arrange in a shallow dish and garnish with the chopped parsley.

Hummus

A quarter of a pound/125 g of chick-peas makes a surprising amount of hummus. The Cypriot restaurant variety often contains too much *tahina* (sesame paste) whose tacky texture can take over. This recipe is deliberately low on *tahina*, so add more if you like it. Serve with hot pitta bread and perhaps a few thin slices of aubergine, salted, left to sit, blotted, floured and quickly fried in vegetable oil to a crisp.

Serves 4

4–6 oz/125–180 g chick peas,
    soaked overnight
juice of 1 large or 2 small lemons

2 tablespoons tahina
2 fat cloves garlic, crushed
salt

GARNISH:

1 tablespoon olive oil
1 teaspoon cayenne pepper

ground cumin (optional)

This recipe can be made by hand or by using a mouli and would probably be all the better for it, but a food processor makes it the work of minutes and if you don't over-process, you will retain a desirable slightly rough texture.

Put the soaked chick-peas into fresh water and bring to the boil. Simmer for about 1 hour or until they are tender. It is hard to over-cook chick-peas. Drain, but reserve some of the water. Put the chick-peas in the bowl of the food processor with 1 tablespoon lemon juice, 2 tablespoonfuls of the cooking water, the *tahina* and crushed garlic. Whizz to a purée and taste. If it needs more lemon juice, use this to thin the consistency. If not, use more cooking water until you have a fairly thin paste. Taste for salt.

Pour the hummus into a serving dish. Mix the oil with the cayenne and dribble it on in a pretty pattern. To complete the Persian carpet effect, make lines or streaks of ground cumin.

Smoked Haddock Soufflé

Of all fish soufflés, we think this is the best because the soufflé process tends to have a slightly deadening effect on flavour but gutsy smoked haddock pulls through. Also, the process of cooking the fish in milk gives you a flavoured stock for the soufflé base. The best smoked haddock is Finnan haddock, properly cured, not dyed, and sold on the bone. Try to get this. Because a contrast in textures is desirable with soufflés, a garnish of crunchy, deep-fried sprigs of parsley is a nice idea.

Serves 4

8 oz/250 g smoked haddock	*4 eggs separated + 1 extra white if*
½ pint/300 ml milk	*that is easy*
2 oz/60 g butter	*2 tablespoons grated hard cheese*
2 tablespoons flour	*freshly ground black pepper*

Either in the oven or on top of the stove, simmer the fish in milk, plus enough water to just cover it for about 10 minutes or until it flakes easily. Remove the fish; skin and bone it if that is pertinent. Strain its cooking liquid into a measuring jug.

Turn the oven to 200°C/400°F, Gas 6 and put a baking sheet on the oven shelf you are going to use. Melt the butter in a fairly large saucepan. Add the flour and cook, stirring, until you have a smooth paste. Add the haddock milk slowly, stirring, until you have a thickish roux. You will probably need almost ½ pint/300 ml of liquid. Let it bubble a few minutes to cook out the taste of flour. Remove from the heat and beat in the egg yolks one by one. Stir in the flaked fish, 1 tablespoonful of cheese and some black pepper. Butter a soufflé dish and dust with the remaining cheese.

Beat the egg whites in a large clean bowl until they hold stiff peaks. Fold a quarter of the egg whites gently into the haddock mixture to lighten it. Now fold that, still with a light touch, into the remaining egg whites. Turn into the soufflé dish. With a knife, make a circular indentation in the mixture about 1½ inches/4 cm from the edge of the dish, which should result in a cottage loaf effect. Put the soufflé in the oven, and immediately turn the heat down to 190°C/ 375°F, Gas 5. Cook for about 30–35 minutes or until well risen, golden brown and not too wobbly, though a slightly sloppy centre is desirable.

Breast of Lamb Stuffed with Spinach and Kasha

The most important thing here, in order to avoid any gibes about cheap cuts, is to spend time removing practically every scrap of fat from the lamb breasts and, if you have time, the bones; though this is not essential. Dedication and a small sharp knife will do it. Kasha is roasted buckwheat and is available at health food stores and enterprising shops.

Serves 4–6

2 breasts of lamb
mustard powder
salt and pepper
1 onion
olive oil

1 lb/500 g fresh spinach or 1 packet
frozen leaf spinach
4 oz/125 g kasha
1 egg

Turn on the oven to 220°C/425°F, Gas 7.

Season the breasts of lamb enthusiastically with mustard, salt and pepper and roast them skin-side up in a hot oven for about 20 minutes or until the skins look brown and appetizing. It is important to the look and texture of the finished dish. You could also cook them under a large grill. Turn the oven down to moderate; 180°C/ 350°F, Gas 4.

Peel, finely slice and sauté the onion in a little olive oil until it is golden. Trim and wash the fresh spinach and cook it in the water that clings to the leaves. Drain firmly and chop. Or cook the frozen spinach according to the packet instructions, drain and chop. Mix the spinach with the onion.

Put the kasha into a saucepan. Break in the egg; cook gently stirring all the while until the grains are coated with the egg. Add boiling water to come just above the grains, season with salt and with the lid firmly on, cook the kasha for 15 minutes or until tender but still nutty. Check from time to time to see if more water is needed.

Place one breast of lamb, skin-side down, in a clean roasting pan. Cover with a layer of spinach. Cover the spinach with the kasha. Place the other lamb breast, skin-side up, on top. You now have a sandwich. Roast your lamb sandwich for 30–45 minutes, depending on how long was the first cooking. Serve in slices which you cut at the table.

Feuilleté of Kidneys

Frozen pastry is a perfectly respectable commodity and using it one can fashion delicious containers that 'stretch' whatever is your main ingredient, be it a luxury vegetable like asparagus or seafood or meat. Kidneys are not, in any case, expensive and whilst they are good, no one wants to eat masses of them. They are, therefore, a particularly suitable passenger for this carriage.

Try to buy fresh lambs' kidneys – amenable butchers will some-times tear them directly from the carcasses.

Serves 4

6 lambs' kidneys
1 8-oz/250-g packet frozen puff
   pastry
2 oz/60 g butter
2–3 shallots or 1 onion, peeled
   and finely chopped
1 clove garlic, peeled and finely
   slivered

1 tablespoon sherry vinegar or wine
   vinegar
¼ pint/150 ml chicken stock
1 egg yolk
2 tablespoons double cream
1 generous dessertspoon Dijon
   mustard
salt and freshly ground black pepper

Trim the kidneys of any gristle or membrane and winkle out the fatty core, leaving the kidneys whole. While you cook the puff pastry in the shape you fancy and according to the instructions on the packet, start on the sauce.

Melt the butter and gently sauté the kidneys for about 5 minutes. You want them to stay a little pink in their hearts. Remove them and keep warm. Sauté the onion or shallots and garlic until softened. When the shallots are golden, add the vinegar and bubble fiercely (a splash of Madeira or port would only improve matters). Add the stock and then simmer for about 15 minutes.

Beat the egg yolk and cream in a small bowl. Add 2 tablespoonfuls of the stock to the mixture. Return this, well combined, to the stock and cook over a low heat until it is thickened. Stir in the mustard and seasoning, and beat through. Slice the kidneys, add them to the sauce and warm through gently.

Split the pastry horizontally, place the bottom half on the serving dish, pour on the kidney mixture, then cover with the top of the puff pastry. Serve at once.

Chicken Liver Risotto

Serves 6

2 large onions
3 peppers (preferably one of each
   colour)
1 lb/500 g chicken livers
12 oz/375 g mushrooms
butter

sunflower seed oil
a pinch of ground coriander
1 lb/500 g brown rice
2 oz/60 g walnuts
1 small bunch of parsley
black pepper

The good thing about this dish is that you can prepare it all before-hand, and then heat it up – gently in a slow oven.

Put whatever dish you want to serve your risotto in (ovenproof with a lid) beside the stove. Chop the onions and peppers. Trim all greeny, yellow bits from the livers and chop them roughly – not too fine. Peel and slice the mushrooms. Next, set a large pan of cold water on the stove to boil for rice. Sauté the onions in ½ oz/15 g butter and 1 dessertspoon of oil. When they are softened, add the peppers and cook until the peppers are just *al dente*. Strain the vegetables from the pan and put into the ovenproof dish; leave as much liquid behind in the pan as you can. Put the mushrooms in the pan; you may find you need more oil for them, but use as little as possible – a non-stick pan helps this. Fry the mushrooms lightly, adding black pepper and a good pinch of ground coriander. Add the mushrooms to the ovenproof dish.

By now, the water for the rice should be boiling. Just before adding the rice, add a teaspoonful of salt – this will raise the tem-perature of the water and help the rice to come to the boil quickly. Brown rice takes far longer than white to cook – the length of time depends upon the variety of rice used – and you should start testing after 15 minutes: it must not be over-cooked as it has to stand being reheated. Test it not by squeezing it between finger and thumb, but with your teeth.

While the rice is cooking, sauté the chicken livers. The mush-rooms will have made a good deal of liquid – this can be added to the main dish if liked. Start the chicken livers in a clean pan with the minimum of butter. They should be cooked until they are just pink on the inside.

When the rice is cooked, carefully drain it and then stir it into the big dish so that everything is well mixed up. Chop up the walnuts and stir in. Just before serving add the parsley, chopped roughly.

Curried Parsnips

If you haven't already done so, this would be the moment to visit an oriental supermarket or grocery shop and stock up on Indian spices in their whole form. They are cheaper this way, keep better and can be ground as needed. A cheap electric coffee grinder kept for this purpose is a sensible investment.

Serves 4

1 lb/500 g parsnips	*1 scant teaspoon black mustard seeds*
1 oz/30 g butter	*1 dried red chilli*
1 tablespoon vegetable oil	*1 teaspoon ground turmeric*
1 teaspoon cumin seeds	*salt and pepper*
1 teaspoon coriander seeds	*lemon juice*
½ teaspoon fenugreek	*finely chopped parsley or fresh*
the seeds of 5 cardamom pods	*coriander or watercress leaves*

Peel the parsnips and cut as if you were making chips; in half horizontally, then quarter vertically. Heat the mixture of butter and oil in a frying pan on which you can fit a lid. When the oil is hot, add the cumin, coriander, fenugreek, cardamom, mustard seeds and chilli and stir-fry until the seeds begin to pop, which they quickly do. Add the turmeric and stir again. Now put in the parsnips and turn in the spices until the parsnip pieces are coloured. Add two tablespoonfuls of warm water and cook, covered, testing frequently and adding more water a little at a time if the mixture begins to stick. Continue cooking until the vegetable is tender, which should take 10 to 15 minutes.

Squeeze on a little lemon juice, season and garnish with chopped parsley.

So good is this that it can be a meal in its own right with the accompaniments of Basmati rice, poppadoms and plain yoghurt.

Note: If you cannot find all the spices, don't abandon the recipe, just use your imagination. Having said that, it should be pointed out that turmeric is essential for the colour and flavour.

Rösti

The essence of this dish is its simplicity and the care you take in putting it together. Amusing ideas like tossing in a handful of chopped ham, a tablespoonful of peas or even some grated cheese should be resisted. The counsel of perfection is to parboil the potatoes for 7 minutes, drain them and allow them to cool overnight in the fridge. This makes a difference to their texture which makes the difference to the finished dish, but if it is not possible just try to cook the potatoes until nearly done somewhat ahead of time.

Rösti makes a superb accompaniment to simple grilled or roasted meat or poultry and we have even dined on it by itself with just a salad to follow.

Serves 3–4

1½ lb/750 g large potatoes
1 tablespoon vegetable oil

1 oz/30 g butter
salt and pepper

Grate the parboiled potatoes using a coarse grater. Heat the oil and butter in a 9-inch/22.5-cm diameter non-stick frying pan, or one more or less that size. Spread the grated potatoes evenly in the pan without pressing them down too harshly. Sprinkle with salt and pepper. Find a plate that will fit over the potatoes and cook them gently for 10 minutes.

Turn the Rösti out of the pan by putting a wooden board or similar over the plate and pan and turn the whole thing over. You should now have a potato cake sitting neatly on the plate ready to be sliced. You could slip the Rösti back in the pan to fry what was the top side, but we like the contrast of crisp and soft that results from the original method.

Gujerati Carrot Salad

This recipe of Madhur Jaffrey's is delicious and moreish. The nuttiness of black mustard seeds (available at oriental grocers) tones well with the inherent sweetness of carrots.

Serves 4

1 lb/500 g carrots
1 tablespoon lemon juice
sea salt

2½ tablespoons vegetable oil
1 tablespoon black mustard seeds

Clean, peel and grate the carrots, then toss in a bowl with the lemon juice and salt. Heat the oil in a small frying pan, add the mustard seeds and wait for a few seconds until they begin to pop. When they do, pour the contents of the frying pan on to the carrots and mix well.

This salad is equally good as a first course or as a vegetable accompaniment.

Marlborough Tart

Serves 6

8 oz/250 g puff pastry (bought or
   made: that's up to you)
6 oz/180 g butter

6 oz/180 g brown sugar
4 egg yolks
2 oz/60 g mixed peel, chopped small

Turn on the oven to 200°C/400°F, Gas 6.

Line a 10-inch/25-cm flan tin with pastry and put in the fridge.
Mix butter, sugar and the egg yolks in a double saucepan very
thoroughly until the sugar is melted. Put the chopped peel on to the
pastry and pour the mixture over it. Bake in the oven for about 30
minutes.

This tart can be served hot or cold.

Pierre Martin's Apple Tarts

The phenomenally economical thing about these delicious tarts is
that one apple will make four of them. Use a crisp dessert apple such
as Cox's or Laxton's and do not be tempted to load the pastry with
more than one layer of paper-thin slices, albeit overlapping ones, as
they will not cook in time. This restaurateur's dream, as far as profits
are concerned, was first tasted at Lou Pescadou, Pierre Martin's
Brasserie/Restaurant in the Old Brompton Road in London. It is
imperative that the tarts are cooked in an extremely hot oven, and
that you work quickly to prevent the apples browning.

Serves 6

1 8-oz/250-g packet frozen puff
   pastry, defrosted
1–2 dessert apples
butter

caster sugar
loosely whipped cream
if affordable, a splash of Calvados

Turn on the oven to 240°C/475°F, Gas 9.

Roll out the defrosted pastry very thinly. Cut out rounds using a
tea saucer as a guide. Place these on a wetted baking sheet (oddly
enough pastry rises crisply in a damp atmosphere). Peel the apple(s),

cut very thin slices and lay them on the pastry rounds in slightly overlapping pieces. Dot each tart with about a teaspoonful of butter and sprinkle with caster sugar. Cook for 15–20 minutes or until the pastry has risen and is crisp.

Serve immediately with the whipped cream, and a splash of Calvados if you have it.

Brandy Snaps

Serves 6

4 oz/125 g sugar
4 oz/125 g butter
*4 oz/125 g Golden Syrup (see
    page 97 for measuring tip)*
4 oz/125 g plain flour

1 tablespoon ground ginger
juice of ½ lemon
*½ pint/300 ml cream flavoured with
    real vanilla essence and ground
    ginger, whipped*

Turn on the oven to 180°C/350°F, Gas 4.

Melt the sugar, butter and syrup in a double saucepan, add the sieved flour, ginger and lemon. Stir well. Then, in teaspoonfuls, put the mixture on a non-stick baking sheet, placing the dollops well apart as the mixture will spread widely. Put in the oven and bake until golden brown, about 8–10 minutes.

Remove from the oven, leave to cool for a few moments and then roll each piece round the handle of a wooden spoon. (This is not difficult: the secret is to get the mixture exactly at the right temperature: too soon and it will not stay rolled; too late and it will become rigid and crack.) Lay each rolled snap on to a wire rack to cool.

You can then fill them with whipped cream, but we think it nicer to serve the cream separately in a bowl. That way the snap doesn't get sodden by the cream, which tends to happen in 2 or 3 hours.

Oat Cakes

1 oz/30 g lard or *dripping*
1 lb/500 g medium oatmeal plus
    extra for the rolling process

½ teaspoon bicarbonate of soda
½ teaspoon salt

Turn on the oven to 150°C/300°F, Gas 2.

Melt the chosen fat (bacon fat is good) in ½ pint/300 ml hot water. Mix the oatmeal in a bowl with the bicarbonate of soda and salt. Make a well in the oatmeal, pour in the melted fat and water and mix with a knife to a fairly moist dough. Dust a surface with oatmeal and roll out the dough, using plenty of oatmeal to prevent any sticking. Cut in rounds with a pastry cutter.

Bake for about 20 minutes on an ungreased baking sheet, turning several times, until the oatcakes are crisp and golden.

Water Biscuits

8 oz/250 g plain flour
½ teaspoon salt
1 teaspoon baking powder
2 oz/60 g butter or *margarine*

sea salt and/or *poppy seeds* or *sesame*
seeds or *caraway seeds (depending*
on the cheeses these will
accompany)

Turn on the oven to 150°C/300°F, Gas 2.

Sift the flour, salt and baking powder together. Rub in the butter or margarine conscientiously and add enough water to make a firm dough. Roll out thinly on a floured surface. Prick all over with a fork and cut out circles with a large scone cutter or a tea cup. Sprinkle with whatever seed you choose or just sea salt. Bake on a lightly oiled baking sheet for 20 minutes or until crisp and faintly brown.

These are best served almost straight from the oven. If you make them ahead of time, store in a tin with a tightly fitting lid, and crisp in a low oven when you need them.

Fried Cheese Sandwiches

Providing a cheese course is not a very budget-conscious thing to do. It is difficult to judge the right amount to buy and almost invariably there are left-overs which will be wrapped, stored and eventually thrown out. These sandwiches, which need a specific amount of cheese, are also a good way of using up any bits you might already have. They will perk up a straightforward supper and go well with any remaining red wine.

Serves 4–6

3 oz/90 g grated hard cheese e.g. Cheddar or Caerphilly (for extra sharpness add in some grated Parmesan)
freshly ground black pepper
1 oz/30 g soft butter

8 thin slices of white bread (slightly stale is an advantage)
¼ pint/150 ml of milk
1 large egg, beaten
a pinch of salt, cayenne pepper and mustard powder
butter or vegetable oil for frying

Mix together the grated cheese, a generous amount of pepper and the butter. Thinly spread four slices of the bread with the cheese mixture. Cover with the remaining slices. Press down hard, trim off the crusts and cut into quarters. Put the milk in a shallow bowl. In another similar bowl mix the beaten egg with the seasonings. Heat gently the butter or oil in a large frying pan. Dip each sandwich briefly into the milk, then the egg mixture, and fry them on each side until the cheese begins to melt and the bread is a light golden-brown. Drain on kitchen paper and serve quickly.

Devils on Horseback

Unexpected courses provide a luxury of their own. After a light meal, a savoury is a great treat and a reason to keep going with the wine and wit.

On the Russian Doll principle of cooking, this version of Devils on Horseback is fun. For 4 people, take 8 large prunes and pour boiling water over them. Leave for half an hour and then simmer them in this liquid until tender. When cool, carefully stone the prunes and stuff them with the sort of olive that, in its turn, has been stoned and filled with pimento.

Take a half-rasher of thinly sliced bacon for each prune. Stretch and flatten it and wrap it round the prune. Set on a baking tin and bake in a hot oven until the bacon is crisply cooked – about 10 minutes. Let each Devil on Horseback ride on a piece of thin, hot buttered toast.

Welsh Rabbit

Correctly, Welsh Rabbit is made on the principle of fondue, with the cheese being slowly melted into brown ale with butter and seasoning and the whole being poured over toast. This is a simpler way that can be prepared ahead of time. However, Worcestershire sauce should still be served. The correct way to apply it is to press a knife criss-cross fashion into the hot cheese and shake on the sauce so that it dribbles into the runnels.

For 4 people, grate 4 oz/125 g of Cheddar and mix with a little butter and a little beer to a spreadable paste. Season with black pepper and made mustard. Spread on to buttered toast and grill.

CHAPTER FOUR

Dull People

'The capacity of human beings to bore one another seems to be vastly greater than that of any other animal. Some of their most esteemed inventions have no other apparent purpose; for example, the dinner party of more than two, the epic poem, and the science of metaphysics.' Some entertaining that, for one reason or another, is thrust upon you makes one empathize deeply with H. L. Mencken's view.

We have all been faced with those evenings where the cooking seems so much more fun than the prospect of the arrival of the guests. The sister of one of the authors once gave her an apron bought in Los Angeles which she is often tempted to wear to open the door to guests. It says on it, 'Who invited these tacky people anyway?' which, when tired and frazzled and consumed with doubts about the meaning of life, is a thought which flits through the mind of even the most munificent hostess.

And, on the whole, if this is how you feel, it will be because somebody else, not you, has initiated the event. Why invite people if that is how you feel, you might be thinking. But that is a naïve response, dear reader. Entertaining, the noun, has its own stringent by-laws, one of which is that it often bears very little relation to entertaining, the adjective. Duty dinners, business contacts, family and in-law coddling, return matches, can all conjure the prospect of a dreary evening. However, we have to add here that frequently, almost uncannily frequently, a dreaded evening turns into the jolliest of occasions. Conversely, you can invite six people celebrated for their wit and charm and needle-sharp intelligence and the evening can be a complete frost, so furious and sulky is each one to find someone else telling jokes or looking devastating.

But given that you suppose that the lunch or dinner is going to need kindling, that it is not going to be an affair of spontaneous combustion, the following ideas will help to what we believe is known as break the ice. Many of them involve the participation of the eaters, and if conversation flags, and new topics are elusive, they can always resort to squabbling over whose piece of beef it is skating round the fondue pot.

<table>
<tr><td>Stilton Soup</td><td>Individual Crème Brûlées</td></tr>
<tr><td>Lettuce Packets</td><td>Baked Alaska</td></tr>
<tr><td>Tacos</td><td>Crêpes Suzette</td></tr>
<tr><td>Lamb Cutlets in Filo Pastry</td><td>Iced Camembert</td></tr>
<tr><td>Fondue Bourguignonne</td><td></td></tr>
</table>

Stilton Soup

This rich soup makes an impressive start to the meal. You may think it is a dubious notion, but it is actually delicious. Beth Coventry, who serves it at Green's Champagne Bar in Duke Street, St James's, in London, says that Americans love it and ask for the recipe. So if you are having dull Americans to dinner . . .

Serves 4

2 oz/60 g butter
1 onion, peeled and finely
   chopped
1 fat clove garlic, peeled and
   finely chopped
2 stalks celery, de-stringed and
   diced
1½ oz/45 g flour

1 teaspoon ground coriander
½ chicken stock cube, crumbled
½ pint/300 ml milk
8 oz/250 g Stilton cheese, broken up
   with a fork
1 sherry glass of port
pepper
2 tablespoons double cream (optional)

Melt the butter and cook the onion, garlic and celery very gently – just let them soften. Stir in the flour and cook for a minute or two to lose any raw taste. Add the ground coriander and the crumbled stock cube. Add the milk and when the mixture is smooth add enough water to achieve a consistency of thin cream – something in the region of 1½ pints/1 litre. Simmer for 15 minutes. Add the crumbled Stilton and, off the heat, beat the soup with a whisk. Add the port, mix again, grind on some black pepper, taste for seasoning and whisk in the cream. Reheat, but gently, since the soup must not be allowed to boil.

Serve with wholemeal toast.

Lettuce Packets

Alongside the illusion of healthiness, there is an 'involving' quality about this dish, helpful if conversation is limping. Each guest takes a lettuce leaf, adds a spoonful of the pork mixture, makes up a parcel as neatly or as messily as they are capable and proceeds.

The recipe below is a simplified version of a Chinese idea, but once you have grasped the concept you will be able to improvise with your own mixtures. Cooked root vegetables diced finely, spiked with chilli, is one thought.

Serves 4

2 tablespoons vegetable oil or
    lard, according to preference
12 oz/375 g minced pork
salt
sugar
1 tablespoon chopped onion
1 teaspoon grated fresh root ginger
4 stalks celery, de-stringed and
    diced
1 tablespoon soya sauce

2 tablespoons dry sherry
3 tablespoons chicken stock (from a
    cube will suffice)
½ cucumber, diced
½ tablespoon cornflour, whisked into 2
    more tablespoons stock
2 teaspoons sesame oil (optional)
1 Iceberg lettuce or Webbs Wonder,
    the leaves separated, washed and
    dried

Heat the oil or lard (the latter gives a more unctuous effect) in a large frying pan or wok. When hot, add the pork. Sprinkle with a good pinch of salt and a teaspoonful of sugar and stir-fry for 2 or 3 minutes or until there is no trace of pink in the meat.

Add the onion and ginger; stir-fry for 2 minutes. Add the celery, soya sauce, sherry and stock. Fry for 1 minute, then add the cucumber and cook until it is heated through but still crunchy.

Give the cornflour mixture a stir to create a cloudy liquid and pour on to the meat. Stir-fry for 1 minute. Finally glaze the meat by dribbling on the sesame oil (or a little vegetable oil if that is all you have to hand).

Serve on a heated dish with the lettuce leaves stacked on a separate plate.

Tacos

Like the Lettuce Packets, this is another involving course. The taco shells (which you buy in a packet made by the company Old El Paso since they taste all right and it is difficult, if not impossible, to buy *masa harina* to make your own) are filled first with spiced beef and then garnished with various sauces and substances. Each taco that a guest assembles can differ a little from the one before. If you are feeding serious numbers, then you might consider offering a variety of meats, for example shredded cooked chicken or fried crumbled sausage of a spicy variety as well as the beef.

Serves 6–8

2 onions, peeled and finely chopped	a hefty pinch of chilli powder or 1 small green chilli, de-seeded and finely chopped or 1 teaspoon chilli sauce
2 cloves garlic, peeled and finely chopped	
2 tablespoons vegetable oil	soya sauce
2 lb/1 kg minced beef	salt and pepper
2 teaspoons ground cumin	a pinch of sugar
2 teaspoons dried oregano	1 packet Old El Paso taco shells

Fry the onion and garlic in the vegetable oil. Add the minced beef and stir until browned. Season with cumin, oregano, chilli and a dash of soya sauce. Season with salt, pepper and a pinch of sugar. Add a cup of water and simmer for 20 minutes.

Heat the taco shells for 2–3 minutes in a moderate oven.

PREPARE BOWLS OF:

shredded lettuce	an avocado mashed with a peeled, seeded and diced tomato and seasoned with lemon juice, salt, pepper and chilli sauce
grated hard cheese	
yoghurt or soured cream	
Salsa Cruda (see page 48)	

Offer the taco shells with the minced beef and the garnishes.

Lamb Cutlets in Filo Pastry

This is made on the same principle as Beef Wellington, the dull person's favourite dish, but we think it better as it is somewhat easier to get the timings right; the pastry puffed and golden, the meat cooked but rosy pink.

Filo pastry, available at Cypriot bakeries and some delicatessens and supermarkets, is a great conversation piece so long as you conceal its origins and just look faintly smug as though rolling out paper-thin dough is something you do every day. If you fail to find filo pastry, use defrosted frozen puff pastry, rolled out thinly.

It is important to buy small, neat cutlets, well trimmed of fat and with a long bone protruding. Inform the butcher that you want best end cutlets prepared in the French style.

Serves 4

1 oz/30 g butter or 1 tablespooon vegetable oil
1 Spanish onion, peeled and finely chopped
2 cloves garlic, peeled and finely chopped
4 oz/125 g mushrooms, wiped clean and finely chopped

1 tablespoon chopped parsley
salt and freshly ground black pepper
1 8-oz/250-g packet frozen puff pastry (defrosted) or 8 oz/250 g filo pastry
8 best end of neck lamb cutlets
1 egg, beaten with a pinch of salt

Turn on the oven to 220°C/425°F, Gas 7.

Heat the butter or oil and sauté the onion and garlic until softened. Add the mushrooms and stir around until cooked. Mix in the parsley and season enthusiastically.

If you are using puff pastry, roll it out thinly and cut into 8 triangles, each one just large enough to wrap around the meat. If you are using filo pastry, cut strips about 5 inches/12.5 cm wide, one for each cutlet, and brush on one side with oil or melted butter. Cover strips with a damp tea towel to keep the pastry pliable.

In the cleaned out sauté pan, seal the chops quickly in a little more oil or butter. Remove, let any fat drain off, and then season the meat. Drain off any liquid from the onion/mushroom mixture. Put a heaped teaspoonful into the centre of each pastry triangle or at one end of your filo pastry strip. Place a cutlet on the stuffing and, with the puff pastry, pinch the pastry around it making a firm seal and aiming for the look of a three-cornered hat. With the filo pastry, wrap it loosely round the meat rather as if you were bandaging it. Brush the pastry with the egg wash. Place the parcels on a wet baking sheet and cook for 15 to 20 minutes, or until the pastry is flaky and golden.

Serve with redcurrant jelly.

Fondue Bourguignonne

For this you need a fondue set with a burner to keep the oil hot or you could use an electric frying pan. The long-handled slender forks that come with fondue sets are useful but not imperative; ordinary forks will do. Use good quality meat, as it is subject to very brief cooking. Serve a selection of sauces from the ideas given below in small bowls and bake small potatoes in their jackets for 45 minutes to hand round afterwards as a vehicle for left-over sauces.

8 oz/250 g steak per person (rump or sirloin)

1¾ pints/1 litre vegetable oil or if you wish to add some flavour, substitute butter or olive oil for one-third of the quantity

Cut the meat into bite-sized pieces and pile up attractively in two dishes.

Make a selection of the sauces below:

Aïoli

Crush 3 cloves of garlic and stir into 2 egg yolks. When that is well blended, add 1 teaspoonful made mustard. Slowly begin to add vegetable oil, drop by drop, stirring all the while until the sauce thickens and the emulsion seems reliable. Add more oil (in total about 8 fl oz/250 ml) until you have a sauce with the consistency of ointment. Flavour with salt, pepper and a squeeze of lemon juice.

Avocado Sauce

Purée the flesh of an avocado with a little oil, lemon juice, salt, pepper and a dash of chilli sauce. If you wish, thin with 2 heaped tablespoonfuls natural yoghurt.

Salsa Cruda

2 large ripe red tomatoes, skinned
   and finely chopped
1 onion, peeled and finely
   chopped
2 small green chilli peppers de-
   seeded and cut into fine threads

1 tablespoon chopped fresh coriander
   or substitute parsley
a pinch of sugar
1 tablespoon oil
1 dessertspoon red wine vinegar
salt and pepper

Mix all ingredients together and leave at room temperature.

Parsley Sauce

4 fl oz/125 ml vegetable oil
2 tablespoons white wine vinegar
1 teaspoon mustard

1 clove garlic, peeled and crushed
4 oz/125 g parsley, finely chopped
salt and pepper

Mix the oil and vinegar and seasonings and stir in the parsley, adding
more if necessary to obtain a cohesive sauce.

Remoulade Sauce

8 fl oz/250 ml mayonnaise
2 oz/60 g chopped gherkins
1 tablespoon capers, finely
   chopped
2 hard-boiled eggs, finely chopped

1 teaspoon chopped tarragon – if
   available
1 dessertspoon chopped parsley
   and/or chives
salt and pepper

Mix together thoroughly.

Satay Sauce

1 onion, peeled and finely
   chopped
1 tablespoon vegetable oil
finely chopped chillis or chilli
   sauce to taste

6 oz/180 g crunchy peanut butter
1 teaspoon sugar
juice of ½ lemon
1 tablespoon soya sauce

Fry the onion in the oil until golden. Add some finely chopped chilli
or ½ teaspoon chilli sauce, the peanut butter, about 6 fl oz/180 ml
water and the sugar. Stir well and simmer until you have a thick
mixture. Stir in the lemon juice and soya sauce and taste for further
seasonings, if any.

Chinese Dipping Sauce

4 tablespoons soya sauce
2 tablespoons rice vinegar
  (available from oriental
  grocers) or use 1 tablespoon
  sherry plus 1 tablespoon
  vinegar

a good pinch of sugar
1 fat clove garlic, peeled and crushed
1 dessertspoon sesame seeds, lightly
  roasted in a dry frying pan
2 spring onions, very finely chopped

Mix all the ingredients together. Threads of fresh root ginger, if you have some, can be added.

Yoghurt Mint Sauce

1 small tub Greek (strained)
  yoghurt
salt and pepper

1 dessertspoon mint sauce base (not
  jellied mint sauce)

Mix together.

Guests spear a piece of meat, cook it to their liking in the bubbling oil and dip it into their choice of sauces, which should first be spooned on to their plates to avoid a messy ending.

Individual Crème Brûlées

Serves 6

1 pint/625 ml double cream
1 tablespoon caster sugar: if you
  keep a jar of caster sugar with a
  vanilla pod in it, use it; if not
  use 1 vanilla pod, split, or a
  few drops vanilla essence

4 egg yolks
more caster sugar for the brûlée

Butter 6 cocotte dishes, and turn on the oven to 140°C/275°F, Gas 1.
  Put the cream and sugar (plus pod or essence) in the top of a double saucepan and heat to scalding point. Remove from the heat, and pour in the egg yolks in a thin stream, stirring vigorously all the while. Remove the pod if you were using one, and strain the mixture into the buttered cocotte dishes. Put the dishes in a baking tin half

full of warm water and bake in the oven for half an hour or until the custard is just firm. Leave to cool, and then put in the fridge.

Before serving, heat the grill, sprinkle caster sugar ⅛ inch/0.3 cm thick over the top of the custards and grill until caramel-coloured. Remove. A few minutes later, the caramel will have cooled and should be like very thin glass.

Baked Alaska

You can count on the fact that there will always be someone thrilled and startled to find that a dessert can come out of the oven and yet still have firm ice-cream at its centre. The trick is to cover the sponge base and the ice-cream lavishly with meringue so there is no crack to let the heat through, and to have the oven well pre-heated, so that the meringue crisps quickly.

Serves 6

1 layer of sponge cake – home-made or bought	3 egg whites
¾ pint/475 ml good quality vanilla ice-cream	salt
	6 oz/180 g caster sugar
fresh soft fruit in season	2 tablespoons brandy or rum, if you want to flame the pudding

Put the cake on an ovenproof serving dish. Cut up the ice-cream and arrange in one layer, leaving about ½ inch/1.25 cm sponge cake around the edge. Put in the freezer for 1 hour.

Turn on the oven to 230°C/450°F, Gas 8.

Arrange your choice of soft fruit, e.g. raspberries, blackberries, peaches or currants, on the ice-cream. Whisk the egg whites with a pinch of salt until stiff. Whisk in 2 tablespoonfuls of the sugar and continue until you have glistening snowy peaks. Carefully fold in the remainder of the sugar. Spoon the meringue over the fruit, ice-cream and cake leaving no patch uncovered. Bake in the oven for about 3 minutes or until the tips of the meringue are browned.

Crêpes Suzette

The flames of ignited alcohol will brighten the eyes of dull guests and they can exclaim over how some of the best cooking ideas are the traditional ones and how these days they tend to get ignored.

Serves 4
Crêpes (to be made in advance)

5 oz/150 g plain flour
a pinch of salt
2 eggs
12 fl oz/350 ml semi-skimmed
    milk

1 dessertspoon caster sugar
2 tablespoons melted butter or
    vegetable oil
butter or oil for frying

Sift the flour and salt into a bowl. Beat together the eggs and milk. Make a well in the flour and gradually whisk in the egg/milk mixture until you have a smooth batter. Stir in the sugar and butter or oil. Let rest for at least an hour but preferably longer. Before frying the *crêpes*, thin the batter if necessary with more milk to the consistency of single cream. In a frying pan about 7 inches/18 cm in diameter heat a dab of butter or a teaspoon of oil. When the pan is hot and covered with a thin film of grease, add a coffee cup of batter and tip the pan until the base is covered. Cook over medium heat until the edges of the *crêpe* curl in. Turn over with a spatula and brown the other side. Remove the *crêpe* to a plate and carry on. It is safest to separate each *crêpe* in the pile with a sheet or a couple of strips of greaseproof paper.

TO SERVE:

4 oz/125 g butter
4 oz/125 g caster sugar
grated rind of an orange

2–3 tablespoons Grand Marnier
2–3 tablespoons brandy

Cream 2 oz/60 g of the butter with the sugar and orange rind and beat in 1 tablespoon of the Grand Marnier. You can use a food processor or a hand-held electric whisk if you wish. Spread a little of the mixture on the more aesthetically pleasing side of each *crêpe*. Heat the remaining butter in a large heavy frying pan. When melted add a *crêpe*, butter/sugar side down. Heat for 30 seconds; fold in half, then in quarters. Push to one side of the pan. Continue in this fashion until all the *crêpes* are neatly folded and the butter and sugar in the pan have caramelized. Heat the brandy gently in a small saucepan. Pour over the *crêpes* and, at the table, carefully put a match to it.

Iced Camembert

This recipe dates from the Thirties. The combination of cold cheese and hot biscuits is a good one. Look on page 39 for the recipe for home-made Water Biscuits and Oat Cakes and make one or other as the accompaniment.

Serves 6

1 Camembert cheese – it should be
ripe but not 'humming' with
ripeness
¼ pint/150 ml single cream

¼ pint/150 ml double cream
salt and pepper
cayenne pepper

TO SERVE:

crushed ice
few sprigs parsley

hot biscuits (see above)

Pare the rind from the cheese, wasting as little as possible. Mash the cheese with the single cream using a fork, or you could whizz it in the food processor or liquidizer. Beat the double cream until it just holds its shape and fold in the cheesy mixture. Season to taste with salt, black pepper and cayenne. Freeze in a shallow dish until firm, but not rock hard.

Set a serving dish in crushed ice. Slice the Camembert, and arrange on the dish with sprigs of parsley. Hand hot biscuits separately.

CHAPTER FIVE

Ladies' Lunch

In the bad old days, ladies' lunches were regarded with patronizing indulgence by the male sex and with various feelings ranging from anxiety to boredom by the lunch goers. One of us, old enough to remember those times, can recall that it was a way for bored middle-class women, who were not allowed by their husbands to engage in any profession or work, to pass the time between shopping at Daniel Neal for their children and running the First Aid classes for the Red Cross.

They were also a part of the old London Season: mothers met at lunch to plan the dinner and cocktail parties surrounding the dances, and the débutantes met to go over the fun and games of the night before. We can be fairly sure that the food on these occasions was either dull – nursery food but with smaller helpings – or downright awful, on the premiss that if something was nasty enough you would not eat very much of it and so preserve your figure. One such lunch can indeed be remembered, where all three courses were some kind of (different) mousse or pâté, dun-coloured and running the spectrum of taste between cheesy face flannel to saccharine-flavoured lemon. The middle course defied description until one more outspoken guest described it as near mouse paste. Food to toy with, you might say.

People mind more about what they eat these days and the only two things that have changed about ladies' lunches is the (almost) universal desire not to become fatter as a result, and the more serious fact that instead of sending for Cook after breakfast and ordering the meals – in the Thirties that was regarded as a terrible chore – you have to do it all yourself. Two courses should suffice, and simplicity and the minimum of last-minute cooking should be the keynote on the principle that you ask women to lunch with you because you really like them and actually want to talk to them.

Gazpacho

This dish, practically a liquid salad, is not only palpably good for you but must have an almost minus quantity of calories. There is much discussion over what is and what is not an authentic gazpacho. This is not. In fact, the recipe emanates from Fire Island in New York, but it is so good that authenticity seems suddenly irrelevant.

Serves 4

14-fl oz/425-ml tin, bottle or
   carton good quality tomato juice
2 green peppers, cleaned and
   roughly chopped
4 tomatoes, skinned and quartered
2 cloves garlic, peeled
1 stalk celery, trimmed

1 large or 2 small cucumbers, roughly
   chopped
2 fl oz/60 ml olive oil
4 fl oz/125 ml wine vinegar
a pinch of salt
a pinch of cayenne pepper

GARNISHES:

1 green pepper, cleaned and finely
   chopped
2 hard-boiled eggs, finely chopped

1 Spanish onion, peeled and finely
   chopped
2–3 slices of bread, cubed and fried in
   olive oil until golden

Using small amounts of tomato juice, blend together the next six ingredients in the list. Pour into a bowl, thin with 4 fl oz/125 ml more tomato juice and stir in the oil and vinegar. Season with salt and cayenne pepper. Decide on the consistency of soup that you like, and add more tomato juice if necessary. Chill thoroughly.

Just before serving, prepare the garnishes and serve them in small bowls beside the soup for people to help themselves.

Watercress Soup

Serves 4

1 large onion
2 bunches watercress
1 oz/30 g butter or 1 tablespoon
  sunflower seed oil

1½ pints/1 litre good chicken stock
salt and pepper

Peel and chop the onion finely. Wash the watercress and chop roughly. Melt the butter or heat the oil in a pan. Add the onion and cook gently for a few minutes, adding a little salt to make the onions sweat. Add the watercress, and cook, stirring, for two minutes, then add the stock. Simmer for half an hour, then pass through mouli, liquidize or whizz in the food processor. Return to the pan, and season.

Note: With soups, there is always the choice between using a hand mouli or liquidizer: the latter is quicker, but the former produces a more interesting texture.

Caesar Salad

The method below is for the 'classic' Caesar salad, made famous by a restaurateur in Tijuana in the Twenties. It may strike you as simplistic, but its restraint is what makes it so good, provided you take no short cuts in the preparation. Success depends on the last-minute coming together of the constituent parts.

Serves 4 as a first course

1 large Cos lettuce or 2 smaller
  ones
juice of ½ lemon
2 oz/60 g Parmesan cheese,
  freshly grated
2 eggs
white bread from a proper loaf

Worcestershire sauce or 1 tin
  anchovies
2 fat cloves garlic
olive oil
sea salt and freshly ground black
  pepper

Pick over the lettuce and use only the unblemished leaves. Wash them, dry them thoroughly and put in a plastic bag in the refrigerator.

Towards the time of serving, assemble all the other ingredients, squeeze the lemon half, grate the Parmesan if you have bought it in a lump and set water to boil for the eggs. Trim the crusts from three slices of bread and cut into cubes. Open the anchovies if you are using then; Worcestershire sauce is, apparently, authentic.

Crush the garlic into 3 tablespoonfuls olive oil and fry the croûtons (bread cubes) in this, turning and stirring the while to ensure they are evenly browned. Place the lettuce in a large salad bowl and add 2 tablespoonfuls olive oil. Toss to coat the leaves. Sprinkle on some sea salt and freshly ground black pepper and toss with another tablespoonful of olive oil – imagine you are a Mexican restaurateur.

Pour on the lemon juice and a couple of splashes of Worcestershire sauce (or the drained and chopped anchovies) and break in the yolks of the eggs which you have plunged into boiling water for just one minute. Toss once. Sprinkle on the Parmesan. Toss again and add the croûtons which should first be drained on kitchen paper. Serve immediately.

Delancey Salad

Serves 6

1 lb/500 g fresh prawns	½ large cucumber
1 bunch watercress	1 box mustard and cress
12 oz/375 g mushrooms	2 avocados

FOR THE DRESSING:

1 teaspoon salt	2 tablespoons best olive oil
1 teaspoon sugar	1 tablespoon tarragon vinegar
freshly ground black pepper	

This salad can all be prepared beforehand, except for the avocado which should be added just before serving.

Peel the prawns. Wash and roughly chop the watercress, peel and slice the mushrooms, cut the cucumber into thick slices and chop into pieces. Cut the cress from its box. Combine all the ingredients in a large salad bowl. Before serving, halve the avocados and scoop out pieces with a teaspoon.

Dress the salad in the following manner. Scatter the salt over the salad and mix. Add the sugar and mix. Add several good screws of black pepper and mix. Add the olive oil and mix. And finally, 1 tablespoonful of tarragon vinegar and mix. Italians very often dress salads in this manner and the result is very fresh and appealing. Naturally you may want to adjust the ingredients of the dressing to suit yourself. Taste the salad in any case to see whether more of anything should be added.

Korean Egg Bundles

This recipe, taken from Madhur Jaffrey's *Eastern Vegetarian Cooking*, is a dainty dish fit for ladies. Rectangular egg pancakes are cut into thin strips and the strips tied into bundles with blanched spring onions. It is the dipping sauce that makes the dish.

Since, unless you are Korean or Japanese, you are unlikely to have a rectangular frying pan, use a 6-inch/15-cm omelette pan or non-stick frying pan and be prepared either for some waste or curvy sticks.

Serves 4–6

5 *large eggs*
2 *teaspoons vegetable oil*

12 *spring onions, trimmed and washed*
2 *teaspoons salt*

FOR THE SAUCE:

4 *tablespoons Japanese soya sauce*
2½ *tablespoons rice vinegar*
1 *teaspoon sugar*
1 *tablespoon very finely sliced*
   spring onion

1 *clove garlic, peeled and crushed*
1 *teaspoon sesame seeds, roasted and*
   lightly crushed

Beat the eggs but not to a froth. Put 1 teaspoonful of oil into the frying pan. Spread it around and heat it over a medium-low heat. When hot, pour in half the beaten eggs. Turn heat to low and cover loosely (with aluminium foil, if necessary). Cook for 5–6 minutes or until the bottom of the pancake is no longer soft. Ease a spatula under the pancake and turn it over. Cook the other side for 2–3 minutes or until it, too, is firm. Remove the pancake. Add another teaspoonful of oil to the frying pan and make the second pancake the same way. Allow both pancakes to cool, then cut them into strips that are about 2½ inches/6 cm long and ¼ inch/0.6 cm wide.

Bring 2 quarts/2.3 litres of water to a rolling boil in a 4-quart/5-litre pot. Add the salt. Put the spring onions, bulbs first, into the water; like spaghetti, the upper ends of the spring onions will have to be eased into the water as they soften. Boil rapidly for 2 minutes. You may have to hold the spring onions down with a spoon so they stay submerged. Drain the spring onions in a colander and rinse immediately under cold running water, then pat them dry. Split each spring onion lengthways into two or more strands by first cutting the bulb with a knife and then tearing upwards.

Now put four egg strips together to form a neat bundle. Place the bulb end of the spring onion strip on the centre of the bundle and then wrap round and round over it. Tuck the end of the strand underneath the binding. It will hold. Make as many bundles as you can this way. Arrange bundles prettily on a round or rectangular platter. If not to be eaten immediately, cover with cling film and refrigerate for a few hours. Mix together the sauce ingredients and serve in small bowls for dipping.

Egg Mousse

Serves 6

6 hard-boiled eggs
3 tablespoons mayonnaise
⅝ packet of gelatine
2 tablespoons light stock

6 anchovy fillets
2 tablespoons cream, whipped
fresh parsley and, if possible, fresh
   coriander

Chop the eggs and mix with the mayonnaise. Dissolve the gelatine thoroughly in the stock (the best way of doing this is to put it in a small bowl in a saucepan of boiling water and stir with a fork), and add to the mixture. Chop the anchovies finely and add. Finally, fold in the cream, put the mixture into a cold mould, and put into the fridge. Turn out before serving, and garnish with parsley and/or coriander.

Spinach Soufflé with Anchovy Sauce

The way to serve this dish is to bring the soufflé to the table, whereupon your friends will 'ooh' and 'aah' as people invariably do when confronted by a soufflé. Boldly thrust a spoon down into the centre and pour in the hot anchovy sauce, keeping the rest to serve separately. Any dryness or monotony in the soufflé will be obviated by the tingling, creamy anchovy.

Serves 4

1 lb/500 g spinach
3 oz/90 g butter
3 tablespoons flour
½ pint/300 ml milk
4 oz/125 g double cream cheese

1 oz/30 g Parmesan cheese, grated
  (optional)
salt and freshly ground black pepper
4 eggs, separated
1 tin anchovies
¼ pint/150 ml double cream

Turn on the oven to 190°C/375°F, Gas 5.

Wash the spinach leaves, trim off any hard stalks and cook, in only the water which clings to the leaves, until it is tender. Drain in a colander and when it is cool enough, squeeze it with your hands to get it as dry as possible and then chop it finely.

Melt 2 oz/60 g of the butter, stir in the flour to make a roux (see page 5). Slowly add the milk until you have a thick smooth sauce and then beat in the cream cheese, bit by bit. Add the Parmesan if you are using it. Stir in the spinach and season quite vigorously. Let it cool a little and then beat in the egg yolks one by one.

This can be done ahead of time. When ready to cook, whisk the egg whites until stiff. Fold about a quarter of them into the mixture to lighten it, then the rest with an even gentler hand. Pour into a buttered soufflé dish and bake for 25–30 minutes.

To make the sauce, briefly soak 5–6 anchovy fillets in warm water and then pat them dry. Melt the final 1 oz/30 g butter, add the fillets, stir around until they break up and then pour in the cream. Bring to the boil, give a quick bubble and serve.

Pigeon Breasts

Contrary to many pigeon recipes, lightning cooking of the pigeon flesh gives far better results than long stewing. Even if you are nervous about techniques like boning or, indeed, dealing with raw meat at all, do not be afraid of the notion of removing the pigeon breasts from the carcass. They scoop off easily and neatly. The skinny legs and the carcass are then used for the stock.

Serves 6

1 pigeon per person   *ground ginger*
olive oil   *1 teaspoon arrowroot*
lemon juice or wine   *port or red wine*
salt and pepper

VEGETABLES FOR STOCK:

1 carrot   *3 cloves of garlic per person, trimmed*
1 onion, stuck with a clove   *but unpeeled*
1 stalk celery   *peppercorns*
bay leaf

Using a sharp, cunning little knife, take off the pigeon breasts by working the knife between the flesh and breast bone; they practically slide off. Trim any gristle or skin that overhangs the 'supreme'.

Mix together some olive oil, a little lemon juice or wine, and salt and pepper. Turn the breasts in this and leave to marinate. Use the carcasses and vegetables to make the stock, adding some peppercorns and the garlic cloves. Simmer for as long as time allows, up to 1½ hours. Strain the stock and put aside the garlic cloves. Continue to boil the stock until it is well reduced. You want only a couple of tablespoonfuls per person. Mix the arrowroot with a little port (or red wine) and stir it into the stock to make it glossy.

Remove the pigeon breasts from the marinade. Sprinkle with a little ground ginger and some black pepper. Grill the breasts under a moderate heat for a few minutes on each side and then leave to rest under the switched-off grill for 10 minutes.

To serve prettily, slice the breasts across, and fan out the slices on a warmed plate. Surrounded with the sauce. If you like garlic (after cooking in the stock, it will now be mild and nutty), sauté the cloves briskly in a little butter and serve alongside.

Hot Fruit Salad

This recipe comes from Elizabeth David's *Summer Cooking*. She says that it is important to use red gooseberries – not green ones – and also that one must stick to the proportions.

Serves 6

1 lb/500 g red gooseberries   *sugar*
4 oz/125 g redcurrants   *8 oz/250 g raspberries*

Stew together gently for 5 minutes (without water) the gooseberries, redcurrants and sugar. The sugar has to be used in quantities depending upon how sweet or sharp you like your summer fruit: start with 2 tablespoonfuls and add more if you feel the fruit needs it. Add the raspberries and cook for a further 2 minutes. Serve very hot with fresh thick cream; the cream should be served separately, so that those who don't want it may have the fruit by itself.

This recipe can also be adapted, using loganberries instead of the gooseberries, and blackberries instead of the raspberries. Redcurrants are desirable for both dishes.

Iced Coffee Granita

A granita should not be smooth like a sorbet but composed of fine-grained frozen crystals, in this case of strong coffee. It makes an excellent finish to a lunch. True coffee lovers eat an iced coffee granita whilst drinking a cup of hot espresso. The coffee should preferably be made in an Italian Moka coffee pot, the kind where hot water is forced up from the bottom of the pot through the coffee and into the top. For preference, use freshly ground high roast Continental beans.

Serves 4

¾ pint/475 ml strong coffee   *double cream, freshly whipped*
2 tablespoons sugar, or more to   *(optional)*
  taste

Pour hot coffee into a jug and dissolve the sugar in it. Taste for sweetness but do not make it very sweet as sugar weakens the flavour. Pour the coffee into metal ice cube trays from which you have removed the grids, or similar containers. When the coffee is cold, put the trays into the freezer and leave for 15 minutes, then stir the contents to break up the ice crystals and to turn the mixture sides to middle. Repeat the operation 15 minutes later and after that stir regularly until you are ready to serve it. It will take up to 3 hours in total to freeze properly.

Serve in individual glasses with whipped cream as an optional topping.

CHAPTER SIX

Abandoned Man

A man accustomed to being cooked for is a helpless thing. Abandoned by his cook, either temporarily or permanently, his first instinct is to find someone else to make his meals. This conditioned response may be because women, from his mother onwards, have not only spoiled him, but woven an air of mystery around cooking. They have whispered of barding and basting and double boilers. Like cats, they have spat at frying pans to test the heat or, in apparent ungovernable rage, flung strands of spaghetti at the wall to see if they would stick. The whole performance, from the shopping that seems to require arcane and distressingly female talk – phrases like a pound of skirt or a bag of Desirées – to choosing the one dish of the thirty available, that in some talismanic way his cook will have decreed the only one suitable, could have made a man craven in the kitchen.

On the other hand, he may just have been arrogant and idle or simply not interested. But friends will soon tire of providing for him and he must turn to the fridge and stove and think conscientiously about cooking for himself and for others, because nothing is more lowering than too many solitary meals, and a man left to cook for his children will find they grow fractious on uninterrupted junk food.

Men who cook, particularly those new to the activity, want to make dishes that either have the quality of immediacy, or ones where alchemy in the oven will transform them. Men, on the whole, are not good at diddling about waiting for one thing to happen before proceeding with the next. For this reason, a stew which can be left alone to cook for hours and requires no cosseting is a favourite. Most men, even abandoned ones, believe it improves with keeping and that it can be jazzed up with curry powder and raisins towards the end of its life. This is not so, although the sauce of a stew does mellow when it is cooked on one day, heated up and eaten the next.

Fundamental Beef Stew	Baked Potatoes with Soured
Steak Tartare	Cream and Caviare
Hamburgers Chic or Childish	Salad Dressing
Kidneys en Pyjama	Omelette Soufflé au Grand
Grilled Kidneys	Marnier

Fundamental Beef Stew

This recipe contains the basic steps of any stew or casserole, i.e. preparing the meat, sealing it and browning it, adding flavourings and spices, making a stock and, where appropriate, thickening or reducing the sauce. Once the steps have been understood, they can be applied to any resilient cut of meat or tough game bird or fowl. Beef, especially the cheaper cuts, is particularly suitable for stewing, and the first recipe serves as a good model for all stews. Details in flavouring must be followed to avoid any risk of a school dinner result but they can of course be varied according to whim.

Serves 4 (Quantities can be doubled easily)

2 lb/1 kg stewing beef – referred to
  at the butcher's as braising
  steak or stewing steak
1 tablespoon flour
1 teaspoon ground ginger
salt and freshly ground black
  pepper
1 oz/30 g butter

2 tablespoons olive or vegetable oil
2 medium-sized onions, peeled and
  chopped
4 carrots, peeled and chopped
1 pint/625 ml Guinness or red wine
1 tablespoon soya sauce
2 cloves garlic, peeled
4 strips of orange rind

Turn on the oven to 170°C/325°F, Gas 3.

Trim any obvious fat from the meat and cut the meat into cubes about 1½ inches/4 cm square. Pieces on the large side emerge looking appetizing rather than bitty. Spread the flour on a plate. Sprinkle it with the ginger, a good pinch of salt and eight turns of the pepper mill – if you have no pepper mill, substitute two pinches of pepper and buy one. Coat the meat lightly with the flour which, when you come to fry the pieces, will help them brown and provide a foundation for the sauce.

In a large frying pan, or cast-iron casserole, melt the butter in the oil and let them get hot. The oil stops the butter burning at the temperature it normally would. Fry the onion and carrot until they take on a colour. Remove them to an ovenproof dish or on to a plate if you are cooking in a cast-iron pot.

Brown the meat carefully on all sides. This is an important step which, if done half-heartedly, will spoil the colour of the finished product. Don't cook for more than about 4 minutes, or the meat will begin to seize up. Take out the meat and add to the vegetables. Pour off any fat remaining in the pan before adding the Guinness or red wine and the soya sauce. Stir vigorously with a wooden spoon, scraping all the crusty bits off the bottom of the pan into the liquid. Bring to the boil. Pour on to the meat and vegetables (or return them to the pan). Add the garlic cloves which you have flattened with the blade of a knife, and the orange rind. This flavour gives a lift to the stew and blends with beef particularly well. Tangerine rind works too.

Cover the casserole and place in the oven, and leave to cook for 3–4 hours. Or part cook it one day and finish the next. If the liquid is at all copious when you come to serve the dish, pour it off and boil vigorously to reduce. The meat should not be swimming – just lying back – in the sauce. Taste the sauce and add more salt or pepper or perhaps a pinch of sugar if you have cooked with a ropey red wine. Pour back on the meat.

Triangles of fried bread are an easy and appropriate accompaniment to beef stew – or any stew – as they provide a desirable crunch.

To Fry Bread: Cut slices diagonally to give two large triangles and then cut each in half again so that one slice of bread gives you four triangles. Heat 1 tablespoonful of vegetable oil plus 1 tablespoonful of butter in a frying pan until hot but not smoking. Lay in as many slices of bread as the pan will accommodate. Fry until they are brown and crisp on the base (lift up to look), turn over and fry the other side. Drain on kitchen paper.

Steak Tartare

Abandoned men do not feel threatened by mince. It is agreeably malleable and requires no cutting or trimming. It also doesn't resemble the beast from whence it came.

An ideal meal for two, or even one, poor pet, is Steak Tartare. It is important that this is made from high quality beef with little fat, and if there is no mincer or food processor in the house, the best tactic is to buy porterhouse, rump or sirloin steak. Having thus pleased the butcher by your largesse, ask him to mince it. Then proceed as follows.

Serves 2 as a main course, 4 as a first course

8 oz/250 g minced or finely chopped (e.g. in a food processor) steak
1 small onion or 2 shallots, very finely chopped
1 dessertspoon capers
3–4 anchovy fillets
Worcestershire sauce or Tabasco
1 tablespoon olive oil
salt and pepper
egg yolks (optional)

There are two approaches to this. One is to serve a patty of the raw chopped meat for each person with, alongside, small mounds of finely chopped onions, capers and anchovies; the oil, Worcestershire sauce or Tabasco and seasoning should be close by. Each person mixes up the meat according to preference. The other approach is to do the mixing first. One school of thought is that steak tartare is raw meat and should taste of meat. Another attempts to disguise that stark fact.

Therefore, for a main course, it is probably better served on a DIY basis. For a first course, mix it first, going easy on the capers which can be overwhelming.

Steak tartare is often served with a raw egg nestling on top, but we think olive oil in the mixture is preferable and would make the heart beat a little more healthily. Black bread goes well with the dish.

Hamburgers Chic or Childish

Less marvellous mince can be turned into hamburgers which, made according to the following method incorporating a tip known so far only to few, can be served to adults and children with equal success. Children, conditioned by fast food chains, will stipulate a sesame seed bun. Others might prefer the simple pan sauce described below.

Serves 4

1 lb/500 g minced beef
1 egg yolk
1 large onion, finely chopped
   (optional)

pepper
coarse sea salt

Mix the meat with the egg yolk, onion if you fancy it, and pepper – but *no salt*. Shape the mixture into four or six patties depending on the thickness preferred. Sprinkle sea salt generously into a thick-bottomed frying pan, preferably made of iron. When the pan is hot and the salt practically jumping, sear the hamburgers on both sides. You need no fat in the pan. A tasty crust will form, a pleasing contrast to the yielding, and if you like it that way slightly rare, centre. Children usually prefer the hamburgers cooked further to a consistent grey/brown.

Serve the burgers in a bun or make a sauce as follows: clean out the excess salt from the pan but leave the juices which will have come from the burgers. Shake in a teaspoonful of plain flour and stir around quickly until it browns. Add single or double cream and stir until you have a pale brown sauce. Taste for seasoning and serve separately. You may also use soured cream or, if on a health kick, yoghurt.

Kidneys en Pyjama

Kidneys en Pyjama is absurdly simple and the name will find favour with a lonely chap. By now the butcher should have become a friend and can be persuaded to rip kidneys still encased in their suet (fat) from lamb carcasses. If not, this dish requires not so much skill in preparation as in shopping, since more depradations from the EC mean kidneys in their suet are not available everywhere.

Serves 2

4 even-sized potatoes, not too
   large
a little oil

4 lambs' kidneys encased in their own
   fat
Dijon mustard
salt and pepper

Turn on the oven to 200°C/400°F, Gas 6.

Wash the potatoes, dry them, rub them with a little oil and

sprinkle them with salt. Put them on the middle shelf of the oven, two on each side. Put the kidneys in their fat in a baking tin and place it on the same shelf in the oven. Leave for 1 hour.

Trim any remaining fat away from the kidneys, which are now perfectly cooked, having been self-basted throughout the hour. Split open the potatoes, or take a slice off the top of each one and scoop out a hole. Place a teaspoonful of Dijon mustard, then a kidney, in each potato. Add a dribble of the hot fat and a little salt and pepper and serve.

Grilled Kidneys

Here is a way with kidneys sold innocent of their fat. Kidneys lend themselves well to grilling and are done in double-quick time.

Serves 3–4

8 lambs' kidneys	a good pinch of dry mustard powder
3 oz/90 g soft butter	a pinch of ground cinnamon
2 large garlic cloves, crushed in a press or finely chopped	a pinch of salt and freshly ground black pepper
1 small onion or 2 shallots, finely chopped	2 tablespoons Madeira or strong red wine
1 teaspoon Worcestershire sauce or Tabasco (if you want hotness)	2 tablespoons chopped parsley

Cut each kidney through the gristly core keeping the kidney shape, i.e. ending up with a long half rather than a squat half. Carefully peel off the membrane that covers the meat and tidy up the core, cutting off as much fat and gristle as you can. Scissors are best for this. Turn on the grill to high. Place kidneys core side up in a lightly oiled pan that can go under the grill; either the grill pan without its rack or a large frying pan. Mix together the butter, garlic, onion and seasonings. Spread the result evenly over the kidney halves. Grill for about 5 minutes. Remove them to a plate and keep warm in the oven. Put the grill pan on top of the stove. Turn on the gas or electricity under it. Pour in the Madeira or wine and scrape about with a wooden spoon until you have a little sauce. You might want to add more wine or a little water to eke it out. Taste to see if it needs more of any of the seasonings. Pour on to the kidneys, sprinkle on the parsley and serve. A triangle of fried bread (see page 65) makes a good base for each kidney. You might also like to grill flat field mushrooms alongide the kidneys to provide an instant vegetable.

Baked Potatoes with Soured Cream and Caviare

If you only have potatoes in the house, buy a jar of Danish lumpfish roe (or caviare if you can run it) at the late-night delicatessen, plus a carton of soured cream. Bake the potatoes as in Kidneys en Pyjama and, when cooked, split them open and serve with the soured cream, caviare and perhaps a small jug of melted butter; a seductive meal.

Salad Dressing

The problem of serving vegetables with a meal, which involves feats of timing that the newcomer cook might shy from, can be avoided by serving a salad. A mixture of green leaves is both the simplest and the nicest – forget those terrible English salads with tomato quarters, beetroot, cucumber and hard-boiled egg jostling one another in the bowl – but it stands or falls on its dressing. A vinaigrette should be freshly made, not shaken in a bottle like a can of emulsion paint. It will taste subtly different every time but that is only an advantage.

It is worth purchasing the best ingredients: extra virgin olive oil, wine vinegar, sea salt, freshly ground pepper. The ratio of oil to vinegar should be about 4 or 5 to 1 and it is best to dissolve the salt first in the vinegar before stirring in the oil. Crushed garlic, powdered mustard and fresh herbs can be added to taste. Dress the salad just before it is to be eaten.

Omelette Soufflé au Grand Marnier

It is unlikely that an abandoned man, having managed to make one or two courses, will feel like making dessert. It is possible nowadays to buy exotic fruits, excellent sorbets and reasonably good *pâtisserie* that will stand in. However, if the meal itself has been purchased at the delicatessen and has been served cold, the following will redeem any flatness. It is a culinary ace up a man's sleeve.

Serves 2

2 eggs
2 heaped dessertspoons caster
  sugar

2 tablespoons Grand Marnier (or
  other liqueur)
½ oz/15 g butter

Separate the eggs, putting the yolks in one medium-sized bowl, the whites in another. Add the sugar to the yolks and mix well. Stir in the Grand Marnier. This can be done before dinner. Just before you want to eat dessert, whisk the egg whites until they stand in peaks. Fold in the yolk mixture. Heat the butter in an omelette pan until it is foaming, then pour in the egg mixture and, after a few minutes, attempt to turn the whole thing over. It won't work but that doesn't matter. It simply gives more delicious crisp sugary cooked brown surface to eat. Wait another minute or two and serve.

CHAPTER SEVEN

After-Theatre Supper

Because most plays, concerts or operas start at a time that makes it impossible, or anyway unappealing, to eat beforehand, there is nearly always a moment when, during a dull monologue or less than perfectly sung aria, your thoughts turn to food. When they do, it is comforting to know that something has been prepared; that you are not reliant on restaurants which are invariably hazardous late in the evening. Also, should the performance give rise to combative discussion, as all good performances should, then it is helpful to be at home where no waiter is going to interrupt your most trenchant observation with 'Who's the *vichysoisse*?'; for a waiter's timing in this respect is always perfect.

Back home, hungry and thirsty, it is possible to have a drink instantaneously and with the first course ready and waiting, to eat fairly immediately, two conditions restaurants frequently fail to fulfil. You, the host, will not want at this point to tie on a pinny and start flurrying around, so it is vital that, apart from easy tasks like heating a soup or grilling a brochette, the work is all done.

Supper is a word we use advisedly. Even though you have been deprived of food, if not drink, for the past three hours or so, it is late and would be a mistake to consume a heavy dinner. The least appetizing after-theatre meal we know was one of roast beef and Yorkshire pudding timed to be perfect at approximately the end of Act Two. By the time the play was over and the members of the party had taken themselves across London to eat it, stern dry meat and rigid batter was the none too festive greeting.

The recipes below have been designed as menus: the one with kedgeree more suited to winter, the one featuring cold turbot composed with summer in mind.

There are also suggestions for simply an array of dishes, similar to a Greek or Middle Eastern *meze*, from which people can help themselves as they wish. We feel that this is a particularly agreeable form of eating. It promotes relaxation and strolling. When you have been sitting pinned to your seat for some time, you do not wish to be stuck with what may well turn out to be another drama, albeit a domestic one. Also, the sight of a spread of food is a cheering one. With the help of a food processor, it is now easy to make interesting dips and also items like fish pâté. The recipes for a *meze* in this chapter can be embellished with hummus from Budget Dinner Party and practically any of the salads listed in the index. Chicken wings, vigorously seasoned, then fried or grilled, can be prepared at the last minute and are a welcome hot addition.

Naturally, the ideas contained in this chapter are equally well suited to other forms of entertaining, but the concept of an after-theatre supper or, indeed, an after-cinema supper, seems an important one to sustain and promote. With the ticket prices the way they are, it makes an evening of entertainment and eating financially conceivable. Making a meal is also a welcome way of rewarding the purchaser of the tickets.

Bortsch

Grilled Peppers

Ceviche

Kedgeree

Turbot with a Mild Aïoli

Brochette of Lambs' Kidneys with
Chorizo Sausage

Barley Salad

Fennel, Radish and Cress Salad

Fruit Tart

Black Treacle Jelly with Cream

Apple Purée

Ideas for a Meze:

Dolmades

Tabbouleh

Queensberry's Cod's Roe Pâté

Aubergine Pâté

Green Bean Salad

Tomato Salad

Fruit Kebab

Bortsch

Serves 6

1 lb/500 g uncooked beetroot – it
    is best if you can procure them
    with the leaves on – peeled
2 onions
2 large tomatoes, skinned
2 carrots
2 stalks celery
1 lemon

3 pints/1.8 litres beef stock (if you can
    make your own stock from shin of
    beef, this is desirable; failing that,
    you can make an acceptable soup
    with beef cubes)
a little wine vinegar
salt and pepper
8 fl oz/250 ml soured cream

Clean and dice all the vegetables. Prick the lemon all over with a fork, then put the vegetables and lemon in a pan with the stock and simmer until cooked. Pass through a mouli or liquidize. Add the vinegar, salt and pepper to taste. Chill. Serve with a large dollop of soured cream on top.

Grilled Peppers

If you are making this dish as the only hors-d'œuvre, you will need one large pepper per person; if you are using it as part of an array of hors-d'œuvre dishes, half a pepper per person would do.

Serves 6

3 large peppers – one of each
    colour would look prettiest
2 tablespoons olive oil
1 tablespoon tarragon vinegar

½ teaspoon salt
½ teaspoon sugar
freshly ground black pepper
fresh parsley

Quarter the peppers and remove all the seeds. Flatten the strips even if this means slightly breaking them. Put the strips, skin side up, under a hot grill, and grill until they are black and blistering. Then skin the peppers carefully. You may need to return odd pieces to the grill, so don't turn it off.

Arrange the peppers in a flat dish and pour over them the amalgamated mixture of oil, vinegar, salt, sugar and black pepper.

Garnish with parsley. This is good eaten with hot pitta bread or crisp French rolls.

Ceviche

The main point of this recipe is that the fish should be as fresh as possible. Monkfish, turbot, halibut, even fresh haddock or cod can be used.

Serves 2

2 fresh green chillies
1 small piece of fresh root ginger
4 limes (if unavailable, use 3
    lemons)
1 onion
8 oz/250 g white fish (see above)

1 tablespoon olive oil
a small pinch of cayenne pepper
1 good sprig fresh coriander (optional,
    but nice if you can get it)
salt and freshly ground black pepper

First of all, prepare the vegetables. De-seed the chillies and cut them into strips like matchsticks, only thinner; cut the root of ginger in a similar way. The rind of the limes or lemons should also be cut into matchsticks, and the juice squeezed. The onion should be very finely chopped.

Put the fish with all these prepared ingredients in a shallow dish, together with the oil, cayenne and finely chopped coriander. Leave in a cool place for at least 3 hours, turning the fish occasionally. It should end up looking milky – as though you had cooked it.

Before serving, season with salt and black pepper.

Kedgeree

Kedgeree, the anglicized version of the Indian dish of rice and lentils called *khichri*, is altogether an amenable dish. The constituent parts can be prepared some time before assembling and, once assembled, the dish can be cooled and then successfully reheated in a double saucepan. For the purposes of after-theatre eating, it would be a good idea to hard-boil the eggs while you are heating up the otherwise completed kedgeree, then chop them and scatter on just before serving. Try to buy Finnan haddock on the bone; it is infinitely preferable to the dyed fillets.

Serves 4–6

12 oz/375 g smoked haddock
milk to cover the fish (approx. 1
    pint/625 ml)
8 oz/250 g rice (preferably
    Basmati)
1 tablespoon vegetable oil

2 oz/60 g butter
2 onions, peeled and thinly sliced
1 dessertspoon ground turmeric
salt and freshly ground black pepper
3 eggs, hard-boiled

Turn on the oven to 180°C/350°F, Gas 4.

Put the haddock in an ovenproof dish, add enough milk to come level with the top surface of the fish and cook for about 20 minutes, until the fish flakes easily. Strain off and reserve the fish-flavoured milk, then remove the skin and bones. Cook the rice using your preferred method. In the oil and butter, fry the onions until golden. Add the turmeric, season and cook gently, stirring, for a few minutes.

Add the haddock and rice, and season; mix gently until the rice is coloured a rich saffron yellow. Use some of the milk to moisten the mixture and more butter if you want richness. Taste for seasoning and be generous with the pepper. Scatter the dish with chopped hard-boiled eggs.

Turbot with a Mild Aïoli

Serves 6

2 lb/1 kg turbot or other firm
    white fish (haddock is very
    good)

3 shallots or a bunch of spring onions
½ cauliflower

COURT BOUILLON:

1 onion
1 lemon
1 large carrot

1 bay leaf
8 peppercorns
1 glass white wine

AÏOLI:

1 fat clove garlic (or more
  depending on preference)
2 egg yolks

½–¾ pint/300–475 ml oil – half olive
  and half vegetable
salt and pepper
lemon juice

In a pan large enough to hold the turbot in one piece, put the *court bouillon* ingredients. Put in the trimmed fish, and add cold water until the fish is covered, just. Bring the pan slowly to the boil and when it has reached boiling point, give it one or two definite bubbles, cover the pan and turn off the heat. Let the fish become completely cold in its liquid by which time it should be perfectly cooked.

Make the aïoli by mixing the crushed garlic into the egg yolks. Slowly start to add oil, mixing with a wooden spoon. As each bit of oil is incorporated, add some more. When you have a definite stable-looking emulsion you can add the oil with a freer hand. Season with salt, pepper and lemon juice.

Flake the fish and fold it into the mayonnaise with the shallots which should have been peeled and finely sliced into crescents (or the spring onions, cleaned and chopped) and sprigs of cauliflower which should have been boiled for no more than 4 minutes. Pile the mixture into a pretty dish. The recipe given for grilled peppers (*see* page 73) goes well with this dish.

Brochette of Lambs' Kidneys with Chorizo Sausage

This recipe was invented for a barbecue, but it works almost as well using a domestic grill, the richness of the *chorizo* (a spicy paprika-red Spanish sausage available in delicatessens) offsetting the compact quality of kidneys. Assemble the dish on stainless steel or wooden skewers and grill when you return from the theatre.

Serves 4–6

8–10 lambs' kidneys
1 lb/500 g chorizo sausage
1 Spanish onion or 3 shallots

8–16 fresh sage leaves or, if
  unobtainable, 8 bay leaves
vegetable oil
salt and freshly ground black pepper

Chop the kidneys into three and remove any gristle and the hard core. Chop the sausages into lengths slightly shorter than 1 inch/ 2.5 cm. Peel the onion or shallots, quarter, and separate the layers so you have pieces roughly the size of the meat. Thread the skewers alternating the kidneys and sausage and interspersing them with onion and the occasional sage or bay leaf. Dribble oil rather scantily on to them.

When the time comes for the main course, grill the skewers fiercely, for a total time of about 8 minutes, turning frequently. Season with salt and pepper.

Serve with barley salad (*see* next recipe) and lemon quarters to squeeze over.

Barley Salad

Victor Gordon, author of *The English Cookbook*, is keen to revive the use of barley in forms other than barley water. It has a good taste, a distinctive texture and is full of goodness. The snag about barley is the cooking time needed. A pressure cooker can reduce it or you can blanch it with three successive kettles of boiling water, allowing it to soak 3 minutes in each water before being drained ready for the next. This is Victor Gordon's recipe.

Serves 4–6

7 oz/200 g pot barley
4 tablespoons olive oil
4 tablespoons sunflower seed oil

salt and freshly ground black pepper
4 tablespoons chopped parsley
4 spring onions or 2 shallots
lemon juice to taste

Boil the barley in salted water – it could take up to 3 hours without the blanching described above. Take it off the heat when it is yielding, but still slightly *al dente*. Drain it patiently, removing as much water as the absorbent cereal will allow.

Put the barley into a salad bowl. While it is still hot, add the oils, pepper and a little salt; mix well. When it has cooled down to tepid, add the parsley and chopped spring onions or shallots. When it is cold, add the lemon juice gradually, tasting until you have the right acidity. 'Much nicer than boring old rice salad, this stands comparison with the cracked wheat salads of Levantine cooking.'

Fennel, Radish and Cress Salad

Serves 4–6

1 large fennel root
1 bunch radishes
1 tablespoon olive oil
juice of 1 lemon

½ teaspoon salt
pepper
2 boxes cress

Slice the fennel as thinly as possible, and trim and slice the radishes horizontally in thin rounds. Mix in a salad bowl with a dressing of oil, lemon juice, salt and pepper. Before serving, add the cress and toss the salad well.

Fruit Tart

Serves 4–6

5 oz/150 g butter
8 oz/250 g plain flour
salt
1 egg yolk

2 large cooking apples
4 large tablespoons apricot jam
juice of ½ lemon

Rub the butter into the flour throughly; add a pinch of salt. Make a well in the centre of the flour: mix a little water with the beaten egg yolk and add to the flour until you have a soft dough; you may not need all of the egg, so add it by degrees. Roll out the pastry and line a buttered 10-inch 25-cm tart tin or dish. Put this in the fridge for at least 2 hours.

Turn on the oven to 180°C/350°F, Gas 4. We find it better to bake the pastry blind, which means putting some butter beans on a piece of foil into the tart to hold down the centre of the pastry. Bake until the tart is a pale biscuit colour, then take out and cool, turn off the oven. While it is baking, you can prepare the fruit.

We are suggesting apples because they are obtainable all the year round, but of course a wide variety of fruit could be used.

Peel, core and quarter the apples and then cut them into thin slices and lay between two damp cloths. Do use a stainless steel knife for this.

Make the apricot glaze as follows: put the jam with 2½ fl oz/75 ml water into a pan, bring gently to the boil and cook for 5 minutes. Add the lemon juice, stir and cook again until the glaze just drops from the spoon. When the tart is cool, remove the butter beans, and paint glaze all over the bottom of the pastry; this helps to prevent the juice from the fruit soaking into the pastry.

Turn on the oven to 150°C/300°F, Gas 2. Lay the apple pieces slightly overlapping round and round until you have entirely covered the tart. Paint generously with more glaze and return to the oven for about 20 minutes. Serve cold.

Black Treacle Jelly with Cream

Serves 4–6

4 oz/125 g black treacle
2 lemons

¾ packet gelatine
½ pint/300 ml whipped cream

Put the tin of treacle in a saucepan of boiling water so that it becomes easy to pour. Squeeze the lemons. Dissolve the gelatine in a bowl with a little hot water, stirring it with a fork until it is thoroughly melted. Pour black treacle into a pint jug, add the strained lemon juice, gelatine and as much hot water as necessary to fill the jug. Stir the mixture well and pour into a shallow dish and, when cool, put into the fridge.

Serve with whipped cream.

Apple Purée

This is a very simple pudding, but light and refreshing.

Serves 4–6

2 lb/1 kg cooking apples
3 oz/90 g brown sugar

3 oz/90 g unsalted butter
a pinch of ground cinnamon

Peel, quarter and core the apples, making sure that there is no core left. Put the quarters into an enamel pan with about 2 tablespoonfuls of water – just enough to stop them sticking before they start to exude their own juice – and the sugar. Stew very gently until soft. Then add the butter and let it melt into the purée, and finally add the pinch of cinnamon.

Put the purée into a large bowl and beat with an egg whisk until smooth. (You can put it in the food processor, but the texture is mysteriously not the same and, in our view, inferior.)

This should be eaten cold – with whipped cream or yoghurt if liked.

Ideas for a Meze

Dolmades

This can either be absolutely delicious or taste like a wet school mackintosh down which school lunch has dribbled. To achieve the first effect, you need either fresh young vine leaves or small ones put up in brine or tins, good olive oil, fresh lemon juice, pine kernels and no meat in the mixture. We are adamant on that point.

The quantities below would serve 8–10 people as part of a buffet, but *dolmades* keep well and are hardly worth making in a small quantity.

olive oil	parsley, chopped
2 large onions, peeled and chopped	a few fresh mint leaves
	salt and freshly ground black pepper
6 oz/180 g Basmati rice	30 vine leaves
2 oz/60 g pine kernels	2 lemons
a handful of currants	

In about 4 tablespoonfuls olive oil, gently fry the chopped onion until soft and slightly tinged with colour. Wash the rice, swirling it round to float off any starch. Drain and add to the onions, stirring it round until it glistens. Add a cup of water, the pine kernels and currants, and bring to the boil. Simmer gently until the water is absorbed. It is not necessary for the rice to be completely cooked. Mix in a handful of finely chopped parsley and a few mint leaves, chopped. Season with salt and pepper and allow to cool.

If you are using tinned or packet vine leaves, rinse them well and blanch for 5 minutes in boiling water. If you have fresh leaves, cut out the hard part of the stalk and blanch in boiling water for at least 5 minutes. Drain them on tea towels.

Lay a spoonful of stuffing near the base of a leaf. Fold in the sides and roll into a neat parcel, but not too tight as the rice will swell in the cooking. Squeeze the parcel gently in your hand to seal the envelope. Put any spare leaves in the bottom of a large shallow pan with a lid. Place the stuffed leaves on top with the join of the parcels downwards. Pour on 4 tablespoonfuls olive oil, the juice of 1 lemon and enough water to bring the liquid level with the *dolmades*. Weight them down with a plate and simmer with the lid on gently for about 1 hour, checking from time to time that they have not dried out, but you should end up with the water absorbed and the little parcels shining with oil.

Cool and then remove carefully to a large pretty plate, and if you think they need more lemon, squeeze on the juice of the other lemon.

Tabbouleh

This Middle Eastern dish actually improves by being made some time ahead, as it gives time for the flavours to permeate the bulghur (sometimes called burgul, but otherwise known as cracked wheat). It is important to use the kind that looks like tiny grains and not an English variety that is flaky. Good delicatessens and health food shops will stock it. It is one of these gratifying dishes that is both good for you – think of the iron and vitamin C in the parsley – and delicious.

Serves 4–6

4 oz/125 g bulghur
1 bunch spring onions, cleaned
   and finely chopped
2 large tomatoes, skinned, de-
   seeded and finely chopped
3 tablespoons finely chopped fresh
   mint, (use less mint if dried)
3 oz/90 g fresh parsley, washed and
   finely chopped
3 tablespoons lemon juice
3 tablespoons olive oil
salt and freshly ground black pepper
crisp lettuce leaves or radicchio for
   serving

Pour cold water on to the bulghur and leave to soak for 20 minutes. Drain in a sieve and then squeeze with your hands to remove the water completely. Put in a bowl, add the spring onions and mix very thoroughly, crushing the onions slightly. Add the chopped tomato, mint, parsley, lemon juice, oil and salt and pepper to taste. Mix and try a spoonful to see if you wish to emphasize any flavour.

Serve heaped on to a pretty dish with the lettuce leaves served alongside to be used as scoops or wraps.

Queensberry's Cod's Roe Pâté

The Marquis of Queensberry evolved this recipe and it is far superior to most of the pink emulsions that go by the name of taramasalata. The important point is that the roe should be mixed with a fork and not in a food processor, which breaks up the eggs and creates a paste. Serve it, as they do at Green's Champagne Bar and Restaurant in London's Duke Street, St James's, in white china egg cups with triangle of brown toast alongside and a lemon section for squeezing on.

Serves 4

8 oz/250 g moist smoked cod's roe (bought as a piece)

3 fl oz/90 ml high quality olive oil
fresh lemon juice
freshly ground black pepper

Scrape the roe from its skin and membrane using a sharp little teaspoon. Discard any hard pieces. Put the roe into a bowl and add the oil slowly, mixing all the while with a fork. Squeeze in lemon juice to taste and add a good deal of freshly ground black pepper, but no salt.

Aubergine Pâté

Serves 6

2 large aubergines
1 clove garlic
1 medium-sized onion
1 tablespoon chopped parsley

3 tablespoons olive oil
juice of 1 lemon
salt and pepper

Bake or grill the aubergines until soft – about half an hour. Then scoop out the insides and combine the flesh in the food processor with the other ingredients. Put into shallow bowls.

Green Bean Salad

Serves 6

1½ lb/750 g French beans (the
  younger and smaller, the
  better)

DRESSING:

2 teaspoons caster sugar   *1 small clove garlic, crushed*
1 teaspoon mustard powder   *1 tablespoon tarragon vinegar*
1 teaspoon salt   *3 tablespoons best olive oil*
black pepper

Make the dressing first so that it has time to dissolve and settle. Mix all the dry ingredients and garlic with the vinegar. Then add the oil and mix very thoroughly.

Tail the beans but leave them whole. If you have a big enough steamer, this is the best way to cook them. If not, put them into a pan one-third full of boiling salted water and boil gently until the beans are just *al dente*. Drain thoroughly and then put into a serving bowl. Let them cool a little, but while they are still warm, pour over the dressing to which you have given a last minute stir, and mix well.

The garlic can be omitted if it is unpopular, but this would be a pity.

Tomato Salad

This is a simple dish, but it is often so carelessly made that its pleasure is spoilt. We know that tomatoes have largely lost their personality, but occasionally it is possible to come across a variety that has some taste left. If you feel as gloomy as we do about the likelihood of this, here is a way to make them taste slightly more.

Blanch tomatoes first by dropping them into boiling water for 1 minute. Tomato skins are utterly indigestible. When you have skinned them, cut them in fine slices with a serrated knife, keeping all the juice that runs out. Lay the slices in a flattish dish; sprinkle with a pinch of salt and rather more caster sugar and leave them for an hour or two. Meanwhile, mix one part vinegar to two parts of olive oil, add sugar and salt and generous screwings of black pepper. Add any juice left from the cutting and pour over the dressing. If you have chives, cut a large bunch into small pieces and scatter thickly. If you don't have chives, use 2 or 3 spring onions chopped very finely.

Before serving, baste the tomatoes with the dressing and the extra juice that they will have made.

Fruit Kebab

Because you are making these in advance, sprinkle them lavishly with lemon or lime juice and wrap the dish you lay them on in clingfilm, tightly sealed. Chill in the refrigerator. The fruit you use will depend on what is in season, so the recipe below is a guideline only. Currants or pomegranate seeds can punctuate the skewers and the more exotic the fruit, usually the better. Slender wooden skewers, the kind sold for satay, are the best.

Serves 4–6

½ pineapple	8 oz/250 g strawberries
1 apple or 1 pear	2 kiwi fruit, peeled and thinly sliced
1 small bunch grapes	1 starfruit, thinly sliced
½ melon, shaped into balls or cubes	fresh lemon juice or lime juice
1 mango	

SHOULD YOU WANT TO FLAME THE KEBABS:

granulated sugar	2 tablespoons Cognac or Grand Marnier or other fruit-based alcohol

Prepare the fruit in pieces as much the same size as possible, but using the grapes whole – or halved if they have big seeds – and strawberries whole or halved depending on size. Thread a selection of fruit on to each skewer. Sprinkle with lemon or lime juice, paying special attention to apple or any fruit that discolours in contact with oxygen. Cover with clingfilm and chill until needed.

If you want to flame the kebabs, sprinkle them with granulated sugar and turn them quickly under a hot grill. Heat your chosen alcohol in a small pan. Pour on to the hot kebabs which have been arranged on a serving dish. Take quickly to the table and set the alcohol alight.

CHAPTER EIGHT

Weekend Entertaining

The secret to successful weekend entertaining that does not leave you a wreck is *planning*. You really need to design all your menus on Wednesday so that you can shop either that day or on Thursday. If you leave the planning until Thursday or Friday, you may find that you simply cannot get some vital ingredient, or you may have to spend a disproportionate amount of time searching for such items as pheasant or hare even when they are in season. Not finding them may throw everything else out. We have tried to present you with a choice that both covers the seasons and enables you to do most of the cooking before your guests arrive. This means that you will spend most of Friday in the kitchen (how much depending upon the number of your guests), but it should leave you free to enjoy them when they *do* arrive.

The most relaxed way of dealing with breakfast is to have all ingredients for it laid out, and then to let guests boil themselves eggs if they want to and make toast as they require it. Home-made muesli and yoghurt, a large bowl of fresh fruit, a choice of jam and marmalade, coffee and various teas will do very well, but if you feel that a hot breakfast dish is *de rigueur,* you could make the kedgeree from our After-Theatre Supper section.

Unless the weather is icy, we think a simple and light lunch is desirable: one main course followed by salads and a good cheese board. Dinner can then be the main thrust. A point about dinner is how many you are expected to provide. We think of weekends as beginning on Friday evening and ending some time on Sunday, but it is important to find out whether your guests intend staying for Sunday night supper or not. Whichever they do can turn out to be tiresome if you aren't prepared for it.

If guests are bringing children, it is advisable to keep some emergency food in the fridge or freezer. If they are too young for grown-up dinner you may, in any case, be giving them a separate, earlier supper. Food that is generally popular with children includes pasta, sausages, fish fingers, ham, hamburgers, cheese, bananas, ice-cream – all easy things to have available.

A word must be said about tea – the afternoon meal that used to be an integral part of English life, lurched out of fashion and is now creeping back. The less people have tea in their ordinary lives, the more they seem to love waking with a start from an afternoon snooze over the Sunday papers and finding themselves ambushed by a tea trolley reeking of hot crumpets and chocolate cake. If afternoon tea *happens* to people, they put up little or no fight, and *all* children need a good shot of carbohydrates by late afternoon. We have provided for this in the menu.

But food is not the only weapon in the armoury of the successful weekend entertainer. Comfort, enough privacy and freedom to choose how guests will spend their time are all important attributes. Remember that other people's houses nearly always seem colder than your own, so provide flexible warmth accordingly. Bedrooms and bathrooms should be places that can be lingered in. Electric blankets are one of the cheapest luxuries available. Do sleep occasionally in the spare room beds: if you find you have spent the night at what feels like the bottom of the Grand Canyon, or perched upon some padded toast-rack, it is time you got some new mattresses. Proper reading lights are also a priority. Our test is that you should be able to read a wartime Penguin in bed without strain. If you can't, then change the lighting. It is also deeply depressing for guests to open wardrobes and find them full of clothes you haven't yet sent to Oxfam. Some space and some decent coat hangers should be provided.

Do not have a lavatory whose flushing practices are so wilfully eccentric as to require desperate handwritten notices. Have it mended. Curtains should draw, taps should turn off; in fact things should work in spare rooms much as you would expect them to do in the rest of the house. There is also a curious myth perpetrated by some hostesses to the effect that if you are only staying two nights in a place, you will need a much smaller bath towel and will hardly notice nylon sheets and pillow, the latter seemingly stuffed with an uninviting mixture of rubber and straw, and blankets better suited to a horse. Also, people over sixty tend to loathe duvets – it is kind to provide an alternative.

Apart from creature comforts, it is desirable to provide varied and good reading matter, flowers – even the tiniest vase with a few sprigs can give great pleasure – a bottle of water and glasses. Tins of biscuits are optional, but if you provide them, do *change* them at regular intervals.

Generally speaking, there are two aims about having people to stay – your enjoyment and theirs – but as these are remarkably interdependent, here for your side of it are a few stones you can turn.

Smoked Trout Pâté
Celeriac Remoulade with
Anchovy Toasts
Egg and Spinach Pie
Chinese Noodle Salad
Crab Mousse
Fish Kebabs
Beth's Shepherd's Pie
Normandy Pheasant
Jugged Hare
Raj Chicken Curry

Bread and Butter Pudding
Toffee Sponge Pudding
Winter Fruit Salad
Brown Bread Ice-Cream
Tea Bread
Mary Coventry's Coffee Cake
Panscones
Making Yoghurt
Muesli
Mrs Howard's Marmalade

Smoked Trout Pâté

Serves 4–6

2 smoked trout
4 oz/125 g unsalted cream cheese

juice of 2 lemons
freshly ground black pepper

Take all the flesh from the trout and put into a liquidizer with the cream cheese and lemon juice. Season with freshly ground black pepper.

This very simple pâté should be made at least 24 hours before it is to be eaten.

Celeriac Remoulade with Anchovy Toasts

Some cookery books tell you to blanch grated raw celeriac, but in our experience, the only result of this is a subsequent watering down of the mayonnaise. What is important is to mix the celeriac into the mayonnaise immediately after the grating, to avoid it taking on a brown hue. The spirited flavour of anchovy toasts complements the creaminess of the celeriac well.

Serves 4

1 large celeriac

FOR THE MAYONNAISE:

2 egg yolks　　　　　　　　　　*a squeeze of lemon juice*
vegetable oil　　　　　　　　　　*salt and pepper*
2 dessertspoons Dijon mustard

FOR THE ANCHOVY TOASTS:

1 tin anchovies　　　　　　　　　*slices of bread*
butter

Make the mayonnaise (a blender or food processor speeds things up) by dribbling the oil on to the well-beaten egg yolks until the emulsion thickens. Flavour it strongly with mustard, a splash of lemon juice and salt and pepper.

Peel and then grate the celeriac and mix with the mayonnaise immediately, giving it no time to discolour. Taste and adjust the seasoning if necessary.

Mash 3 or 4 anchovies into about 2 oz/60 g butter. Toast slices of bread on one side, spread the untoasted side with the anchovy butter and put, anchovy butter-side up, under the grill until the butter is melted and the bread crisp. Cut into fingers and serve with the celeriac.

Egg and Spinach Pie

Serves 6

12 oz/375 g shortcrust pastry (see　　*1 tablespoon sunflower seed oil*
　page 78)　　　　　　　　　　　*12 oz/375 g Ricotta cheese*
1½ lb/750 g spinach　　　　　　　*salt and pepper*
1 large sweet onion　　　　　　　*6 eggs*

For this dish you need a medium-sized pie dish of the kind that you would use for apple pie. Make the pastry, then, reserving one-third for the top of the pie, line the bottom and sides of the pie dish and put it in the fridge.

Turn the oven to 180°C/350°F, Gas 4.

Wash the spinach and cook it in the water that clings to the washed leaves. Chop it well, drain and leave to cool in a large bowl. Fry the peeled and finely chopped onion in oil until it is beginning to go brown. Mix the Ricotta cheese into the spinach, adding some salt and pepper. When thoroughly mixed, add the fried onion.

Now put this mixture into the pie dish, and in the mixture make 6 fairly deep indentations with your knuckles; each must be deep enough to accommodate an egg. Carefully break each egg into position. Roll out the remaining pastry fairly thinly and place on top of the pie. Score the pastry with a knife to mark the position of the eggs; each person should get one.

Bake in the oven for 25 minutes and serve hot.

Chinese Noodle Salad

It is important to find the right noodles for this dish. They are called bean thread noodles and are obtainable at an oriental supermarket or grocer. They need no cooking, just boiling water poured on to them. They will turn soft and transparent and have a unique slippery, sensual texture. They make a perfect summer dish.

Arrange the various garnishes to look aesthetically pleasing on top of the noodles and mix only at the time of serving. When you are in the Chinese supermarket, try to find a pack of wind-dried sausages, as their aniseedy flavour adds a special piquancy to the mixture.

Serves 4–6

8 oz/250 g bean thread noodles
1 dessertspoon sesame seed oil or
 vegetable oil
2 oz/60 g dried Chinese
 mushrooms
1 bunch spring onions
½ cucumber

8 oz/250 g cooked chicken, cut into
 fine strips or 8 oz/250 g steamed
 prawns, finely sliced or 4 Chinese
 wind-dried suasages, sliced on the
 diagonal and steamed or a
 combination of these

FOR THE SAUCE:

2½ tablespoons soya sauce
1 tablespoon wine vinegar
1 tablespoon peanut butter
2 teaspoons sugar
1 teaspoon chilli oil

1 tablespoon dry sherry
2 tablespoons vegetable oil
1 fat clove garlic, finely chopped
salt and freshly ground black pepper

Put the noodles into a large bowl and cover them with boiling water. Leave them for 5 minutes until they are soft and translucent. Drain well and toss in the sesame oil. Soak the dried mushrooms in hot water for 15–20 minutes or until they are tender; drain and cut into thin strips. Clean the spring onions and slice finely lengthways. Cut the cucumber into matchsticks. Prepare your chosen protein, but if using the sausage, steam it close to the time of serving.

Mix together the ingredients for the sauce, then toss the noodles in half the sauce and arrange them on a large flat serving dish. Place heaps of the garnish on top of the noodles and bring to the table in this manner. At the moment of serving, toss everything together with the remaining sauce.

Crab Mousse

Serves 4–6

1 lb/500 g crabmeat
¾ pint/475 ml fish aspic (see below)
2 tablespoons mayonnaise

2 tablespoons double cream
1 teaspoon curry powder
1 teaspoon tomato purée
1 tablespoon lemon juice

FISH ASPIC:

It is much better to make the fish aspic yourself and it's not at all difficult. Ask your fishmonger for the fish trimmings and you can also add the peelings from prawns if you happen to be using them for something else.

1 lb/500 g fish trimmings and scraps
¼ pint/150 ml white wine
1 onion
1 carrot

2 bay leaves
1 sprig of thyme
2 sprigs of parsley
½ oz/15 g gelatine

Put everything for the fish aspic except the gelatine into a pan together with 1¾ pints/1 litre water, and bring slowly to the boil. Simmer for 20 minutes, strain through muslin and return to the pan. Boil to reduce to ¾ pint/475 ml.

Melt the gelatine in a little of the hot fish stock, then stir this into the rest of the stock and leave in a separate bowl until it is beginning to set.

Mix the crabmeat very thoroughly in a bowl. Add the mayonnaise and double cream, then add the curry powder, tomato purée and finally the lemon juice.

Stir this into the crab mixture, and put into a lightly oiled mould or dish, and place it in the fridge. When it has set, you can turn it out and garnish it.

Fish Kebabs

Serves 6

2 lb/1 kg firm white fish: we think turbot, halibut or monkfish are particularly good

12 oz/375 g small button mushrooms

2 medium-sized onions

8 oz/250g streaky bacon, cut finely

3 peppers – ideally one each of yellow, red and green

24 bay leaves

¼ pint/150 ml olive oil

juice of 1 large lemon

1 tablespoon crushed coriander seeds

salt and pepper

You need to prepare each ingredient and lay it on a separate dish. Allow 2 skewers per person.

Chop the fish into 1-inch/2.5-cm cubes or as near that as anatomy will allow. Wipe the mushrooms with a damp cloth and plunge them in boiling water for a minute (this helps to stop them splitting when you skewer them).

Peel the onions and then ease off their outer skins, cutting them into pieces slightly larger than your fish pieces. Cut the bacon in 1-inch/2.5-cm length pieces. Halve the peppers, remove all the seeds and cut into pieces the same size as the onion.

Now, skewer a piece of onion, fish, bay leaf, mushroom, bacon and pepper, easing each piece along the skewer. Continue until the skewer is full.

Make a marinade with the oil, the lemon juice, the crushed coriander, salt and pepper and put this in a large shallow dish long enough to accommodate the skewers. Lay the kebabs in it and roll them over gently until everything is coated. The kebabs can be left like that in the fridge overnight.

Turn the kebabs in the marinade once more before you grill them. They will need turning once under the grill, and should be grilled just long enough to cook the fish – about 10 minutes.

Beth's Shepherd's Pie

The best shepherd's pie is made with minced raw lamb. You can, of course, use left-over cold meat – the original intention of the dish – but it is unlikely, these days, that one has a big enough joint to have a couple of pounds of left-overs. You could use beef, but it tends to go into little pellets in an oily sauce whilst lamb manages to keep its unctuousness to itself. The mint is an important ingredient, naturally suited to lamb.

Serves 6–8

4 oz/125 g bacon, finely chopped
1 tablespoon olive oil
2 large onions
3 carrots
4 stalks celery
3 cloves garlic
2 lb/1 kg minced raw lamb
4 fl oz/125 ml milk
1 14-oz/425-g tin tomatoes

1 dessertspoon dried oregano
1 teaspoon ground cinnamon
1 tablespoon Worcestershire sauce;
1 tablespoon chopped fresh mint
2 lb/1 kg potatoes (cooked and mashed
  with milk and butter)
2 oz/60 g Cheddar or Gruyère cheese,
  grated

Fry the bacon gently until the fat runs, then add the olive oil. Clean and chop the onions, carrots and celery, or shred all three in a food processor. Sauté the vegetables and finely chopped garlic in the oil until softened. Stir in the meat and brown it carefully. Next add the milk and let it bubble away. This is always a good tip with mince as it lends a desirable sweetness. Whizz the tomatoes in a liquidizer or food processor, and add them to the meat together with the seasonings.

Simmer everything gently on top of the stove or in the oven (set at 150°C/300°F, Gas 2) for at least 1 hour, preferably longer, then turn into a pie dish. Cover with mashed potato, sprinkle with grated cheese, and heat through in the oven (set at 200°C/400°F, Gas 6), or under the grill if the meat and potatoes are still hot. You can, of course, make the pie in advance, chill or freeze it, and heat through when wanted.

Normandy Pheasant

This simple method of cooking pheasant results in a silky, luxurious dish, the cream and the apples doing the work themselves in melting down into a sauce. A nice accompaniment would be puréed Jerusalem artichokes, enthusiastically seasoned with freshly ground black pepper. If you wish to avoid using quantities of double cream, substitute *fromage blanc* or *petit-suisse* for half the amount of cream. For greedy guests, allow one pheasant for two people, although the richness of this dish means that you should be able to stretch one bird to three.

Serves 6

2 oz/60 g butter
2 tablespoons oil
2 plump pheasants
4 dessert apples, peeled, cored and
   sliced

4 tablespoons Calvados or 1 pint/625
   ml dry cider, reduced by vigorous
   boiling to 4 tablespoons
½ pint/300 ml double cream or ¼ pint/
   150 ml double cream plus a petit-
   suisse or some fromage blanc
salt and freshly ground black pepper

Turn on the oven to 190°C/375°F, Gas 5.

In half the butter and the oil, sauté the trussed pheasants (without their pork back fat, if provided) until golden on all sides. Remove from the pan and in the remaining butter and other pan juices, gently fry the apple slices.

Find an earthenware casserole or similar ovenproof dish with a lid that will hold the pheasants quite snugly. Place the apples in the bottom, and the pheasants on top. Add the Calvados or cider to the pan juices, bubble them a minute or two and then pour them on the pheasant. Cover and cook in the oven for about 30 minutes. Remove the casserole from the oven, and add the cream. Season with salt and freshly ground black pepper. If you are wanting to use less cream for health reasons, do as the French do and put a *petit-suisse* cheese inside the bird and pour in the smaller amount of cream.

Take this opportunity to turn the pheasants over, i.e., breast-side down. Return the casserole to the oven for another 15 minutes.

Place the birds on a warmed serving dish. Stir the contents of the casserole until well amalgamated, reducing the sauce, if necessary, by boiling for added thickness. Pour it around the pheasants, and serve.

Jugged Hare

When you buy the hare, the blood should be kept. A hare is often sold with a bag over its head into which the blood has dripped. If the hare has been frozen, it will be in a sealed bag and the blood should also be contained in the bag. In either case, reserve the blood carefully; it is essential for the sauce. A medium-sized hare will serve 6.

Joint the hare and place in a marinade made as follows:

MARINADE:

1 tablespoon redcurrant jelly	*1 teaspoon thyme*
3 fl oz/90 ml mushroom ketchup	*2 bay leaves*
1 onion, cut into thin slices	*2–3 sprigs bruised parsley*
3 fl oz/90 ml port	*½ teaspoon allspice*
3 fl oz/90 ml medium sherry	*6 bruised peppercorns*
3 fl oz/90 ml good olive oil	

Melt the redcurrant jelly in the ketchup and add to the other marinade ingredients. Put the hare pieces in the marinade and leave for 24 hours.

Then assemble the rest of the ingredients, which are:

4 oz/125 g bacon or pork fat	*1 bouquet garni*
2 medium-sized onions, peeled	*½ teaspoon sea salt*
and stuck with 4 cloves each	*juice of 1 lemon and 1 orange*
2 stalks celery, diced	*2 pints/1.1 litres stock*
2 carrots, scrubbed and sliced	*1 wine glass of port*
6 peppercorns	*1 tablespoon redcurrant jelly*
1 teaspoon allspice	

Turn on the oven to 150°C/300°F, Gas 2.

Dry the hare pieces and fry them in bacon fat until brown all over. Then put them into a deep casserole with the vegetables, spices, bouquet garni, salt and fruit juices. Cover with the stock, cover the casserole tightly and cook in the oven for 3 hours, or until the hare is perfectly tender (the time will depend upon the age of the hare).

Take out the hare pieces and then the onions and other vegetables. Thicken the gravy with enough *beurre manié* (1 oz/30 g butter to $\frac{3}{4}$ oz/20 g flour kneaded together with a fork) until the gravy is like thin cream. Allow it to boil, then set aside.

Add spoonfuls of the gravy by degrees to the retained blood, then pour it gently into the remaining gravy and add the port and redcurrant jelly. Taste for seasoning – adding salt, pepper, redcurrant jelly or port until you like the flavour: it should be very rich and smooth.

At this point, you can choose whether you will bone the hare or simply put the pieces into a fresh casserole and pour sauce through a strainer on to them. We favour boning, as this makes the eating much easier for your guests, but the classic method is to leave the pieces intact.

We suggest serving this with mashed potatoes or noodles.

Raj Chicken Curry

With the publication of dozens of Indian recipe books, the success of television programmes about cooking Indian food, and the increasing sophistication of Indian restaurants, there is probably not a soul left without an array of whole spices in the kitchen cupboard and some recipe in their head for their personal *garam masala*. Remember, though, when 'curry' meant a jolly good pinch of Vencat and 'exotic' meant adding apples and sultanas and 'condiments' meant sliced bananas, grated coconut and Green Label Mango Chutney? Don't you sometimes long for those uncomplicated days?

This recipe will stir fond memories in anyone over a certain age – who knows, maybe curry is still made this way in schools and canteens – and is ideal for weekend entertaining as it improves upon being reheated; in fact, it should be made one day and served the next. Serve with it a large bowl of Basmati rice (see the Vegetarian section) and little bowls filled with cashew nuts, sliced bananas sprinkled with lemon juice, Bombay duck heated through in the oven, mango chutney, lime pickle, wedges of tomato, cucumber cut into sticks, onions cut into rings and dressed with oil into which you have stirrred some cayenne pepper, and poppadums bought in a packet and fried or grilled.

Serves 4–6

1 tablespoon flour
salt and pepper
1 large roasting chicken, cut into
  about 10 pieces
2 tablespoons oil or 2 oz/60 g
  ghee
4 oz/125 g onions, peeled and
  thinly sliced
2 dessert apples, peeled and
  chopped

2 cloves garlic, peeled and crushed
2 tablespoons curry powder from a
  recently purchased tin
8 oz/250 g ripe tomatoes, skinned or 1
  small tin tomatoes
1 tablespoon redcurrant jelly or
  similar
juice of ½ lemon
2 oz/60 g Sharwood's creamed coconut

Season the flour and roll the chicken pieces in it. Heat the oil and brown the chicken pieces carefully; remove. Add the onions, apple and garlic and more oil if you need it and cook them gently until they begin to colour. Stir in the curry powder and cook for a few minutes, stirring constantly to remove the 'raw' taste. Next add the tomatoes, and enough water to make a thin sauce. Stir until smooth. Add the redcurrant jelly and lemon juice. Return the chicken pieces to the sauce and cook extremely gently for 45 minutes.

About 5 minutes before the end of the cooking time, add the creamed coconut broken into small pieces and shake the pan until it dissolves. Taste for seasoning and adjust as necessary. You might want to add more lemon juice or sweeten a little with a spoonful of mango chutney. Let it cool, then refrigerate. The next day, heat through gently, cooking for a further 15 minutes.

Bread and Butter Pudding

Chef Anton Mosimann of the Dorchester Hotel can be credited with the fashionable revival of bread and butter pudding. His approach is not that of making a virtue out of left-overs, but creating a light and delectable dish in its own right.

It is very rich, so serve only small helpings.

Serves 6–8

8 fl oz/250 ml milk
8 fl oz/250 ml double cream
vanilla pod
¼ teaspoon salt
3 large eggs
4 oz/125 g sugar

white bread, sliced
1 oz/30 g butter, softened
fine-shred marmalade
½ oz/15 g sultanas, soaked in water or
  whisky (see recipe)
icing sugar

Bring the milk, cream, vanilla pod and salt slowly to the boil. Beat together the eggs and sugar in a large bowl and add the milk mixture, combining well. Pour the liquid through a sieve into a bowl.

Butter the slices of bread and, here is a tip from Beth Coventry, who serves the pudding at Green's Champagne Bar, spread with the thinnest possible coating of marmalade. Butter a shallow ovenproof dish of a size that will hold the bread only just, and arrange the bread slices in the dish.

Scatter the sultanas around (soaking in whisky rather than water gives a more dynamic result). Pour in the custard and, if it suits your plans, leave for 1–2 hours.

Turn on the oven to 170°C/325°F, Gas 3.

Cook the pudding in a *bain-marie* in the pre-heated oven for 40 minutes. Remove it from the oven, crisp the surface under the grill, sieve on a small amount of icing sugar and serve.

Toffee Sponge Pudding

Serves 6

1 small stale loaf white bread
4 oz/125 g butter
4 oz/125 g Demerara sugar

8 level tablespoons Golden Syrup
grated rind and juice of 1 lemon
¼ pint/150 ml milk

Cut the crusts off the bread and dice into 1-inch/2.5-cm cubes.

Put the butter in a non-stick frying pan and, when melted, add the sugar, lemon juice and rind and the Golden Syrup (warm the syrup tin in a saucepan of hot water to make it easy to measure). Boil this mixture until it is caramel-coloured. While it is boiling, dip the bread into the milk. Fry the milky bread in the sticky mixture, turning the pieces until they are clearly browned. Serve at once, preferably with some whipped cream.

This dish can be prepared up to the boiling mixture being ready, which you can then keep warm in a low oven or on a hot plate: the frying takes about 3 minutes. It is *not* a dish for the figure-conscious, but very popular indeed with children, men and all those nostalgic for good nursery food.

Winter Fruit Salad

Serves 6

1 lb/500 g mixed dried fruit:
  apricots, apples, pears,
  peaches, prunes and figs
3 tablespoons dark brown sugar
2 tablespoons raisins

grated rind and juice of 2 oranges
grated rind of 1 lemon
1 oz/30 g almonds, coarsely chopped
2 oz/60 g walnuts, coarsely chopped

Cover the fruit with water and soak for 1 hour. Then put the fruit and enough of the water you soaked it in to cover in a saucepan and stew fairly quickly until the fruit is soft, but not disintegrated (about 15 minutes, but this does depend a little on the quality of the fruit). Add the sugar the moment you take the pan from the heat and stir it in gently to dissolve. Then add the raisins and the grated rind. Leave to cool and finally add the orange juice and chopped nuts.

This dish can be eaten warm, but in our opinion it is better cold, but not chilled.

Brown Bread Ice-Cream

Recipes for brown bread ice-cream have been around since the late nineteenth century. It may sound an odd notion; but have faith, the crunch of the crumbs contrasts well with the creamy ice and the whole has a surprising nutty flavour.

Serves 4–6

3 oz/90 g wholemeal breadcrumbs
2 oz/60 g butter
4 oz/125 g brown sugar
½ pint/300 ml double cream

½ pint/300 ml single cream
2 eggs, separated
1 tablespoon sherry or rum or brandy
   (all optional)

Fry the breadcrumbs in the butter until crisp. Add 2 oz/60 g of the sugar and cook gently until it caramelizes and coats the crumbs. Whisk the double cream until thick and then beat in the remaining sugar, the single cream, the egg yolks and sherry, rum or brandy if you are using it.

Whisk the egg whites in a clean bowl until stiff, and gently fold them and the crumbs into the ice-cream mixture. Freeze in a suitable container. It is a good idea to stir the mixture after it has been in the freezer for an hour and also remember to remove the ice-cream from the freezer at least 1 hour before you mean to eat it

Tea Bread

4 oz/125 g soft brown sugar
4 oz/125 g margarine
4 oz/125 g sultanas
2 large eggs

1 tablespoon honey
1 teaspoon mixed spice
6 oz/180 g self-raising flour
2 oz/60 g wholemeal flour

Turn on the oven to 180°C/350°F, Gas 4.

Beat the sugar and margarine together and add the eggs, honey and spice. Then add the flours. Put the mixture into oiled tins and bake for 1 hour, then reduce the heat to 160°C/325°F, Gas 3 and cook for a further 15–20 minutes.

Mary Coventry's Coffee Cake

This is a recipe from the mother of one of the authors. It is much enjoyed by her church discussion group when it is Mary's turn to provide the tea. Camp coffee essence is still available and is by far the best coffee flavouring for cakes, even if it does make a rather dubious hot drink.

8 oz/250 g Krona margarine   8 oz/250 g self-raising flour
   (works better than butter)   1 teaspoon baking powder
8 oz/250 g caster sugar   a pinch of salt
4 eggs   2 tablespoons Camp coffee essence

FOR THE FILLING:

1 egg yolk   2 oz/60 g plain chocolate
2 oz/60 g butter, softened   2 dessertspoons Camp coffee essence
2 tablespoons icing sugar

Turn on the oven to 190°C/375°F, Gas 5.

Cream together the margarine and sugar with a wooden spoon (much better than using a food processor in this instance). Beat the eggs in a bowl. Sift together the flour, baking powder and salt, then alternately add the flour and eggs in small quantities to the creamed margarine. Halfway through, beat in 2 tablespoonfuls warm water. When all the eggs and flour have been incorporated, stir in the Camp coffee essence. Divide the mixture between two sandwich tins which have been lightly greased and floured. Bake for 30 minutes.

To make the filling, beat the egg yolk with the softened butter. Add icing sugar to the desired sweetness. Over hot water, melt the chocolate and stir into the mixture, then stir in the Camp coffee essence. When the cake is cool, spread the bottom half with the filling and place the other cake on top. It needs no further icing.

Panscones

These are quick to make, practically foolproof and, served warm, are wonderful with butter and homemade jam. It is worth aiming to have left-overs as they can be fried in bacon fat at breakfast time – a very popular move.

Serves 6

8 oz/250 g plain flour   1 egg
1 teaspoon bicarbonate of soda   ½ pint/300 ml milk
1 teaspoon cream of tartar   1 tablespoon sugar
a pinch of salt   ½ oz/15 g butter, melted

Sieve together the dry ingredients, except for the sugar. Beat together the egg, milk and sugar, and then stir in the melted butter. Add the wet to the dry slowly as if making pancake batter, which you are doing, but aiming for a consistency that drops fairly reluctantly from a spoon. Leave to stand for about 15 minutes.

Heat a griddle or heavy-bottomed frying pan. Rub with butter or vegetable oil. Drop spoonfuls of the mixture which should spread out to scones about 3 inches/7.5 cm in diameter. When bubbles appear on the surface, flip them over and cook the other side. Serving them hot in batches is preferable to keeping the panscones warm in the oven or wrapped in a napkin, as they quickly lose their perkiness.

Making Yoghurt

A large bowl of yoghurt on the breakfast table with, to add to it, some fresh fruit, good honey or just Demerara sugar for crunch, satisfactorily symbolizes health consciousness in what can often be a meal that is a riot of fats and carbohydrates if it is the egg and bacon, toast and marmalade variety. Do not be tempted to use more than a heaped teaspoon of commercial yoghurt as your starter, as using too much can give a sour, grainy result. The second batch of yoghurt is invariably better than the first.

1 quart/1 litre milk (whole, skimmed or reconstituted powdered milk)

1 heaped teaspoon commercially made natural yoghurt (preferably a 'live' yoghurt)

Bring the milk to the boil over a high heat. Watch it carefully and when it starts to rise in the pan, take it off the heat and allow to cool until you can keep your finger in while you count to ten. Should you have a thermometer, this is 43°–49°C/110°C–120°F.

Put the starter yoghurt in a bowl and pour in the milk, mixing well. Put cling film over the bowl, wrap the bowl in a towel and put in a warm place, such as an airing cupboard, or the back of a solid fuel stove, for 6–8 hours or overnight.

Pour off any watery liquid and chill the yoghurt. A wide-necked Thermos jar is a good container for making yoghurt, a glazed earthenware crock lends it a nice folksy feel.

Muesli

8 oz/250 g All-Bran   4 oz/125 g prunes, stoned and chopped
8 oz/250 g crushed oats   4 oz/125 g dried apricots
8 oz/250g bran flakes   8 oz/250 g sultanas
4 oz/125 g almonds, chopped   4 oz/125 g sunflower seeds
4 oz/125 g hazelnuts, chopped

Mix all the ingredients very thoroughly in a large bowl and then
transfer to an airtight container. Stir up again before serving as the
heavier items tend to sink to the bottom.

Mrs Howard's Marmalade

4 lb/2 kg Seville oranges   5 lb/2.5 kg preserving sugar
4 pints/2.3 litres cold water

Slice the oranges, first cutting each fruit into four pieces and extrac-
ting the pips. You can then put the orange segments into a Magi-Mix
for slicing, or continue by hand. Put all the pips into a muslin bag (or
piece of muslin) laid upon a saucer. Put the sliced oranges into a large
bowl with 3½ pints/2 litres of the water. Soak for 24 hours with the
bag of pips.

Bring slowly to the boil in a preserving pan and simmer for
about 2 hours or until the peel is really soft. Put into the bowl again
and leave for up to 48 hours.

Take out the bag of pips, squeezing out the liquor. Add the other
½ pint/300 ml water to make up for the loss in the previous boiling.
Heat the sugar in its bags in the oven. Bring the oranges slowly to
the boil in the pan and then add the warmed sugar. Take off the heat
and leave until the sugar is completely dissolved. Then bring to a fast
rolling boil and after 15 minutes test for setting. (The best way to do
this is to put a saucer into the freezing compartment of the fridge, so
that a sample sets fast when you put it on the saucer. It should
wrinkle and a drop should stay on your finger if it is setting.)

Pot up into heated pots.

This recipe, by one of the author's mothers, makes a good classic
marmalade. We have varied it by adding 1 lb/500 g grapefruit to

every 3 lb/1.5 kg oranges, which gives it a delicious sharp tangy taste. You can also use 1 lb/500 g black treacle to every 4 lb/2 kg sugar to make it darker with a rich taste.

Note: When marmalade is boiling, it is important to watch it and stir it occasionally, to make sure it is not sticking to the bottom of the pan. It is easier to make all jams in small batches.

CHAPTER NINE

Impressing People

One of the things that makes impressing people difficult is that we don't often admit that this is what we want to do. Where meals are concerned, a lot of 'they must take me as they find me' goes on, while the owner of this rugged and unrealistic dictum wrestles with some covert pioneering – such as making their own hot water crust pastry for the first time, 'we just have a bit of pie and salad in the evenings'. Wanting to impress other people carries with it the notion that one is giving a false impression, trying to suck up, wanting to appear grander than one is – or cleverer, or more interesting; this is ignoring the fact that if one wants to *be* cleverer or more interesting, one has to practise. 'Pot luck' always reminds us of the witches in *Macbeth*, whose ingredients for a wicked brew seemed pretty haphazard rather than necessarily efficacious.

Possibly, some of the dishonesty about wanting to impress comes from the sad fact that we *do* sometimes want to impress people whom we don't much like or are afraid of – an uncomfortable feeling. People have been known to feel something of the sort about their in-laws, or their employer; of course, one doesn't have to stand in some formal relationship to somebody before disliking them, but it is the formal relationship that often pre-empts one cutting them out of one's life. We all find ourselves faced with having to cook for such people from time to time. Then there are the people who seem potentially powerful in our lives, whom we hardly know, or do not know at all. If faced with cooking for them, we call it 'wanting to make a good impression', by which we mean we want to impress them with cuisine and general hostmanship. One way and another, practically all of us fall into the trap.

It is worth beginning with two rules. The first is that if one is going to cook a rather splendid – even pretentious – meal, one might as well enjoy it. If that is agreed, the second rule is never to cook anything that you haven't cooked before: you can't enjoy an evening if you are anxious about the food. So we suggest that you select from the following menus and *practise*. You don't need to cook the whole dinner for one family meal: you can take each course separately for practising. The most expensive course is probably the sea bass; if you don't want to afford that for a rehearsal, buy a fresh haddock or a large trout – the principle is the same. Truffles are expensive, but what you need to learn is how to put things under the skin of a bird.

Finally, the best way of impressing people is to look as though you have tried – and succeeded. If you simply succeed without seeming to have tried at all, your efforts will be undervalued, or incur resentment – the one hand tied behind one's back syndrome is always irritating, except to another virtuoso.

Smoked Eel Fillets with Sweetcorn Pancakes and Pancetta	Braised Chicory
	Paillasson
Broad Bean and Artichoke Salad	Grilled Goat's Cheese with
Filo Pastry Pies	Prestigious Salad
Sea Bass Poached with Sauce Verte	Individual Cheese Soufflés
	Raspberry Soufflé
Capon Stuffed under the Skin	Pistachio Parfait

Smoked Eel Fillets with Sweetcorn Pancakes and Pancetta

'But how did you *know* these things would go so well together?' said a guest when served this first course. This is just the sort of question you are hoping for.

Serves 4

6–8 fresh or frozen (preferably fresh) corn on the cob
3 tablespoons double cream
2 tablespoons sifted plain flour
1 tablespoon melted butter
1 egg, well beaten
salt and pepper

8 fillets of smoked eel
8 thin slices of pancetta (if you cannot get pancetta from a delicatessen or Italian grocery substitute thinly sliced streaky bacon)
1 tub crème fraîche

Remove the husks and silk from the corn on the cob or let frozen corn defrost. With a sharp knife cut down the centre of each row of kernels and then scrape down the cob to push the kernels off. Do this for each corn on the cob and collect the result in a bowl. Stir in the cream, flour, melted butter and egg. Season with salt and pepper. Arrange two fillets of eel on each plate. Gently fry the pancetta or bacon until crisp, and while it is frying make the corn pancakes. Oil or butter a separate heavy frying pan and drop spoonfuls of the mixture on to it. Cook over medium heat turning once until the pancakes are delicately browned. If you are doing them in batches keep the pancakes you have made in a warm oven along with the pancetta/bacon when that is ready. Divide the bacon and pancakes – perhaps holding some pancakes back for a second serving – between the plates. Add a spoonful of *crème fraîche* and serve.

Broad Bean and Artichoke Salad

This is a starter, and can only be made when the vegetables are in season. The broad beans should be as small as possible; the artichokes can be small or large.

Serves 6

4 lb/2 kg broad beans in their pods   *6 globe artichokes if large or 9 small*
salt   *ones*

Put a large pan of water on to boil. Cut off the artichoke stalks and when the water is boiling, add a good teaspoonful of salt and then the artichokes. They will take approximately 20 minutes to cook (longer for large ones), but you will have to test them, by pulling off an outer leaf and tasting it to see if the fleshy part is cooked. When they are cooked, drain them in a colander.

Meanwhile, pod the beans and steam them gently for about 6 minutes. They should be just *al dente*. While they are still warm, slough off the grey skins between your first finger and thumb.

Pull the leaves off the cooled artichokes (don't waste them, they are delicious to eat with vinaigrette), and cut out the choke with a sharp knife. Then slice the hearts thinly. Put the broad beans and sliced hearts in a dish and pour over them the following mixture.

DRESSING:

2 tablespoons best olive oil   1 teaspoon salt
juice of 1½ lemons   several good screws of freshly ground
1 teaspoon caster sugar   black pepper

Mix this dressing very thoroughly, making sure that the salt and
sugar are dissolved. Toss the beans and artichokes gently until they
are coated with dressing.

Filo Pastry Pies

Filo pastry (paper thin leaves of dough available from Cypriot bakeries and some enterprising delicatessens and supermarkets; usually
sold by the pound (in 500 g quantities), rolled up and sealed in
cellophane) is one of your best weapons in the battle of impressing
people. If your guests have never encountered it before, they will
assume you have at your fingertips the talents of an Austrian strudel-
maker and you, of course, will just cast your eyes down and let a
little smile play round your lips.

Having mastered the technique of assembling a filo pastry pie
(which basically means separating each sheet with melted butter and
keeping the spare pastry under a damp tea-towel while you work to
prevent it becoming brittle and crackly) you can invent your own
fillings.

Spinach and cheese is a traditionally Greek one. We find that a
mixture of Ricotta and Feta works with the spinach. The two ideas
below make a delicious and quite sustaining first course which you
could follow with something cold and luxurious, such as the
poached sea bass (page 109) or the cold wild duck, which appears in
the chapter Dîner à Deux.

Having prepared the filling, assemble the pie according to the
instructions on page 109.

Hard-boiled Egg and Mushroom Filling

2 oz/60 g butter
1½ oz/45 g flour
1 pint/625 ml skimmed milk
salt and freshly ground black
   pepper
4 eggs, hard-boiled

8 rashers streaky bacon, crisply fried
12 oz/375 g mushrooms, wiped clean
   and sliced
1 dessertspoon vegetable oil
2 tablespoons chopped coriander or
   parsley (preferably coriander)

Melt 1½ oz/45 g butter in a heavy-bottomed pan, stir in the flour, and cook gently for 5 minutes. Add the milk slowly, stirring until you have a smooth, thick sauce. You may need to adjust quantities of milk up or down. Season. Chop the eggs, crumble the bacon. Sauté the mushrooms in a mixture of oil and the remaining butter until they are softened. Strain carefully, leaving the mushroom juice in the pan unless you want to thin your sauce some more, but it will turn it a dull grey colour.

Add the mushroom, eggs, bacon and coriander/parsley to the mixture and stir sensitively, but thoroughly. Let it cool. This preparation may be done in advance if you wish.

Fish Filling

Serves 6–8

1½ lb/750 g firm white fish such as
   haddock or cod (this is not the
   moment to lash out on turbot or
   halibut)
8 oz/250 g peeled prawns – the
   best you can find

1½ oz/45 g butter
1½ oz/45 g flour
1 heaped teaspoon ground turmeric
½ pint/300 ml skimmed milk
salt and pepper

FOR THE COURT BOUILLON:

1 carrot, peeled
1 onion, peeled
1 bay leaf
a few sprigs of parsley

fennel leaves if you have them
6 black peppercorns
1 glass white wine

Poach the fish in a *court bouillon*, which you do by covering it with water, adding the *court bouillon* ingredients, and bringing it very slowly to the boil. Let the liquid only shudder until the fish is opaque right through – depending on your cut of fish, this could take 5–10 minutes. Remove the fish and let it cool. Continue to simmer the court bouillon to extract the maximum flavour from the vegetables.

Meanwhile, melt the butter in a heavy-bottomed pan. Stir in the flour and turmeric and cook over a low heat for a few minutes. Start your sauce by adding some milk and then more, and when you have a very thick, smooth mixture, use the fish stock to obtain a less thick texture, but with still enough body to act as a binder for the fish and prawns. Season to taste with salt and pepper.

Mix the flaked, cooked fish and the prawns gently into the sauce and let the mixture cool. This can be done hours in advance of dinner if you wish.

TO ASSEMBLE:

Turn on the oven to 190°C/375°F, Gas 5.

Decide whether you wish to separate your pastry leaves with melted butter or warm vegetable oil. Butter obviously has the better flavour, but you might be feeling health-conscious. Find a roasting tin or ovenproof dish about the size of one of the sheets of pastry. Melt 4 oz/125 g butter or heat up 4 fl oz/125 ml vegetable oil. Using a pastry brush, paint the base of the pan with butter or oil. Lay in a sheet of pastry. Brush this with your chosen fat and repeat with another four or five sheets. Spread your choice of filling on the pastry. Cover with another five sheets, separating each one with melted butter or oil. Brush the top sheet with oil or butter. Using a knife with a sharp point, score the pastry into diamond shapes, cutting down through quite a few layers. Think about the look of baklava.

Bake in the oven for 45 minutes by which time the pastry should look flaky and the top golden and crackling like autumn leaves. The pie can be served hot or warm.

•

Sea Bass Poached with Sauce Verte

This dish is delicious cold, and as a main course has many advantages. Ideally, you need a fish kettle, but if you don't have one, then substitute a very large pan in which the fish can lie curved. For 6 people, you need a 4 lb/2 kg fish, cleaned, but with the head left on.

First of all, make the *court bouillon*.

COURT BOUILLON:

½ bottle white wine (preferably
   dry)
1 teacup/180 ml tarragon vinegar
2 onions, peeled and sliced
2 carrots, scrubbed and sliced
½ lemon, cut in slices
1 bouquet garni

1 bay leaf
12 peppercorns
1 blade of mace (you can tie the
   peppercorns and mace in a bit of
   muslin if you like, but this is not
   essential)

Put all the ingredients into a large pan together with 3 quarts/3.5 litres water and simmer for 50 minutes. Strain and cool.

Put the fish into the kettle or pan, pour over the cool *bouillon*, and bring gently to boiling point. Then, turn off the heat and leave the fish to cool in the *bouillon*. This method has the advantage that whatever size your fish, it will be cooked when the bouillon is cool. Lift it carefully out of the pan, put it on a board and remove the skin. Then put the fish on a serving dish; it can be garnished with lemon, parsley or any greenery that makes it look attractive.

SAUCE VERTE:

3 egg yolks
1 pint/625 ml olive oil (see
   below)
tarragon vinegar or lemon juice
salt and paper

½ bunch watercress
6 good sprigs parsley with stalks
   removed
a little fresh tarragon or fresh
   coriander if you can get either

Make a mayonnaise with the egg yolks and a light olive oil. Some people prefer to use sunflower seed oil for this; it makes a much lighter mayonnaise, but on the other hand it doesn't have the same taste. Season with tarragon vinegar or lemon juice, black pepper and salt.

Place the greenery in the liquidizer with a tablespoonful of water and whizz until you have a smooth green paste. Add this to the mayonnaise by degrees, until you have the colour that you like. Taste the sauce for final seasoning; a little sugar is often an improvement at this point.

Serve in a sauce boat with the fish.

Capon Stuffed Under the Skin

Once you have learned to stuff a capon (or chicken or turkey) under the skin with butter, or *fromage blanc*, or a purée of vegetables, or truffle slices or whatever, you will probably never roast it straight-forwardly again. There is every possible virtue in the process. The skin is separated from the flesh and so crisps more emphatically, the flavours go into the meat and not the baking dish, the bird is virtually self-basting though with none of the horrid overtones of injections with oil or stock that the phrase can have.

It is rare for the domestic cook to obtain black truffles that have retained worthwhile flavour. Should you do so, then thin slices of truffle slipped under the skin – a dish that rejoices in the name *poulet demi-deuil*, i.e. in semi-mourning – is perhaps the best flavouring. A chicken prepared this way and simmered wrapped up in a roasting bag to catch the juices would be very impressive.

However, we are not presuming upon your powers to obtain black truffles and suggest instead the mixture below:

Serves 6

1 *capon or large free-range roasting chicken, weighting 5–6 lb/2.5–3 kg*	2 *oz/60 g butter, softened* 1 *tablespoon fresh herbs – tarragon is best*
1 *tablespoon vegetable oil* 4 *oz/125 g* fromage blanc or low-fat cream cheese	1 *clove garlic, peeled and crushed* salt and freshly ground black pepper

Turn on the oven to 190°C/375°F, Gas 5.

Rub the chicken with the vegetable oil, giving it a little massage to loosen the skin and make it pliable. Mix together the cheese, butter and seasonings, using more garlic if you like an emphatically garlicky flavour.

Approaching the chicken from the back where there is a loose flap of skin, start to work your hand under the skin. Go gently and pull at the membranes holding the skin to the flesh. You will find there are one or two quite resilient ones, but once these are snapped it is plain sailing. Work your hand up to the tip of the breast bone and over the thighs. Holding a small fork with your fingers over the back and the tines pointing downwards, go in again under the skin and prick the capon flesh in a few places. The skin should now be quite malleable, and you should find it quite easy to spoon in the stuffing and pat it around evenly over the breast and thighs. Spoon any left-over stuffing into the cavity of the bird.

Season with salt and pepper and roast for 1½–2 hours depending on the size of the bird. Baste occasionally towards the end of the cooking time and if the breast is browning too deeply, cover with foil. Serve with the pan juices, which should be like a creamy sauce, and a large bunch of fresh watercress.

Note: To impress people when you are in a hurry, substitute a mashed-up Boursin cheese for the butter, cheese and herb mixture, or even a very mild blue cheese like Dolcelatte.

Braised Chicory

Serves 4–6

2 lb/1 kg chicory (try and get the pieces roughly the same size)
2 oz/60 g butter

½ pint/300 ml chicken stock
juice of 2 lemons

Turn on the oven to 150°C/300°F, Gas 2.

Wipe each piece of chicory with a damp cloth, and trim the ends. Lay the pieces in a shallow buttered baking dish, and pour in the stock and half the lemon juice. Cover the dish with a lid or aluminium foil.

Place the dish in the oven for 1 hour. Transfer to a clean, hot serving dish, with the remaining butter and lemon juice poured over. A little salt may be added at this stage if liked.

Paillasson

It is important to follow the instructions for this potato pancake to the letter, i.e. do not skip the rinsing and drying process. Should you do so, the result could be grey and gluey. It is also important to use a good variety of potato, not some hopeless mealy one suited only to mashing.

Serves 4

1½ lb/750 g potatoes, peeled   salt and freshly ground black pepper
2½ oz/75 g butter

Grate the potatoes, either using a food processor or the medium
blade of a mouli julienne. Rinse potatoes well in two changes of
water. Drain them and spread out on a tea-towel. Roll the towel up
tightly and squeeze the potatoes dry.

Melt 2 oz/60 g butter in an omelette pan, or a pan with a
non-stick surface. Add the potatoes, pressing them down evenly.
Cover and cook over a low heat for 20 minutes, when the potatoes
should be golden and crisp on the bottom.

Turn out on to a large plate. Melt the rest of the butter and slip
the potatoes back into the pan. Cook, uncovered, for another 20
minutes. Slip out on to a hot serving dish and cut as you would a
cake, white side down.

Grilled Goat's Cheese with a Prestigious Salad

This is both a more impressive cheese course than the assembly of a
lot of different varieties, and a more economical one since there
won't be little pieces and wedges left mocking you from the fridge or
larder. If it is not possible to buy whole, small goat's cheese, for
example Chavignol, often sold from a jar of olive oil, use thick slices
cut from a cylinder of *chèvre*.

1 goat's cheese or 1 slice of goat's   a selection of interesting salad leaves,
    cheese, per person   e.g. lamb's lettuce (salade de
1 slice rough country bread per   mâche), frisée, oak leaf lettuce,
    person   raddiccio, watercress
                                             vinaigrette dressing
                                             black pepper

Toast the bread on one side. Put it in an ovenproof dish, untoasted-
side up. Place the cheese on top, trim away the excess bread, and
grind on some black pepper. Cook, either under the grill, or in a hot
oven until the cheese is slightly browned, bubbling and melting, but
not melted.

Arrange a heap of dressed salad leaves on each serving plate with the toasted cheese beside it.

Individual Cheese Soufflés

Despite the fact that soufflés could almost feature in the chapter Foolproof Dinner, they seem always to impress, individual ones even more so, as it looks as if the presumed skill and effort are all directed, channelled and funnelled at one person. What is less well-known about soufflés is that they can be monotonous in texture and, to avoid this, we suggest you bury a (nice) surprise in the centre of each small soufflé which you could be serving either as a first course, a cheese course or a savoury, depending on the structure of your meal.

Possible 'surprises' would be a sun-dried tomato taken with a teaspoon from a jar of sun-dried tomatoes put up in olive oil, an anchovy arranged in a coil, a prawn dusted with chilli pepper, a piece of smoked salmon or smoked haddock, some Parma ham cut into julienne strips and bundled together. Think carefully however about not springing an unwelcome ingredient on one of your guests. A confirmed oyster loather lulled into a sense of security by the sight of a cheese soufflé would be horrified – and unimpressed – to find the mollusc lurking inside.

Serves 4

1 oz/30 g butter	*4 eggs, separated, and 1 extra white*
1 tablespoon flour	*cayenne pepper*
just under ½ pint/275 ml milk	*salt and freshly ground black pepper*
1½ oz/45 g each Parmesan and	*a little extra Parmesan cheese for*
Gruyère cheese, freshly grated	*dusting*

Turn on the oven to 200°C/400°F, Gas 6.

Melt the butter, stir in the flour, and cook very gently for a few minutes. Gradually add the milk, which will be incorporated more easily if you warm it first, and stir until you have a smooth mixture. On the lowest possible heat, or using an asbestos mat – or the equivalent – let the sauce cook for about 10 minutes. Stir in the cheeses, then remove from the heat and, one by one, beat in the egg yolks. Season, remembering that the cheese is already quite salty, but also remembering that egg whites have a deadening effect on flavour. This part of the preparation can be done in advance, as well as deciding on your 'surprise' if you are going to have one.

Near the time of eating, butter individual soufflé dishes and dust them with Parmesan. Whisk the egg whites to firm, snowy peaks. Mix a quarter of the egg whites gently into the cheese mixture to lighten it, then fold in the rest of the egg whites, taking care not to squash the bounce out of them. Spoon into the prepared dishes, adding your surprise in the middle, i.e. spoon in some mixture, lay on the extra ingredient, fill to the top with more mixture. With a knife, cut a small circle about ½ inch/1.25 cm in from the circumference of the pot which will give a nice cottage-loaf look result. Bake for 15–20 minutes until golden brown and risen. Serve immediately.

Raspberry Soufflé

Serves 6

1 lb/500 g raspberries	*juice of 1 orange*
6 eggs	*1 tablespoon gelatine*
3 tablespoons caster sugar	*¾ pint/475 ml double cream*

Reserve a dozen or so of the best raspberries for the garnish. Put the remainder in the liquidizer and pulp very thoroughly. Separate the whites of the eggs from the yolks. Put the yolks, slightly beaten, into a double saucepan with the sugar and the orange juice and whisk until the mixture thickens. Dissolve the gelatine in about 2 tablespoonfuls of hot water in a small bowl in a saucepan of hot water. Add the raspberry purée to the egg and sugar mixture and put it in a large bowl to cool.

Meanwhile, beat the cream lightly, and the whites very stiffly. When the raspberry mixture is beginning to set a little, add the cream, and finally the whites, folded in gently but thoroughly so that there are no lumps of cream or egg white. Put into a serving dish and then quickly into the fridge.

Garnish with whole raspberries before serving.

Pistachio Parfait

Serves 6–8

3 oz/90 g pistachio nuts, chopped   *8 oz/250 g caster sugar*
3oz/90 g almonds, chopped   *3 egg whites*
1 pint/625 ml double cream   *1 tablespoon vanilla essence*
a few drops of green colouring   *1 teaspoon almond essence*

Whip the cream fairly stiffly and add the green colouring, but only a few drops. Boil 2½ fl oz/75 ml water and the sugar together until the syrup threads when dropped from the tip of a spoon. While the sugar is dissolving and coming to the boil, beat the egg whites stiffly, so that you can turn the bowl upside down without the whites moving. We find that a hand electric beater is best for this.

Pour the sugar syrup slowly into the whites, beating hard all the time. Add the nuts and flavourings to the whipped cream, and then fold in the egg white mixture gently but thoroughly so that everything amalgamates. Spoon the mixture into a soufflé dish and put at once into the freezer, and remove 10 minutes before serving.

CHAPTER TEN

Vegetarians

Vegetarian cooking is on the up and up. It needed to be: for years we have watched vegetarians having to put up with anything from grated Cheddar on a baked potato to hastily cooked pulses – murder on the digestion – or draught-excluding quiches made by hostesses who seemed to feel that it was pretty broad-minded of them even to produce that. For years, vegetarians have been covertly regarded as cranks and bores, social nuisances, out to make trouble for their hostess by their irritating whim of not eating as the majority do. Vegetarian food is still pretty awful in a good many places, but people are beginning to recognize that it is, and that is the first step towards it getting better.

Also, the number of vegetarians is increasing. There have always been people who do not eat fish or meat because of religious or humane principles of one kind or another, but as factory farming has increased and has been exposed, more people are unprepared to eat meat at such a cost to the animal. So, far from being cranks, these people (of whom we are not two) should do nothing but inspire respect: many strict vegetarians still yearn for things like prawns or game.

But there is now a new reason for becoming vegetarian, and that is health. People are rightly starting to question what the food they eat contains, and unfortunately a great deal of meat is full of antibiotics, hormones and preservatives, so that much as the Victorians suffered widely from rickets and/or constipation due to a diet that for children of all classes consisted largely of carbohydrates, so children now are getting eczema, are hyperactive, insomniac and aggressive. New allergies are being discovered all the time and seem to be very much on the increase, but it remains to be seen how much and how precisely children – and adults – are being affected by additives to food of all kinds.

Vegetarians are more likely to occur in our social life, and as cooking for them can produce delicious results, you may simply broaden your repertoire by making a vegetarian menu.

First, it is important to know what kind of vegetarian you are cooking for. A surprising number of people who call themselves vegetarian do, in fact, eat fish, or even poultry, but the ones who don't, feel strongly about it. Never cheat – don't make a vegetable soup with a meat stock: they will almost certainly detect this and feel very uncomfortable about it. So, not only don't cheat, but tell them you haven't. Secondly, it is necessary to make the distinction between vegetarians and vegans. The former eat dairy products, as well as cereals, nuts, fruit and vegetables. Vegans are confined to cereals, nuts, fruit and vegetables: no cheese, eggs, milk or butter can be used for them. In the recipes below, we have indicated which would be suitable for vegans. Soya milk and miso – which can be used for stock among other things – have made vegan cooking easier.

Having a vegetarian guest does *not* simply mean providing those parts of a non-vegetarian meal that are acceptable; if everybody else is having roast turkey, you cannot get away with shoving chestnut stuffing and brussel sprouts on to your guest's plate and expect them to feel very welcome or cared for. It is better to provide a vegetarian meal for everyone.

In our experience, most vegetarians love puddings – generally because the main courses presented to them have been so stodgy or dull – so even if you are not ordinarily a pudding eater or maker, do take this part of the meal seriously. They are also too familiar with the omelette/salad meal – often the only reasonable thing on the menu in non-vegetarian restaurants – just as vegans have to resort so often to pasta with a tomato sauce. The following recipes try to widen the field a bit. You will also find a number of vegetarian recipes elsewhere in this book.

Avocado, Celery and Hazelnut Salad
Hot Onion Tart
Stir-fried Vegetables with Bean Curd
Piperade
Dal with Fried Onions and Crackling Eggs
Lentil Dal
Basmati Rice
Curried Spinach

Asparagus and Rocket Risotto
Pasta Sauce No. 1 – For Vegans
Pasta Sauce No. 2 – For Vegetarians
Pasta Sauce No. 3
Raspberry and Hazelnut Crumble
Pineapple and Orange Salad with Toasted Almonds
Baked Apricots with Yoghurt and Cream

Avocado, Celery and Hazelnut Salad

(Vegan)

Serves 4

2 avocados
6 stalks celery

vinaigrette dressing
1½ oz/45 g chopped hazelnuts

Clean, dry and slice the celery. Open the avocados and scoop out pieces with a teaspoon into a bowl with the celery. Dress with a vinaigrette composed of salt, sugar, mustard, pepper, oil and a little vinegar (taste this to be sure it is to your liking). Dry fry the hazelnuts until they are lightly toasted and mix in with the celery and avocado. This makes a delicious starter at any time of the year.

Hot Onion Tart

(Vegetarian)

Serves 4

FOR 8 OZ/250 G SHORTCRUST PASTRY:

3 oz/90 g butter
2 oz/60 g vegetable fat
8 oz/250 g plain flour

salt
1 egg yolk
1 teaspoon lemon juice

You can buy frozen pastry, of course, but it is also very easily made. One secret of light pastry is not to let the flour etc. get beyond your knuckles. Here is our way of making it.

Rub the fats into the flour in a large bowl and add a little salt. You may not need the whole yolk. Beat it in a cup with a little cold water and lemon juice, add to the bowl and mix with a wooden spoon to a stiff paste. Roll out the pastry quite thinly on a floured board and then place it in an oiled 8-inch/20-cm tart or flan tin. Put it into the refrigerator and leave for about 2 hours.

FILLING:

1 tablespoon olive oil
2 oz/60 g butter
1½ lb/750 g onions
salt and pepper

3 egg yolks
6 fl oz/180 ml double cream
freshly grated nutmeg

Heat the oil and butter in a pan. Peel and slice the onions finely, discarding any tough outer skins. Cook the onions gently until they are quite soft – don't fry them: they must not get brown or crisp. Season with salt and pepper.

Turn on the oven to 230°C/450°F, Gas 8. Beat the egg yolks with the cream and add grated nutmeg to taste. Put the onions into the tart case and pour the creamy mixture over them. Bake for about 30 minutes and serve hot.

Stir-fried Vegetables with Bean Curd

(Vegan)

Serves 6

2 onions or 6 shallots
1 lb/500 g mange-tout
1 lb/500 g broccoli
2 blocks of bean curd

1 oz/30 g wholemeal flour
salt
sunflower seed oil
soya sauce (optional)

This dish is most easily made in a wok, using a small frying pan for the bean curd, but if you don't have a wok, you can use a large frying pan or a large enamelled pan. You will use less oil with the wok.

Begin by preparing all your vegetables. It is important that you cut them all to the same thickness. Slice the onions and chop. Cut the mange-tout in diagonal strips. Remove the heavy part of the broccoli stalks and cut the florets into strips. Cut each piece of bean curd into nine pieces and roll in salted wholemeal flour. Heat 2 tablespoonfuls of oil in a small pan. When the oil is really hot, put in the bean curd and turn down the heat a little. Turn the bean curd when it has browned.

Meanwhile, put some oil in a large pan (about 1 tablespoonful for a wok, about 3 tablespoonfuls for a pan), and heat until the oil is sizzling hot. Add the onions to the pan and stir-fry for 3 minutes, then add the mange-tout and continue stirring for 2 minutes. Finally, add the broccoli and stir for 2 more minutes.

This dish should be served at once in hot bowls with the bean curd on top and some soya sauce if liked.

Piperade

(Vegetarian)

Serves 6–8

2 tablespoons sunflower seed oil
    or *olive oil*
1½ lb/750 g onions, chopped
1½ lb/750 g green peppers, de-
    seeded and chopped

2 cloves garlic (optional)
1½ lb/750 g tomatoes, chopped (or one
    20-oz/600-g tin of same)
salt and pepper to taste
8 eggs

Heat the oil and add the onions. When they have begun to cook, add the peppers and garlic. Cook gently until the peppers begin to soften, then add the chopped tomatoes and season. Cook until you have a soft mélange of vegetables. Break the eggs into a bowl, and whisk until the yolks are well broken into the whites. Add this mixture to the vegetables and cook gently, stirring until the eggs are softly cooked.

This dish can be served on lightly buttered slices of wholemeal toast.

Dal with Fried Onions
and Crackling Eggs

(Vegetarian)

The lentils to use for this dish are the small orange variety, sometimes called Egyptian lentils, that cook to a purée in about 15 minutes. In Indian shops they are called Masoor dal. A pool of plain yoghurt goes well with this dish.

Serves 4

12 oz/375 g lentils	garam masala or *your own blend of*
2 onions	*spices*
vegetable oil	*3 hard-boiled eggs*
	salt and freshly ground black pepper

Wash the lentils in a bowl of water to remove any dust or other aliens. Cover the drained lentils with fresh water to a depth of ½ inch/1.25 cm above the lentils, bring to the boil and simmer. Peel and slice the onions, cutting from root to tip to obtain crescents. When the dal has reached a sludgy consistency, start to fry the onions. Depending on the age of the lentils you find, you may need to add more water during the cooking or, conversely, simmer for longer to achieve the correct texture. Fry the onions to a deep golden brown, set aside and keep warm.

Clean the pan, heat up a little more oil and fry the spices. Slice the hard-boiled eggs thickly and cook the slices, turning them once or twice until a bubbly crust forms. Season the dal with salt and freshly ground black pepper. Serve with the eggs, any spicy oil remaining in the pan and the onions.

Lentil Dal

(Vegan)

This is a lentil dal from Madhur Jaffrey's excellent book, *An Invitation To Indian Cooking*.

Serves 4

1 lb/500 g green lentils	*1½ teaspoons salt*
1 cinnamon stick	*⅛ teaspoon freshly ground black pepper*
1 bay leaf	*¼ teaspoon cayenne pepper (optional)*
2 cloves garlic	*3 tablespoons vegetable oil or*
2 slices freshly peeled root ginger	*1½ oz/45 g ghee*
about ⅛ inch/0.3 cm thick	*a pinch of ground asafoetida*
1 teaspoon ground turmeric	*½ teaspoon whole cumin seeds*
¾ lemon	

Wash the lentils well, picking out any stones you can see, then drain. Combine the lentils, 2½ pints/1.5 litres water, cinnamon stick, bay leaf, garlic, ginger and turmeric. Bring to the boil. Cover the pan, lower the heat and simmer gently until the lentils are tender, about 30–45 minutes.

Slice the lemon into 5 or 6 rounds, removing the pips. Add the lemon, salt, pepper and cayenne to the lentils. Stir and cover for another five minutes. Just before serving, heat the vegetable oil or ghee in a frying pan over a medium-high heat. When the oil is very hot, put in the asafoetida and cumin seeds. As soon as the asafoetida begins to sizzle and expand and the cumin seeds darken, pour the contents over the lentils and stir.

Note: Lentils take a varying amount of time to cook, depending upon their kind, and their age. Dal should be quite thick: as Madhur Jaffrey says, 'thinner than porridge, but not quite so thin as pea soup'.

Basmati Rice

(Vegan)

Serves 4

12 oz/375 g Basmati rice
1¼ teaspoons salt

1½ oz/45 g vegetable ghee (or butter if you are cooking for vegetarians)

Wash the rice well in cold water, then soak it in a bowl with 2 pints/1.1 litres water and ½ teaspoonful salt for at least half an hour. Then drain it thoroughly. Melt the butter or ghee in a heavy-bottomed pan. Pour in the drained rice and stir for 2 minutes until the rice is coated with fat. Add 18 fl oz/575 ml water and ¾ teaspoonful of salt. Bring to the boil, cover, lower heat to very low, and cook for about 20 minutes. Look at the rice occasionally, mix it gently and cook until the rice is tender and the liquid has evaporated.

Basmati rice cooked in this manner has a delicious flavour that goes excellently with many of the dishes in this chapter.

Curried Spinach

(Vegan)

Serves 4

3 lb/1.5 kg spinach
2 large onions, finely chopped
1 tablespoon sunflower seed oil
6 cloves garlic, sliced lengthways
a very small pinch of chilli
  powder

1 teaspoon ground cumin
1 teaspoon ground coriander
1 sprig of fennel, chopped
1 teaspoon chopped rosemary
salt

Wash the spinach well in a large bowl of water. Take it out and drop it into a large pan without extra water. Cook it, stirring from time to time for about 8 minutes, by which time all the water on the washed leaves will have evaporated. Strain the spinach and squeeze dry, then chop it roughly.

Fry the onions in the oil until they are transparent. Add the garlic, chilli powder, cumin and coriander and continue to fry for 3 minutes. Add the spinach to the pan together with the chopped fennel and rosemary and a good pinch of salt and cook for a further 3 minutes.

This dish is good with Basmati rice and a dal.

Asparagus and Rocket Risotto

(Vegetarian or Vegan)

Mastering the art of making a classic risotto is an important weapon in the armoury of being or feeding a vegetarian. The different vegetables that can be used are infinite but an important point is to celebrate one flavour rather than making a jumble. For example, capitalize on the short season when peas or broad beans are sold fresh or when courgettes are in flower, and garnish liberally with fresh herbs. It is essential to use risotto rice, often called arborio rice, now easily found.

Serves 4–6 as a first course, 2–3 as a main course

1 lb/500 g asparagus
a handful of rocket leaves
1¾ pints/1 litre vegetable stock
made up in part by asparagus
water
1 onion, finely chopped

2 oz/60 g butter
10 oz/275 g arborio rice
2 oz/60 g butter and 2 oz/60 g grated
Parmesan (or for vegans substitute
something like toasted pine kernels
or toasted sesame seeds) to dress

Trim the asparagus and slice on the bias, preserving the tips whole. Bring a pan of water to the boil and blanch the asparagus for 3 minutes. Strain, reserving the water. Mix this asparagus stock and the vegetable stock about half and half. In a large heavy-based pot or sauté pan, cook the onion in the butter until softened. Add the rice and stir to coat the grains. Add the asparagus and stir. Add a ladleful of stock and stir until the stock is absorbed. Continue in this fashion, ladleful by ladleful, until the risotto is a creamy consistency. This is not a dish that can be left to its own devices. It must be looked after; the result is worthwhile. After about 25 minutes, the rice should be cooked. Bite a grain; it should have resistance only at the core. Stir in butter and the Parmesam if you are using it. Just before serving, roughly tear up the rocket leaves and stir them in, achieving an effect of the rocket streaked through the rice.

Pasta Sauce No. 1

(Vegan)

Serves 6

4 tablespoons olive oil
2 oz/60 g onion, peeled and finely
chopped
2 oz/60 g celery, scrubbed and
finely chopped
2 oz/60 g carrot, finely chopped
2 lb/1 kg fresh tomatoes or one
20-oz/625-g can Italian plum
tomatoes (see below)

salt
1 teaspoon dark brown sugar
12 oz/375 g mushrooms, wiped clean
and roughly chopped
1 teaspoon ground coriander or
1 oz/30 g fresh coriander, chopped

This sauce can be made ahead of time and warmed up, in which case reserve the fresh coriander until the warming-up process. Most of the year, it is better to use tinned tomatoes: fresh tomatoes are seldom worth eating and have no flavour when cooked.

Put 2 tablespoons of the oil into a pan and add the onion, celery and carrot. Fry gently, stirring all the while, for 3 minutes. Add the tomatoes and their juice, salt and sugar, and simmer for 30 minutes. Meanwhile, put 2 tablespoonfuls of oil into a second pan and when it is hot, add the mushrooms and ground coriander. Sauté the mushrooms lightly until the oil is absorbed, then remove from the heat.

When the tomato mixture has finished simmering, put the mixture through a food processor, then return it to a clean pan, and simmer gently for a further 30 minutes. Add the mushrooms to the pan, stir and taste to see if you have added enough salt.

This sauce is good with most kinds of pasta. Buy fresh pasta if you possibly can: you will need about 1¼ lb/575 g for 4 people. Fresh pasta should be cooked in a large pan (or in two pans of you haven't got a really big one) three-quarters filled with water. When the water is boiling, add salt (which will further raise the temperature of the water) just before you put the pasta in the pan. Fresh pasta cooks very much faster than dried – a matter of minutes.

Note: The tomatoes will be greatly improved by the addition of a spoonful or two of sun-dried tomatoes. These come packed in oil in jars and can be obtained from good delicatessens.

Pasta Sauce No. 2

(Vegetarian)

This is a sauce from Delia Smith's book, *One Is Fun*; it is an excellent sauce for a vegetarian – but *not* for vegans.

Serves 6

1¼ lb/575 g green tagliatelle
6 oz/180 g Gorgonzola cheese
8 oz/250 g Ricotta or cottage
  cheese
4 small cloves garlic
12 fl oz/375 ml single cream
4 tablespoons olive oil

1 red or green pepper, very finely
  chopped
8 spring onions including green parts,
  finely chopped
salt and freshly ground black pepper
2 oz/60 g Parmesan cheese

Put the pasta in boiling salted water (with a few drops of oil to prevent it sticking) and when the water has returned to the boil, cook for exactly 8 minutes for dried pasta, and cook until *al dente* with fresh pasta. Meanwhile, put the Gorgonzola and Ricotta cheeses into the liquidizer with the garlic, cream and a tablespoonful of hot water. Season with pepper and blend until completely smooth.

When the tagliatelle is ready, drain it thoroughly in a colander, then return it immediately to its hot pan. Add the olive oil, chopped pepper and spring onions, season with salt and pepper, then toss well. Add the cheese mixture to the pasta, toss thoroughly, then serve straight on to hot plates. Sprinkle with the Parmesan.

Pasta Sauce No. 3

(Vegetarian)

This sauce is not *strictly* vegetarian since it contains a tin of anchovies. However, we have found that many people who say they are vegetarian in fact do eat fish, so if you are feeding them, this is a popular sauce.

Serves 6

1 large Spanish onion, chopped
3 tablespoons best olive oil
5 peppers (try to have yellow, red and green ones), chopped
12 oz/375 g mushrooms, chopped

2 oz/60 g dried wild mushrooms, soaked in ½ cup of hot water
1 large tin chopped tomatoes
1 tin anchovies, chopped
½ pint/300 ml single cream
fresh parsley, chopped

Fry the onion in as little oil as possible. Add the peppers. Fry gently until the peppers are beginning to get soft. Add the rest of the oil and turn up the heat before adding the mushrooms. Stir to get the mushrooms well coated in oil and continue to fry. Extract the wild mushrooms from the water (but reserve it) and chop them up before adding them. Add the mushroom water and chopped tomatoes. Cook very gently for ½ hour. Add the chopped anchovies – drained of their oil – and shortly before serving add the single cream slowly. Serve with chopped parsley.

Raspberry and Hazelnut Crumble

(Vegan)

Serves 4

1 lb/500 g raspberries
4 oz/125 g plain flour
2 oz/60 g sugar

2 oz/60 g margarine (or butter for
  vegetarians)
2 oz/60 g toasted chopped hazelnuts

Turn on the oven to 170°C/325°F, Gas 3.

Put the raspberries in a fairly shallow baking dish. (If you like your fruit very sweet, add a sprinkling of sugar – personally, we don't think this is needed.)

Mix the flour with the sugar and rub in the fat until the mixture is like crumbs. Add the hazelnuts and put the mixture on top of the raspberries. Bake in the oven until the top is golden brown. If you bake it too fast, the raspberry juice will bubble up and spoil the top.

Pineapple and Orange Salad with Toasted Almonds

(Vegan)

Serves 4

1 pineapple
4 oranges

4 oz/125 g toasted almonds

You can tell if a pineapple is reasonably ripe by pulling a leaf from the top. If it doesn't come away from the fruit, don't buy it.

Peel the pineapple carefully, taking away all the husks. Slice thinly and then cut into small pieces. Peel the oranges, removing all the pith, then slice thinly with a very sharp knife on a plate, to catch the juice. Mix the fruit together and leave covered with a damp cloth.

Blanch the almonds and then toast them in the oven on a baking tray until they are a rich brown. Shake them from time to time in order to turn them. Split the browned almonds and chop coarsely. Add them to the fruit salad before serving.

Baked Apricots with Yoghurt and Cream

(Vegetarian)

Serves 4

8 fl oz/250 ml double cream
8 fl oz/250 ml natural live
   yoghurt (see page 101)
3 oz/90 g soft dark brown sugar

1½ lb/750 g fresh apricots
3 tablespoons caster sugar (if you have
   any with a vanilla pod – good)
grated rind and juice of 1 lemon

This is a very simple but delicious pudding. It should be made the day before you eat it.

Mix the cream and yoghurt well together, and put into a shallow dish. Sprinkle the dark brown sugar thickly all over it and leave in the fridge for 24 hours.

Wipe the apricots with a damp cloth and score them with a knife down their crease. Pile them into a baking dish. Add 6 tablespoonfuls of cold water and 3 tablespoonfuls of caster sugar, plus the grated rind and juice of the lemon. Bake in a very slow oven until the fruit is soft. Serve cold with the yoghurt and cream.

CHAPTER ELEVEN

Having a Roux Brother to Dinner

One of the drawbacks about being labelled a good cook is that others are nervous of asking you to their place. If you go to a good deal of trouble to prepare a delectable meal, thinking hard about what might please and surprise, not in order to show off but because you enjoy entertaining and hope that return matches will be arranged, you can find yourself transformed into a social pariah. 'Oh, we can't ask you back,' guests have said to both of us confidently, 'our food wouldn't be good enough for you.'

Famous chefs more rightfully personify this predicament. Imagining having, say, a Roux brother to dinner fleshes out the worry of inviting someone to your house whose knowledge and skills in connection with food you assume to be vastly superior to your own. What you must keep in mind when faced with this scenario is that professional cooks and chefs, perhaps even more than ordinary individuals, value well-sourced, wholesome ingredients treated simply and respectfully. In their own life they come across too much teased and tormented 'luxury' food – and this also applies to those people obliged by their business life to have many meals out in restaurants – and they like nothing better than a dish such as plainly roasted chicken served with its buttery juices and a watercress salad and a homely pudding such as a carefully made creamy rice pudding. Something else to remember is that the world of professional food is on the whole peopled by charming, generous types. They are thrilled to have the tables turned and are usually ready to love everything you put in front of them, exclaiming over perfectly ordinary assemblies as if it had never occurred to them to prepare them. Indeed, the better the cook, having probably suffered from the cold-shoulder treatment mentioned above, the more appreciative he or she will be.

Given that your guest has a genuine love for food, there should not be too much time spent drinking and chatting before getting down to the serious subject of what is for dinner. The first course will be the one where your main impact resides which is why it is worth peeling chestnuts for the chestnut soup or seeking out pink fir-apple, la ratte or another flavourful variety of potato for the first course salad. A main course should either be classic – as in the roast chicken – or feature an item such as skate or tongue that relatively rarely makes an appearance either in homes or restaurants. With tongue it is worth discreetly checking if your guests like it but genuine food lovers invariably adore extremities. Well-bought, well-kept cheese, a pure green salad and a proper pudding should conclude the meal, whereupon satisfaction and even self-satisfaction will reign. Then you wait and hope to be invited back to the Roux brother's place.

Confit of Chicken Livers	Blackberry and Sultana Sauce
Chestnut Soup	Sauté of Baby Vegetables
Salad with Fried Potatoes	Potato, Brussels Sprouts and
Seafood Lettuce Wrap	Celeriac Cakes
Skate with Browned Butter	The Cheese Course
Perfect Roast Chicken	Excellent Green Salad
Quails with Supportive Rice	Sussex Pond Pudding
Hot Ox Tongue	Rice Pudding
Gooseberry Sauce	

Confit of Chicken Livers

Confit refers to meat preserved in its own fat and if you can obtain chicken fat, it is the best medium for this recipe. Kosher butchers often sell chicken fat (schmaltz), or if you buy a boiling chicken from a Kosher butcher there are usually quantities of fat in the cavity of the bird which can be rendered down. Failing that, use duck fat or goose fat, both of these are usually in copious supply after roasting the duck or the goose.

As long as the livers remain covered by the fat, they are preserved, but after the pot is opened they should be eaten fairly quickly. Because this is a rich dish, put it into small jars.

Serves 4 as a first course

8 oz/250 g chicken livers
4 oz/125 g chicken fat or
  alternative such as duck fat
  (see above), or enough to cover
  the livers

1 large onion, peeled and thickly sliced
3 cloves garlic, peeled (optional)
salt and freshly ground black pepper

Pick over the chicken livers and discard any gristle or green bits which, on account of a taint from bile, will be bitter. Separate the livers into their natural portions, i.e. pieces about 1 inch/2.5 cm wide.

Find a glass Kilner jar about the size to hold the livers or, failing that, seek out a clean jam jar. Pack in the livers interspersing the layers with salt and freshly ground pepper. Top with onion slices. Melt the fat you are using and heat the cloves of garlic in it. Pour it on to the livers and, if necessary, add more until the livers are covered.

Turn on the oven to 180°C/350°F, Gas 4, and bring a kettle of water to the boil. Put the glass jar into a larger oven-proof dish. Add boiling water to come at least halfway up the jar, then place them in the pre-heated oven for 1 hour.

Remove the jar from the *bain-marie*, cool, and refrigerate. When you serve the *confit*, we advise mashing the liver and a little of its fat on some brown toast, making sure that it is garnished with some of the onion. It makes an ideal snack or something to serve with drinks.

Chestnut Soup

This soup is quite a lot of trouble, but it is absolutely worth it.

Serves 4

2 carrots
2 leeks
1 large onion
1 small head of celery

a good sprig of parsley
1½ oz/45 g butter
1 lb/500 g sweet chestnuts
salt and pepper

Chop the cleaned vegetables and put them in a pan with melted butter. When they begin to look transparent, add 2 pints/1.1 litres cold water and simmer gently. Meanwhile, score each chestnut on the rounded side with a sharp knife, drop them in boiling water and boil for about 10 minutes. Take the pan off the heat and, taking one chestnut at a time, peel them, removing both outer and inner skins.

Now take half the vegetable liquid and stew the peeled chestnuts in it until they are soft (about 45 minutes). Liquidize the vegetables with the remaining stock with the chestnuts and their liquid. Season when you heat up the soup before serving.

Salad with Fried Potatoes

This is a dish that a restaurant, particularly a highly priced one, might think too humble to serve, but using one of the flavoursome varieties of salad potato now widely available (supermarkets often being the best source) and with careful cooking in a fresh nut oil, it can be sublime. Also the healthiness implicit in a salad first course is what is wanted these days.

Serves 4–6

*a selection of salad leaves
   including some fairly robust
   ones such as cos, young
   spinach, watercress, frisée or
   corn salad*
3–4 cloves of garlic
*3 tablespoons walnut oil or
   hazelnut oil*

2–3 small dried red chillis
*1 lb/500 g new salad potatoes, washed
   or wiped clean*
salt and pepper
2 tablespoons chopped parsley
a dribble of sherry vinegar

Arrange the salad leaves either in one large bowl (best) or on individual serving plates. Leaving the garlic cloves unpeeled, flatten them with the side of a cleaver or heavy knife, just so that the skin splits. Heat the oil gently. Add the garlic and chillis, stir around and add the potatoes. Cook over a medium heat for about 20 minutes or until the potatoes are soft inside when pierced with the point of a sharp knife. Make sure the garlic doesn't burn. If this looks likely, remove the cloves and replace them at the end of the potatoes' cooking time. Season with salt and freshly ground black pepper. Pour the potatoes, garlic, chillis and the oil over the salad leaves. Scatter the parsley over the leaves. Dribble on a little vinegar (no more than a tablespoon). Toss and serve immediately.

Seafood Lettuce Wrap

This recipe was inspired by a meal in a Chinese restaurant specializing in seafood. It is rather more sophisticated than the similar approach to pork which appears in the chapter Dull People, but with enough guests, it is worth offering both fillings with perhaps two varieties of lettuce, say Cos and Webb's Wonder, to act as the packaging.

Serves 4

6 oz/180 g large peeled prawns
6 scallops
8 oz/250 g squid (if unobtainable, use more of the shellfish)
salt and pepper
5 tablespoons vegetable oil
1 cube peeled fresh root ginger about 1 inch/2.5 cm square
1 medium-sized fresh green chilli
4 spring onions

2 cloves garlic
1 large carrot
4 oz/125 g cauliflower or broccoli
2 tablespoons fish or vegetable stock
1 tablespoon soya sauce
1½ tablespoons dry sherry mixed with 1 teaspoon cornflour
1 teaspoon sesame seed oil
1 cos or Webb's Wonder lettuce, separated into leaves for serving

Chop the prawns and scallops into small dice. Clean the squid by pulling out everything inside and peeling off the flaps and purplish skin. Cut off the tentacles and reserve. Wash the 'bodies' and cut down one side giving you a roughly square-shaped white sheet of squid. With a sharp knife, cross-hatch the surface of the squid, making sure you don't cut right through; this tenderizes the flesh. Now chop the squid into small squares. Add it to the tentacles, chopped if large. Mix the fish together and sprinkle with salt, pepper and a little vegetable oil.

Cut the ginger into threads and do the same with the chilli, discarding the seeds and membrane. Cut the cleaned spring onions (including the green part) into small rings, and chop the garlic finely. Peel the carrot and, using a vegetable peeler, take off thin strips which you then cut into ½-inch/1-cm pieces. Break up the cauliflower florets or broccoli head into tiny pieces and discard the stalk. Heat 3 tablespoonfuls of oil in a wok or sauté pan and, when hot, stir-fry the fish for 1½ minutes. Remove and set aside. Add the rest of the vegetable oil, heat up and stir-fry the vegetables for about 30 seconds, pour off any excess oil and add the stock, soya sauce and the

sherry-cornflour mixture, stirring the latter just before you tip it in.
When the liquid comes to the boil, return the seafood to the pan. Mix
well and cook for about 1 minute to ensure that all the ingredients are
well heated through.

Pile on to a warmed serving dish, sprinkle with sesame oil and
offer alongside the lettuce leaves. The guests put a spoonful of the
mixture in a lettuce leaf, make a parcel, and eat.

Skate with Browned Butter

There are certain foodstuffs and dishes that, good though they are,
are rarely offered either in homes or restaurants. It is as if they are not
sufficiently glamorous. A simple dish carefully and correctly cooked
is sure to be received more enthusiastically by someone for whom
food is their work and their life than an imitation of 'smart' food.
Skate is an often overlooked pleasure and anyone truly keen on food
will appreciate its faintly gelatinous quality. The butter needs last-
minute attention but is simple to do.

Serves 4

4 medium-sized wings of skate	1 dessertspoon capers
4 oz/125 g butter	2 tablespoons finely chopped parsley
2 tablespoons red wine vinegar	

COURT BOUILLON:

2 tablespoons white wine vinegar	10 peppercorns
1 onion, peeled and thickly sliced	parsley stalks
1 carrot, peeled and cut into chunks	a pinch of sea salt

In a large shallow pan, put just enough water to cover the skate and
add the *court bouillon* ingredients. Put in the fish and bring it slowly to
the boil. After one eruption of bubbles, lower the heat to achieve the
barest simmering. Cook the fish for 10–15 minutes until the flesh is
opaque beside the main bone. (The second part of this process can be
done in the oven if you prefer, the oven being set at 180°C/350°F,
Gas 4.)

Warm a serving dish and four plates quite thoroughly, and when the fish is cooked, drain it and arrange on the serving dish. Melt the butter in a frying pan and, watching like a hawk, cook it until it goes a deep brown. Pour it over the fish. To the hot frying pan, add the red wine vinegar, swirl it round and let it bubble a few seconds. Pour that over the fish. Scatter on the capers and sprinkle on the parsley.

Sauté potatoes go well with this dish, and they are a great treat in their own right.

Perfect Roast Chicken

We have noticed that the more involved with food you become, the more you gravitate towards simplicity. A well brought up chicken, considerately cooked, becomes a far more beguiling dish than any *nouvelle cousine* flight of fancy, pushed and primped and served in pre-ordained portions, which obviate that pinnacle of eating enjoyment, second helpings.

Serves 4

1 lemon
1 large free-range, grain-fed
   chicken or failing that, the best
   chicken you can buy
1 tablespoon extra virgin olive oil
4 oz/125 g unsalted butter

a few leaves of tarragon (if possible)
sea salt and freshly ground black
   pepper
a bunch of watercress, washed and
   trimmed

Turn on the oven to 180°C/350°F, Gas 4.

Rub the skin of the chicken with one half of the lemon, squeezing it the while. Squeeze a little lemon juice into the cavity as well. Then massage the chicken with olive oil until the skin is supple. Now work your hand under the skin of the chicken, starting at the back where there is a flap of skin; after you have tugged away one or two tough membranes, you will find it quite easy to get your hand between the flesh and the skin over the breast and the thighs. Stop where the skin is attached to the breast bone. If the butter is hard, chop 3 oz/90 g of it into small dice and insert it under the skin, distributing it fairly by pushing it around from above. If the butter is softened, the technique is similar but you may need to spoon it in. If you have tarragon leaves, dot them about under the skin also. Do not use more than about 6 leaves as tarragon can be overpowering and you want the flavour of the butter and chicken to predominate. Place the remaining 1 oz/30 g butter and the intact lemon half inside the bird. Sprinkle the chicken with sea salt and grind black pepper evenly over it.

Place the chicken in a roasting pan which you have lightly oiled with olive oil. Put it in the oven and cook for 60 minutes, beginning to baste occasionally after the first 30 minutes. The separation of the skin from the chicken flesh will render it extra crispy and the butter under the skin will act as a self-basting process, ensuring that the flesh is succulent.

Towards the end of the cooking time, heat a serving dish, a gravy boat and the plates. Remove the chicken to the serving dish. Pour off the accumulated buttery juices into the gravy boat. Arrange the watercress in two bunches on the serving dish, one at either end of the chicken. Carve and serve, and make sure that, as well as chicken, everyone gets some skin and also some watercress wilted by the cooking juices. Keep accompaniments simple; perhaps just some steamed new potatoes.

Quails with Supportive Rice

This dish is inspired by a Greek method of serving the little birds. Spices have been added since quails, by law, are now all farmed and have none of the flavour benefits of an interesting and hazardous life. The amount of meat on a quail is limited to say the least, thus the sausage meat in the rice is a welcome addition. Serve 2 quails per person with a few extra for hearty appetites.

Serves 4

10 quails
½ lemon
1 teaspoon ground coriander
1 teaspoon ground cumin
1 teaspoon ground cardamom
½ teaspoon ground ginger
8 screws of the pepper mill
8 oz/250 g Basmati rice

a good pinch of salt
2 tablespoons vegetable oil
2 oz/60 g butter
6 oz/180 g sausage meat (you can skin high-quality sausages)
¼ pint/150 ml double cream
1 hothouse (Dutch) lettuce cut across into thin ribbons

Rub the quails with the lemon and then with a mixture of the ground spices including pepper; let them sit for as long as possible absorbing the flavours. Wash the rice in several changes of cold water, then drain and put into a heavy-bottomed wide pan (rice cooks more evenly when spread over a large surface, rather than piled up). Add water to come above the rice by a scant ½ inch/1 cm. Add a pinch of salt and put it on the heat. Bring to a simmer and cover.

Meanwhile, heat the oil and butter and sauté the quails in a large pan, turning them until evenly browned. Cook them carefully, turning often, for about 15 minutes. It should be possible to do this without the addition of liquid, but should they be catching, add a tablespoon or two of water. In a separate pan, fry the sausage meat in a little oil, breaking it up with a fork until it resembles browned crumbs.

Test the rice. When it is ready, all the liquid should have been absorbed. Mix the drained cooked sausage meat with the rice. Remove the quails from the pan and keep warm. Add the double cream to the spicy pan juices and stir while it bubbles, to produce a small amount of deep honey-gold sauce.

Arrange the sausage/rice mixture on a warm serving dish, and scatter the strips of lettuce on top. Pile the quails in the centre and dribble the sauce over them. It should cover each quail just a little, not swamp the dish. A salad of lettuce hearts follows this dish nicely.

Hot Ox Tongue

1 salted tongue weighing 3–4 lb/ 1.5–2 kg	2 carrots
3 onions	1 bay leaf
	6 peppercorns

Soak the tongue for 8 hours or overnight.

Put the tongue in cold water to cover and bring to the boil slowly. Discard the water and refill the pan with fresh. Add vegetables and seasoning, and simmer as slowly as possible for at least three hours. Drain the tongue, peel it, remove any extra fat and the small bones and serve with either of the following sauces.

Gooseberry Sauce

½ lb/250 g gooseberries – bottled or
canned will do provided they
are without sugar
2 oz/60 g butter

4 oz/125 g veal stock
3 egg yolks
seasoning to taste (this may include a
little sugar)

Simmer the fruit with the butter for five minutes. Add the stock and continue simmering until the fruit is soft enough to be sieved or pulped. Transfer the pulp to a double boiler and gradually add the beaten egg yolks. Heat while stirring, until the mixture thickens. Season and serve.

Blackberry and sultana Sauce

½ lb/250 g bramble jelly
¼ pint/150 ml water

2 oz/60 g sultanas

Melt the jelly and the water in pan. Add the sultanas and simmer until they are soft. Serve warm or cold with hot tongue.

Sauté of Baby Vegetables

Inevitably, this dish is better in the early summer when broad beans and peas can be obtained young and fresh. It is possible, however, to assemble it with carefully chosen frozen produce. Dill is an important flavouring and if you are unable to obtain it fresh, the freeze-dried variety works perfectly well.

Serves 4–6

3 lb/1.5 kg fresh broad beans
2 lb/1 kg fresh peas
1 bunch spring onions, cleaned
and chopped
1 tablespoon vegetable oil
1 oz/30 g butter
chicken stock

1 hothouse (Dutch) lettuce, trimmed
and cut across into thin ribbons
salt and pepper
sugar
chopped dillweed
cream (optional)

Pod the broad beans and peas. Heat the oil and butter in a heavy-bottomed pan. Cook the onions gently for a few minutes, then add the broad beans and cook for a few minutes. Add the peas. Carefully stir them to glaze them with the buttery oil. (If the broad beans are tiny, they can be cooked with the peas.)

Add sufficient stock to come just level with the vegetables; add the lettuce, a pinch of salt and black pepper and the sugar. Cover and simmer gently until the vegetables are tender – for about 10–15 minutes.

Add the dillweed and the cream if you are using it. If you want a thicker sauce, mix 1 teaspoonful cornflour or potato flour in a little more stock. Add and shake the pan to blend.

Potato, Brussels Sprout and Celeriac Cakes

Serves 4

8 oz/250 g cooked Brussels sprouts	1 egg
8 oz/250 g cooked mashed celeriac	1 oz/30 g seasoned flour
8 oz/250 g cooked mashed potato	salt and black pepper
	3 tablespoons sunflower seed oil

It is important to use fresh vegetables for these cakes, not left-overs.

Chop the Brussels sprouts and mash them with a fork. Then mix the celeriac, potato and Brussels sprouts well together, adding the egg, and salt and pepper. Make little cakes from this mixture with your hands and roll them in seasoned flour. Fry them in hot oil in a frying pan.

The Cheese Course

Your choice of cheese will be dictated to some extent by your sources of supply. These can range from the shelves of a late-night supermarket, apt to provide you with firmly sealed sweaty packs of generic cheeses much favoured by the wretched Milk Marketing Board, through local supplies of farmhouse and cottage industry cheeses, to a shop able to import cheeses from a master *fromagier*, such as Philippe Olivier in Boulogne, and keep them at the optimum temperature. Whatever your scope, remember that a few cheeses, as few as two, in prime condition are much more satisfying and appetizing than lots of different cheeses that will get picked at and leave you with bits of some and triangles of others that are good for nothing but storing in the fridge until it is time to throw them away.

Aim for contrast – a hard cheese and a soft one, a cheese on the bland side and one that is pungent, a white cheese and a blue cheese. We like to theme the cheeses to some extent, making an effort to procure English country cheeses (but beware of the more arcane varieties which can sometimes be quite horrid) if English is the style of the meal; Italian cheeses if, for example, you have decided to serve a Bollito Misto (*see* page 245).

If you know the tastes of your guests and you find that you can buy one cheese that they will like in its whole form without being wildly extravagant, do so as it looks marvellous and in an odd way it encourages people to eat more than if they were faced with a range of cheeses. Cheeses made with unpasteurized milk – *au lait cru* – are invariably superior, if you can find them. A home-made cheese – which can be as simple as mixing fresh herbs and sea salt into a fresh cheese, or dressing half a Ricotta with ground black pepper and virgin olive oil – always has appeal and will invariably be chosen in preference to anything else you provide.

We feel that bread is the best accompaniment to cheese, but offer biscuits as well and celery for those pretending to be on a diet. Cheese boards do not look better for the presence of a tomato or sprig of parsley. Large enough pieces of cheese are beautiful in their own right. Lastly, the cheese course is the moment to open a good bottle of red wine or, should you be serving Stilton, some port. It is now *très snob* to drink a sweet Sauternes or other dessert wine with Gruyère cheese. If you are planning to continue with a dessert wine after the cheese course anyway, why not try?

Excellent Green Salad

A salad that appears either with or after the cheese course should be notable for its simplicity. This is the moment to look for a selection of interesting leaves such as *salade de mâche* (also called lamb's lettuce or corn salad), *frisée*, oak leaf lettuce, baby spinach, *mesclun*

(sometimes available in this country at specialist shops), watercress and so forth. It is not the time for adding cunning or surprising ingredients like chopped green peppers, or cooked peas.

The salad dressing that works best is one made at the moment of serving. Have your leaves and chopped fresh herbs washed, dried, and arranged in a salad bowl. When you want to serve the salad, pour on 2½ tablespoonfuls of the best olive oil you can buy and mix well. When all the leaves seem coated, add a scant tablespoonful of wine vinegar, or balsamic vinegar if you have some, and toss again. Lemon juice could be used in place of vinegar but it tends to do battle with the wine you are drinking. Sprinkle on some sea salt, grind on some black pepper, toss once more and serve. Save more complicated notions of dressings, such as those made with mustards and garlic, anchovies and so on, for first course salads or *crudités*.

A favourite mid-meal salad is just soft lettuce, finely chopped parsley and the dressing outlined above served in a glass bowl the way the French do.

Sussex Pond Pudding

Jane Grigson revived this 'best of all English boiled suet puddings' alongside so many other worthwhile dishes which became muddled and travestied until the publication of her books on the subject of British cookery. As Mrs Grigson says in *English Food*: 'The genius of the pudding is the lemon. Its citrus bitter flavour is a subtlety which raises the pudding to the highest class. When you serve it, make sure that everyone has a piece of the lemon, which will be much softened by the cooking, but still vigorous.'

Actually, no one could fail to be impressed by this cornerstone of serious country house food. The name of the pudding refers to the sauce which runs out of it when it is turned on to a serving dish and provides it with a moat of brown buttery liquid.

Serves 4–5

8 oz/250 g self-raising flour	slightly salted butter
4 oz/125 g fresh beef suet, chopped	soft light brown or caster sugar
	1 large lemon or 2 limes
milk and water	

Mix the flour and suet together in a bowl. Make into a dough with the milk and water, half and half; ¼ pint/150 ml should be plenty. The dough should be soft, but not too soft to roll out into a large circle. Cut a quarter out of this circle, to be used later as the lid of the pudding. Butter a pudding basin lavishly. It should hold about 2½ pints/1.5 litres. Drop the three-quarter-circle of pastry into it and press the cut sides together to make a perfect join. Put about 3½ oz/ 100 g butter, cut up, into the pastry, with the same amount of sugar. Prick the lemon (or limes) all over with a larding needle so that the juices will be able to escape, then put it on to the butter and sugar. Fill the rest of the cavity with equal weights of sugar and butter cut into pieces – at least another 3½ oz/100 g, possibly more.

Roll out the pastry which was set aside to make a lid. Lay it on top of the filling, and press the edges together so that the pudding is sealed in completely. Put a piece of foil right over the basin, with a pleat in the middle. Tie it in place with string and make a string handle over the top so that the pudding can be lifted out easily. Put a large pan of water on to boil, and lower the pudding into it; the water must be boiling, and it should come halfway, or a little further, up the basin. Cover and leave to boil for 3–4 hours. If the water gets low, replenish it with *boiling* water.

To serve, put a deep dish over the basin after removing the foil lid, and quickly turn the whole thing upside-down: it is a good idea to ease the pudding from the sides of the basin with a knife first. Put on the table immediately.

Rice Pudding

To restore delectability to a dish that has been desecrated and damaged by institutional, or simply negligent cooking, is a crafty tactic in the business of feeding a foodie. Rice pudding, sinned against by schools, hospitals, prisons, no doubt, and the nursery, is an ideal candidate. You might think, upon reading the recipe, that such a small amount of rice will not absorb the liquid but it does. Long, slow cooking is the key. The bottom oven of an Aga or other solid-fuel stove or a crockpot are ideal.

Serves 4 with second helpings

generous 2 oz/60 g butter
3 heaped tablespoons caster sugar
4 oz/125 g pudding rice (it is
    vital to use pudding rice)

half a vanilla pod, split lengthways
1½ pints/900 ml creamy milk
½ pint/300 ml double cream
a pinch of salt

Turn on the oven to 150°C/300°F, Gas 2.

In a roomy shallow flameproof dish, melt the butter. Add the sugar and stir around while it froths together. Add the rice and keep stirring until every grain is glistening. Continue cooking for about 5 minutes. The rice should not colour but the sugar and butter will have a slight caramelizing effect apparent in the finished dish. Add the vanilla pod, pressing it against the side or bottom of the pan so that it spills its seeds and its flavour. Add the milk and cream carefully, so as to avoid the spitting butter, and put in a pinch of salt. Bring almost to the boil and then put on the bottom shelf of the oven for at least 2 hours. If the top seems to be browning too deeply, turn the oven lower.

Serve the pudding warm rather than hot and don't hang back from also offering cold, loosely-whipped double cream on the side.

CHAPTER TWELVE

Sunday Lunch

However many conventional mealtimes go by the board as women embark on raw energy diets and men decide to work late at the office, or as men decide to go on raw energy diets and women work late at the office, and as children discover the joys of re-heating a boil-in-the-bag meal, Sunday lunch when friends and family gather tends to go on being prepared. The fact that Sunday lunch has a different image to other sorts of meals is borne out by the fact that restaurants, however chic or modernistic, will abandon their daily menu and put on one that features a joint and a luscious pudding.

One of the attractions of Sunday lunch, quite apart from the shopping which most probably has been done the day before – unless Sunday-opening delicatessens and supermarkets have eroded your efficiency – is that it will be the only meal needing to be prepared that day. Even sticklers for punctuality and conventional mealtimes, even hard and fast believers in breakfast, dinner, lunch and tea being at the very least what the humane frame requires, will accept that Sunday lunch can be served at 2 p.m. or later and take you through the afternoon. A little cold collation of the leftovers at about 10 p.m. can satisfy the greedy or those who panic at the thought of a missed meal.

That said, you do not want to spend the entire morning cooking; there are papers to be read. For this reason, a joint of meat is apt since, along with probably being quite different to anything you have eaten during the week, it takes only minutes in preparation and afterwards more or less looks after itself. We have given a recipe for a slightly unusual way of going about roasting lamb as roasting beef is a matter of timing, instructions for which can be taken from any competent cookery book, and since it is necessary to roast a very large joint of beef to have real success with it, lamb seems more practical. The Chicken pie can be assembled the day before and an advantage is its ease to serve, for unless a born carver numbers among your guests or your family, the dishing out of a roast, though comfortingly symbolic, can involve tedious waits and the food of the polite becoming tepid. Hot plates are essential if you are serving a roasted joint.

The suggestions in each course may seem rather few, but yet another plus of this weekend meal is that guests will not only not mind repetition, they may come to hanker after it. In this mutable world some fixed points, such as a pie with a well-considered lucky dip of ingredients or a dish of delicious potatoes, are important. Recipes with which you become so familiar in the making that you can knock them up without reference to a book or recourse to weighing and measuring can provide soothing occupational therapy, something that is frequently required at the close of an anxious week.

On the whole, the main course of Sunday lunch is recognizable by its substantiality and the pudding by its puddingy quality. Therefore, we feel a first course is inappropriate as well as being a bore to make. Some suggestions for little things on toast to precede the meal and eat with drinks are included. The very nicest drink for Sunday midday is champagne. You may balk at believing this, but it is also one of the cheaper alternatives these days since champagne prices have held pretty steady and some supermarket champagnes are far from negligible in quality. Opening a bottle (or two) of champagne makes guests feel special and saves the host fussing around preparing this, that and the other. If you wish to stretch it or embellish it, depending on your point of view, you could make a Bellini with peach juice, a Kir Royale with cassis, a Paradis with raspberry juice, a rather fashionable mix with the juice of blood oranges, or whatever you will. Establish your own house cocktail.

A further consideration with Sunday lunch is the mix of age groups it usually attracts. Whilst we view the meal as a time to educate the young palates, it should also be a pleasure for children and obviate whining noises about how they don't like salsify and, in the case of separated parents, how Mummy/Daddy never makes them eat polenta. The very old can be similarly difficult and share with children a dislike of strange things sprung on them and can misconstrue a *nouvelle cuisine* purée as a thinly veiled insult. However, the pureé of leeks we have suggested with the lamb is so delicious that it is worth risking the implicit irony.

All the puddings, bar the Jam Roll, can be prepared ahead of time and the Jam Roll will provide you with the virtuous glow that attaches from 'using the oven'.

Anchovy Surprise
Smoked Salmon Pâté
Chicken Liver Pâté
Chicken and Mushroom Pie
Lamb Boulangère
Beefsteak and Kidney Pudding

Pureé of Leeks
Honeycomb Mould
Chocolate Mousse
Treacle Tart
Baked Jam Roll
Apple Charlotte

Anchovy Surprise

Serves 4

4 *thin slices wholemeal* or
  granary bread
1 *tin anchovy fillets*
¼ *pint/150 ml double cream* or
  clotted cream or *soured cream*

vegetable oil
chives or *fresh parsley, chopped*
  (optional)

With a small biscuit cutter, stamp out rounds of bread; you want a size that constitutes one mouthful. Wash the anchovies quickly in warm water to remove excess salt (or don't if you like saltiness), and pat dry. Cut each fillet into three. If you are using double cream, whip it until quite stiff and put it back into the fridge. Leave the soured cream or clotted cream in the fridge until the last minute. Fry the rounds of bread in hot vegetable oil, then drain on kitchen paper. Place 3 pieces of anchovy on each round and cover with a spoonful of cold cream. If you like, sprinkle with chopped parsley or chives. Serve immediately.

The contrasts in this are delectable; hot and cold, crisp and soft, salty and bland.

Smoked Salmon Pâté

It is usually possible to find smoked salmon bits wherever smoked salmon, the whole fish, is sold. They tend to be very good value and used in a pâté, their bitty appearance is not a problem. To forgo the monotony factor in pâtés, this one has three layers, which is less time consuming than it sounds if you have a food processor.

Serves 4–6

8 oz/250 g smoked salmon bits   *freshly ground black pepper*
7 oz/200 g curd cheese   *1 tablespoon chopped fresh parsley*
lemon juice

In a food processor fitted with a steel blade, or in a liquidizer, chop the salmon into small pieces. Remove about a quarter of the salmon and set aside. Add the cheese to the mixing bowl and run the motor until you have a smooth mixture. Flavour with lemon juice to taste and freshly ground black pepper. Switch on the motor for one more second. Remove half this mixture to another bowl and stir in the parsley.

Lightly oil the base and sides of a small straight sided dish, e.g., a small soufflé dish. Into the base evenly press the mixture of smoked salmon and cheese. Arrange on top the smoked salmon pieces and then smooth on the salmon/cheese mixture flavoured with parsley. Chill in the fridge for a few hours or overnight.

To serve, run a knife around the pâté and unmould. Arrange thin slices of hot brown toast in a napkin on a plate and serve with drinks.

Chicken Liver Pâté

Serves 8

1 lb/500 g chicken livers   *1 large clove garlic*
4 oz/125 g butter   *½ teaspoon dried thyme*
2 tablespoons brandy   *salt and freshly ground black pepper*
2 tablespoons medium-dry sherry

Clean the livers, removing any green parts with a sharp knife. Melt half the butter in a frying pan and cook the livers gently for a few minutes: they should be pink inside, but not raw. Remove the livers and put them in a liquidizer. Put the brandy into the pan with the cooking butter, let it bubble and then add the sherry. Add to the livers in the liquidizer the chopped garlic, thyme, the rest of the butter, the salt and pepper, and the liquid from the pan, then whizz until you have a smooth paste. Decant into a bowl or pot. You can, if you wish, melt a further ounce of butter to seal your pâté in its container, in which case it will keep for a week or two in the refrigerator. In any case, the pâté is better if you keep it for a few days before eating it. Serve with hot toast.

Chicken and Mushroom Pie

This recipe, evolved by Beth Coventry, the sister of one of the authors, is influenced by her many stays in Greece. The addition of cheese is a very Hellenic touch; it adds a surprising richness to what is essentially a homely dish.

Serves 6–8

1 chicken, preferably free-range
2½ oz/75 g butter
1½ oz/45 g flour
1 heaped teaspoon mustard
 powder
1 glass dry white wine
4 oz/125 g Cheddar cheese, grated
salt and pepper
2 tablespoons finely chopped
 parsley

1 tablespoon vegetable oil
1 large onion, peeled and finely
 chopped
forcemeat balls made from 8 oz/250 g
 top quality sausage meat (optional)
8 oz/250 g mushrooms, wiped and
 chopped
1 8-oz/250-g packet frozen puff pastry
1 egg, beaten

VEGETABLES FOR STOCK:

1 onion
1 large carrot
1 stalk celery

3 sprigs parsley
1 bay leaf
8 peppercorns

Turn on the oven to 220°C/425°F, Gas 7, 20 minutes before the pie goes in.

Put the chicken in a pan with water just to cover and add the vegetables and seasonings for the stock. Poach until tender, which will be no more than 1 hour for a large roasting chicken but up to 3 hours for a tough old hen.

Melt 1½ oz/45 g butter in a heavy-bottomed pan, stir in the flour and mustard powder, and cook gently until you have a smooth roux. Add up to 1 pint/625 ml of the chicken stock, or more if necessary to achieve a silky sauce of the consistency of single cream. Stir in the white wine and the cheese and cook gently. Taste for seasoning and add salt, pepper and the finely chopped parsley.

Heat the oil and remaining butter, and fry the onion until softened. Add the mushrooms and stir until they, too, are cooked. Remove the flesh from the chicken in fairly large chunks. Mix the chicken, onion and mushrooms into the sauce. (If you are including forcemeat balls, buy the best quality pork sausages you can find, skin them, and roll it into small balls which you should dust with flour and fry until crisp.) Pour the chicken mixture into a pie dish and add the forcemeat balls which have been drained on kitchen paper. Cover with the puff pastry and decorate the pie with any left-over pastry. Glaze with a beaten egg and cook for 30 minutes, or until the pastry has risen and is golden. If you want to make the filling in advance, reheat it before covering with pastry and cooking in the oven.

Lamb Boulangère

The purpose of this recipe is to place the meat straight on one of the racks of the oven and let its juices 'weep' on to a tin of sliced potatoes sitting below. This produces delicious potatoes and crisply cooked meat.

We like to use masses of garlic but you could reduce the quantities if it is not to your taste. If you slash the lamb radically as described below, it will open out during cooking and appear quite different from the usual leg of lamb.

Serves 6

$3\frac{1}{2}$ lb/1.75 kg leg of English lamb
6–8 cloves garlic, peeled and
   chopped
herbs, such as rosemary and mint
salt and pepper

olive oil
3 lb/1.5 kg good quality potatoes,
   peeled and thinly sliced
butter

Turn on the oven to 200°C/400°F, Gas 6.

Make deep diagonal slashes in the lamb, rather as if you were criss-crossing on a baked ham. Push three-quarters of the chopped garlic into the cuts and sprinkle with herbs. Season with salt and pepper and dribble olive oil over the whole leg.

Layer the potatoes in a roasting tin, interspersing the layers with salt, pepper, dots of butter and the remaining garlic. Set the tin on the bottom rack in the pre-heated oven and the meat on a rack above. Roast for about $1\frac{1}{2}$ hours if you like the meat pink, or for another half an hour if you like the meat well done.

Slice the meat and serve on the juice-impregnated potatoes.

Letting the lamb 'rest' in a warm place for 15 minutes is always a good idea. During that time, you can brown and crisp the potatoes on a high rack in the oven.

Beefsteak and Kidney Pudding

Serves 4–6 depending upon appetite

1 lb/150 g suet paste, made as
   below
1 lb/500 g shin of beef

1 lb/500 g ox kidney
1 tablespoon flour

SUET CRUST:

salt and freshly ground black
   pepper
12 oz/375 g flour

6 oz/180 g suet
¼ teaspoon salt
¼ pint/150 ml cold water

To make the crust mix the flour and suet, add the salt and gradually as much water as you need to make a fairly stiff paste. Roll it out and use three-quarters of it to line a pudding basin. Cut up the meat into 1-inch/2.5-cm cubes, and dip in the flour seasoned with pepper and salt. Fill the basin, and then three-quarters fill it with boiling water. Use the remaining crust to make a top for the pudding, sealing it with your fingers. Prick the middle once or twice with a fork. Cover the basin with greaseproof paper, making a pleat in it so that there is room for the suet to rise. Steam for 4 hours.

This is the classic recipe for pudding. We have tried it with cut-up pigeon breasts and kidney and it is very good. (You need kidney because it makes such rich gravy.) The Victorians used to add two or three oysters for flavour.

Purée of Leeks

Serves 4–6

3 lb/1.5 kg leeks
2 oz/60 g butter

freshly grated nutmeg
salt and freshly ground black pepper

Trim and wash the leeks thoroughly. As you are going to chop them up, you can be quite ruthless in the cleaning, pulling them apart to see that no sand or mud is lurking. Chop them into 1-inch/2.5-cm slices using some of the dark green part. Cover the leeks with cold water and bring to the boil. Simmer them for about 15 minutes, or until they are quite tender; this is not a moment to aim for *al dente* veg. Strain the leeks rather carelessly so that some water clings, then empty them into the bowl of a food processor. Add the butter cut in pieces and whizz to a purée: depending on the size of your machine, you may have to do this in two batches. Put the purée back into the cleaned pan, or into the top of a double saucepan if you wish to keep it warm for quite a long period. Season with salt, pepper and a little freshly grated nutmeg.

At the time of serving, dribble some of the meat juices onto the purée.

Honeycomb Mould

This nursery pudding appeals to children and grown-ups alike. The fresh lemons lend a clear singing flavour appropriate after a heavy main course. If you have a fancy jelly mould, this is the moment to use it. The pudding splits into layers providing a summit of lemon jelly and two bands of creamy mousse.

Serves 6–8

3 large eggs
rind and juice of 2 lemons
1 tablespoon gelatine
3 oz/90 g caster sugar

6 tablespoons/90 ml single or double
  cream
¾ pint/475 ml creamy milk

Separate the eggs. Whisk the yolks in a basin and add the lemon rind, gelatine, sugar and cream. Heat the milk to scalding point and whisk it into the eggs. Don't fret if it looks grainy – it will smooth out.

Put the basin over simmering water and cook, stirring, until you have a mixture as thick as double cream that coats the back of a spoon. Mix in the lemon juice. Taste to see if you want more sugar, but try to resist. Beat the whites into stiff peaks and strain the lemony custard on to them, folding it carefully and with a light hand, using a metal spoon. Pour into a 2-pint/1.1-litre mould and chill until set. To unmould, slip a knife round the edge, put a plate on top and turn over. It should plop out pretty as a picture.

Chocolate Mousse

The simpler a chocolate mousse the better. What you need is 1 oz/ 30 g dark bitter chocolate and one egg per person. Melting the chocolate in strong coffee or adding a little grated orange rind are the only flourishes allowed. Forget from here on recipes that include milk, cream, gelatine, alcohol, etc.

Serves 8

8 oz/250 g plain chocolate   *8 eggs*
    (Menier is a good choice or   *2 tablespoons instant coffee*
    Terry's bitter)

Either in a bowl that fits over a saucepan without touching its base, or in a double saucepan, place the squares of chocolate with 3 tablespoons of strong hot coffee that you have made by pouring not too much boiling water on to the instant coffee. Let it melt very gently, preferably in one layer so that you don't have to disturb it. The water in the lower saucepan should just shudder or, if you want to be sure not to overheat the chocolate, which makes it grainy, bring the water to the boil and then turn off the heat. The chocolate will eventually melt. Remove the pan from the heat and stir to blend.

Separate the eggs. Beat the yolks one by one into the chocolate. In a clean bowl, whisk the egg whites until they stand in stiff, dry peaks. Add a quarter of the volume of the beaten whites to the chocolate mixture and fold in with a light hand. Pour this on to the egg whites still in the bowl and fold again, blending carefully so that there are no white 'islands' but not hammering the air out of the mousse. Pour into small ramekins or pretty cups.

Chill in the fridge for a few hours. The chocolate hardening will set the mousse to just the right consistency. If you must serve cream, use single cream.

Treacle Tart

Serves 6

8 oz/250 g self-raising flour
a pinch of salt
3 oz/90 g butter
4 oz/125 g lard (Trex is very
    good)

2 tablespoons Golden Syrup
1½ tablespoons black treacle
4 oz/125 g fresh white breadcrumbs
grated rind and half the juice of
    1 lemon

Turn on the oven to 200°C/400°F, Gas 6.

Rub the fats lightly into the flour to which you have added the salt. The fats should be cold and cut into nut-sized knobs before you start rubbing. When you have a gravelly texture, add a little cold water and bind the mixture with your hands or a wooden spoon. Roll out to ¼ inch/0.6 cm thick and put into a greased tart tin, then put it into the fridge for half an hour.

Put the syrup and treacle tins with their lids off into saucepans of hot water to melt the contents. This makes it easier to measure the quantities you require.

Put the breadcrumbs into the tart tin, and pour over the treacle and syrup. Sprinkle with the lemon rind and add the lemon juice. Bake in the oven for about 35 minutes.

Baked Jam Roll

Serves 4

½–¾ lb/250–375 g blackcurrant or
    raspberry jam

SUET CRUST:

6 oz/180 g self-raising flour
pinch of salt

2 oz/60 g fresh white breadcrumbs
4 oz/125 g finely chopped suet

Put the jar of jam into a saucepan of very hot water to soften it. Turn on the oven to 180°C/350°F, Gas 4.

Sift the flour, salt and breadcrumbs together. Add the suet and rub it in lightly for a minute – use only the ends of your fingers. Add cold water by small degrees until you have a light spongy dough; use a wooden spoon for this. You should end up with a non-sticky ball of pastry.

Roll out on a floured board to a rectangular shape about 8 inches/20 cm wide and ¼ inch/0.6 cm thick. Spread with jam to within 1 inch/2.5 cm of the edge of the pastry. Roll up the pastry, seal the ends and flap together with your fingers. Put the roll on a baking tin and bake for 40 minutes.

Apple Charlotte

Serves 4

1 small white loaf	*2 lb/1 kg cooking apples*
6 oz/180 g butter	*4 oz/125 g Demerara sugar*
rind and juice of 2 lemons	*3 oz/90 g sultanas*

This dish is best made in a fairly shallow baking dish – about 4 inches/10 cm deep. Turn on the oven to 180°C/350°F, Gas 4.

Slice and butter the bread generously. Finely chop the rind of the 2 lemons and squeeze out the juice. Peel, quarter and slice the apples, put them on a damp tea towel and keep covered to prevent discoloration.

Line the bottom of the dish with the bread, butter-side downwards. Put in a layer of apple, a scattering of sugar, sultanas, lemon rind and a little lemon juice on top. Then put in another layer of bread. Continue like this until the dish is full, ending with bread and butter with the butter-side facing upwards. Scatter the remains of the sugar and rind on top and bake in the oven for about 45 minutes. The top should be brown and crisp.

This dish can be eaten either hot or cold, and many people like whipped cream with it.

CHAPTER THIRTEEN

Late-Night Shopping

There was a time when, unless you shopped during the day, which often meant a mad scramble around during an office lunch hour, you were consigned to an evening spent eating in a restaurant, munching take-away food or picking at a meal composed from the dry goods and tins in your store cupboard. Late night supermarkets, Asian grocers – usually one and the same thing – and ambitious delicatessens, have changed all that.

Butchers and fishmongers, however, resolutely believe that the day should wind down around tea-time, so meals shopped for late at night still have certain constraints. Implicit in shopping at this hour is the need to make a meal in a hurry or anyway the wish to assemble food rather than laboriously prepare it. It is here that delicatessens can help out though we feel they must be viewed circumspectly as so often the prepared salads and pâtés are astonishingly nasty. For example, it would be wiser to buy a tin of white haricot beans, a tin of tuna fish and some onions and quickly put together your own Italian salad rather than buy the mixture that has been sitting in the cabinet throughout the day and is feeling, and looking, weary. It will also work out considerably cheaper. A tin of sauerkraut might be a more interesting solution – particularly if you enhance it with some white wine and additional spices when you warm it up – than a carton of cole slaw which invariably seems to be made with malt vinegar and inadmissible amounts of sugar.

Certain items do not exactly benefit from being canned, but adopt a quite distinct personality which can turn out to be pleasing, rather the way the dullest looking person at a gathering can sometimes eventually prove the most diverting. Tinned *petits pois* come to mind in this category and, in a sense, tinned salmon is so unlike its fresh counterpart that it can be considered a whole new fish. Tinned salmon sits perfectly well in fish cakes.

We are not of the school that believes it takes only a spoonful of cream and a dash of sherry to turn a tinned soup into a gastronomic event. The one variety of soup that can provide a useful base are the fish soups put up in France. Often they have an intensity of flavour quite hard to achieve in the domestic kitchen. Such a soup, embellished with prawns and perhaps even some smoked trout, could be served with croûtons, grated cheese and a fiery Sauce Rouille and not be an ignoble thing.

Continental sausages are usually well represented in late night shops. Varieties such as Bratwurst have a high meat content and usually a less harmful fat content than an English breakfast variety. Served with a warm potato salad and a choice of mustards, they make an excellent quick supper. Superior English pork sausages, with a minimum of rusk and some emphatic herbs, could be the springboard for Toad in the Hole, a dish for which most people will reveal an atavistic fondness.

The availability of boxed fresh pasta has been a great boon for the instant cook and this chapter includes two good and slightly unusual sauces. Bought fresh pasta will never quite match pasta made at home, but it is nevertheless delicate and should not be swamped by the more conventional sauces like Bolognese and certainly not by tinned Bolognese. An invaluable item to store in the least chilly part of your refrigerator is a lump of Parmesan cheese well wrapped in layers of foil. Freshly grated Parmesan perks up many a dish, and just butter and Parmesan is a fine dressing for pasta. Packet spaghetti, for which we are developing renewed liking and respect (it seems to have moral fibre), is equally delicious just served with garlic and a good brand of olive oil. Eggs are, of course, the eternal stand-by and the omelette recipe is one thought up at a time of true deprivation when the cupboard resembled Mother Hubbard's, for there are times when, even though shops are open, it is late and you simply don't want to go out at all.

Sardines

Omelette with Spring Onions and Croûtons

Tinned Salmon Fish Cakes with Tomato Sauce

Ham with a Piquant Sauce

Toad in the Hole

Bratwurst with Warm Potato Salad

Fresh Pasta with Mushroom Sauce

Fresh Pasta with Smoked Trout and Fish Eggs

Chick Peas with Spinach and Fried Breadcrumbs

Sauce Rouille

Lemon Syllabub

Black Cherries with Soured Cream

Sardines

There are some people who keep sardines rather as others keep wine, dating the tins and turning them from time to time to keep them thoroughly steeped in oil. Even without going to these lengths a good brand of sardines, preferably a French one with the fish packed in olive oil, is a great pleasure and needs only bread and butter as an accompaniment. When you drain the sardines from their oil, save it for a cat. They like it and it gives gloss to their coats. And maybe yours too. Less perfect sardines, for example Portugese ones packed in vegetable oil, need some help. Drain them, extract any obvious bones – but remember the slight crunch of the spine is full of calcium – and mash with a lump of butter. Flavour with salt, pepper, a dash of vinegar (balsamic is good here) and mix in freshly chopped parsley if it is to hand or some finely chopped spring onion. This spread can be enjoyed on hot toast or let it make the base of an open sandwich topped with thin slices of cucumber and tomato. A different flavour and texture can be achieved using thick yoghurt or soured cream to mix with the mashed sardines.

Omelette with Spring Onions and Croûtons

This dish was invented in a Mother Hubbard situation but turned out to be good enough to suggest even were you to have some mushrooms, bacon, or other conventional omelette fillings to hand. The crunch of the croûtons provides relief from the softness of the egg and if you use wholemeal bread it also lends a nice nuttiness.

Serves 2

4 eggs
salt and freshly ground black pepper
a few sprigs parsley, chopped
1 small bundle chives, finely
    chopped
2 slices brown bread

vegetable oil
1 fat clove garlic, peeled and chopped
1 oz/30 g Parmesan cheese, grated
1 bunch spring onions, trimmed,
    peeled and finely chopped
1½ oz/45 g butter

We like to cook omelettes one at a time. If you are of this persuasion, break 2 eggs into a bowl and add 1 teaspoonful cold water. Season with salt and pepper and add half the herbs. Beat lightly.

Leaving the crusts on, chop the bread into cubes. Heat some vegetable oil in a small frying pan with the garlic and fry the bread, turning until you have croûtons, crisp on all sides. Roll them in Parmesan, then keep warm. In the same oil, quickly fry the spring onions. Drain on kitchen paper and keep warm.

Heat half the butter in an omelette pan. When it is foaming, add the beaten eggs. Push them and lift them, as you do with an omelette, and when it is set on the bottom and tacky on the surface, scatter on half the croûtons and onions. Fold over, tip out and serve with a little butter rubbed on top of the omelette to give it gloss.

Repeat the procedure with the other 2 eggs.

Tinned Salmon Fish Cakes with Tomato Sauce

Tinned salmon is now often more expensive than the fresh variety, but you might be feeling like having fish cakes and find the fishmonger closed. You could use pilchards if you draw the line at paying a lot for tinned fish; they lend themselves to a perfectly good, if different, fish cake. Tinned tomatoes are often considerably better in flavour than the fresh ones on sale nowadays.

Serves 4

1 lb/500 g potatoes, peeled
butter
2 tins (8 oz/250 g) salmon or
    pilchards
1 egg
1 teaspoon dried dillweed
    (optional)
a squeeze of lemon juice

a splash of anchovy essence or
    Worcestershire sauce
1 dessertspoon chopped fresh parsley
salt and pepper
1 egg for coating
home-made breadcrumbs
vegetable oil for frying

FOR THE SAUCE:

1 tablespoon olive oil	*a pinch of cayenne pepper* or *chilli*
1 clove garlic	*powder*
1 14-oz/425-g tin peeled tomatoes	*1 teaspoon sugar*
1 glass red wine	*salt and freshly ground black pepper*

Boil the potatoes until they are cooked through and practically falling apart. Drain them not all that assiduously and mash with a knob of butter, but no milk as you want a stiff mixture. Drain the fish of oil or brine, break it up and mix into the potatoes. Add an egg, stir well, and season with dillweed if you have it, lemon juice, anchovy essence or Worcestershire sauce, parsley, salt and pepper.

Form the mixture into cakes. Chill to firm them while you make the tomato sauce.

In the olive oil, gently heat the finely chopped garlic; don't let it brown or burn as bitterness results. Tip in the tin of tomatoes, and break them up as best you can with a wooden spoon. Add the wine and seasonings including the sugar and let simmer and thicken while you fry the fish cakes.

Beat the egg in a soup plate. Cover the base of another soup plate with breadcrumbs; try not to resort to the packet variety that is bright orange. You can buy more respectable crumbs these days or easily make them in a food processor. Coat the fish cakes in egg, then breadcrumbs. Fry slowly in about ¼ inch/0.6 cm hot vegetable oil until they are heated through and the coating is crisp. Serve with the sauce.

Ham with a Piquant Sauce

This recipe is a simplified version of one given in Elizabeth David's *French Provincial Cooking*. It is considerably finer than ham in white sauce and a good alternative to the sort of meal you *meant* to shop for at the butcher's but when you arrived, found that the butcher had shut up shop.

Serves 4

4 shallots or 1 onion
3 juniper berries
4 tablespoons wine vinegar
2 oz/60 g butter
2 tablespoons flour
8 fl oz stock/250 ml or ½ stock
    cube

a splash of white wine (optional)
¼ pint/150 ml double cream
salt and pepper
4 thick slices ham (from a whole ham,
    not out of a packet)

Turn on the oven to 180°C/350°F, Gas 4.

Peel and chop the shallots finely or, failing shallots, an onion. Put the shallots, the juniper berries and the wine vinegar into a small saucepan. Bring to the boil and reduce until there is practically no vinegar left.

In a larger saucepan, melt the butter, stir in the flour and continue stirring watchfully until the mixture is smooth and a pale coffee colour. Dissolve the stock cube in 8 fl oz/250 ml of water, or heat the same amount of stock should you have some. Add the stock to the flour and butter mixture gradually, stirring until the mixture thickens. Add a splash of white wine if it is around, and then the shallot mixture. Cook gently until there is no taste of flour, about 20 minutes.

Stir in the cream, taste for seasoning and thin if necessary; you want a fairly liquid sauce. Arrange the ham in a single layer in a shallow oven-proof dish. Strain the sauce over the ham and heat through in the oven.

Toad in the Hole

Serves 4

1 lb/500 g best pork sausages you
    can buy

12 oz/375 g streaky bacon, cut finely
1 tablespoon sunflower seed oil

FOR THE BATTER:

8 oz/250 g plain flour
a large pinch of salt
1 egg

½ pint/300 ml skimmed milk or half
    water and half ordinary milk

Make the batter by mixing the flour and salt together in a bowl, then make a hole in the centre and drop the egg into it with one-third of the milk. Beat well, gradually adding the rest of the milk. Beat until perfectly smooth. Leave to stand for at least half an hour in the fridge.

Turn on the oven to 180°C/350°F, Gas 4.

Wrap each sausage in the bacon. Put them in a baking dish and bake for 20 minutes. Take the sausages out of the dish, pour off the fat, then pour in the oil and return the dish to the oven. When the oil is really hot, lay the sausages, brown-side down, along the centre of the dish. Take the batter, beat it briskly for 1 minute, and then pour over the sausages. Return the dish to the oven and bake for 50 minutes; when ready, the batter should be crisp and light brown.

Bratwurst with Warm Potato Salad

This assembly, typical of a meal you might find in a brasserie, makes a most satisfactory supper. Serve it with a selection of mustards, including a grainy one, a German one and English mustard powder made up according to your preference with water, milk or wine vinegar, about 10 minutes before you are going to eat. A really good chilled lager is the appropriate drink.

Serves 4

2 lb/1 kg potatoes – new ones or *a*
waxy variety
8 Bratwurst sausages
6 tablespoons olive oil or *3*
tablespoons olive oil and 3
tablespoons vegetable oil

2 tablespoons wine vinegar
salt and freshly ground black pepper
4 shallots or *1 bunch of spring onions,*
peeled and chopped
1 tablespoon chopped parsley
(optional)

Peel the potatoes and cut them in half if large. Boil them in salted water until just tender. While they are boiling, grill the Bratwurst, starting gently so they remain intact, but increasing the heat to finish with a nice browned surface. Mix together the oil, vinegar, and salt and pepper with the back of metal spoon – you want an amalgamation but not an emulsion. Drain the potatoes, slice immediately and while still hot turn in the dressing with the shallots or spring onions. Sprinkle with parsley and serve warm.

If you like an oily dish as they do, for instance, in Alsace, dress with a little more oil.

Fresh Pasta with Mushroom Sauce

Serves 6–8

2 ½-oz/15-g packets dried wild
   mushrooms
12 oz/375 g fresh mushrooms
1 large sweet onion
2 tablespoons light olive oil
2 cloves garlic
⅓ bunch fresh coriander, roughly
   chopped, or 10 coriander seeds,
   pounded in a mortar or 1
   teaspoon ground coriander

1 teaspoon tomato purée
1½ lb/750 g fresh pasta – tagliolini is
   best, but you may not have a choice
½ pint/300 ml double cream
2 tablespoons chopped fresh parsley
salt and freshly ground black pepper
3 oz/90 g Parmesan cheese, freshly
   grated

Soak the dried mushrooms in ¼ pint/150 ml of water just off the boil. They should soak for at least half an hour, so it should be the first thing that you do when you get back with the shopping.

Peel – or wipe clean – the fresh mushrooms and slice. Peel and chop the onion finely, then heat the oil in a pan and sauté the onions until they are transparent. Add the fresh mushrooms, pressed garlic and coriander and cook gently, stirring often. A little salt may be added at this stage to help the mushrooms sweat.

Add the dried mushrooms, roughly chopped and drained of their juice (but keep it). Stir well, and then add the juice by degrees. Add the tomato purée and leave to simmer for 15 minutes. (You can at this point turn off the heat and leave the sauce until you are boiling water for the pasta.)

While the pasta is cooking, stir the double cream into the sauce, cooking gently as you do so. Just before serving, add the chopped parsley and black pepper. The Parmesan should be in a bowl on the table for people to use as they like.

Fresh Pasta with Smoked Trout and Fish Eggs

Boxed fresh pasta is now easily available, but should you need to buy the packet kind, choose a narrow width, i.e. tagliolini rather than tagliatelle. If you choose green pasta, try to find the red lump fish roe as the colours are pretty together. This idea, as with most ideas about food, came from another cook; in this case Alice Waters who owns Chez Panisse restaurant in Berkeley, California.

Serves 4

4 oz/125 g smoked trout
6 fl oz/180 ml double cream
1 lb/500 g fresh pasta

4 tablespoons fish eggs, i.e., caviare,
lumpfish roe (known as Danish
caviare) or salmon eggs
freshly ground pepper

Skin and bone the smoked trout and carefully flake the flesh; set aside. While a large pot of water is boiling for the pasta, reduce the cream slightly in a small pan over a medium heat. Cook the pasta until it is *al dente* – if it is fresh to begin with, this should be a matter of a minute or two, otherwise consult the packet, but test the pasta some time before the suggested limit.

Add the smoked trout to the hot cream and then mix carefully with the drained pasta. Put the pasta on to warmed plates and crown each heap with a tablespoonful of fish eggs. A pepper mill should be at the ready.

Chick-Peas with Spinach and Fried Breadcrumbs

This is a satisfying dish, and though the ingredients can be assembled by a quick dash around the supermarket, this is not reflected in the taste.

Serves 2

1 onion	1 dried red chilli
olive oil	salt and pepper
1 lb/500 g frozen leaf spinach	1 slice bread
1 14-oz/425-g tin chick-peas	1 large clove garlic

Peel the onion and slice it from tip to base in thin crescents. Fry until golden in 1 tablespoon olive oil. Add the leaf spinach and cook according to the instructions on the packet until softened; drain off any excess water.

Drain the chick peas and stir them into the spinach with a dribble more of olive oil and the crumbled chilli pepper. Season with salt and pepper, cover the saucepan and allow the mixture to simmer. Meanwhile, fry a slice of bread in olive oil into which you have put a finely chopped or crushed large clove of garlic. When the bread is golden brown, drain and crumble it roughly onto the spinach and chickpeas. Put into a serving dish. You could now fry another slice of bread and cut into triangles to serve alongside. Put the dish on the table before the breadcrumbs have lost their crunch.

Sauce Rouille

This sauce will glamorize tinned or bottled fish soup, both of them often surprisingly good. If you also serve croûtons made of slices of French bread fried in olive oil and some grated cheese, you have a real meal on your hands. Try not to resort to bottled mayonnaise as a base. However fancy the label on the jar, it is never much like the real thing. Oddly, mayonnaise in tubes is better.

There are alternative methods to follow:

FIRST METHOD:

2–3 cloves garlic, peeled	3 tablespoons olive oil
2 small dried red chillies	1 dessertspoon of the soup
1 slice white bread, crusts removed	salt and pepper

Pound together the garlic and chillies in a mortar or a small pudding basin. Squeeze out the bread in water and stir into the garlic mixture thoroughly. Gradually add the olive oil as if making mayonnaise and moisten with the soup. Season to taste with salt and pepper.

2–3 cloves garlic
2 small dried red chillies
2 egg yolks
1 teaspoon Dijon mustard

3 tablespoons olive oil
3 tablespoons vegetable oil
salt and pepper
a squeeze of lemon

Pound the garlic and chillies as above. Beat in the egg yolks and mustard. Gradually add first the olive oil and then the vegetable oils as if making mayonnaise. Stop when you have a thick, viscous mixture. Season with salt and pepper and perhaps a squeeze of lemon juice.

Float a piece of fried bread on each serving of soup. Add a dessertspoonful of rouille and sprinkle with grated cheese. Serve the remaining rouille in a bowl on the table.

Lemon Syllabub

Serves 6

1 pint/625 ml double cream
2 oz/60 g caster sugar
grated rind and juice of 1 lemon

¼ pint/150 ml dry sherry
¼ pint/150 ml brandy

Put all the ingredients together into a bowl and, with a hand-held electric beater, whisk until very thick; this will take about 20 minutes. Pour into small glasses and put in the fridge until serving.

Black Cherries with Soured Cream

Serves 4

1 tin (14 oz/425 g) black cherries
2 oranges
1 lemon

½ pint/300 ml soured cream (if you cannot get soured cream, buy fresh double cream and sour it with a small squeeze of lemon juice)

Drain the cherries and reserve the juice. Grate the orange and lemon rinds and squeeze the fruit.

Put a small amount of cherry juice into a small pan with the orange rind and simmer for a few minutes. Put the cherries into a serving bowl with the rest of the cherry juice, add the orange and lemon juice, then the contents of the pan. Finally, add the grated lemon rind. Serve with dollops of cream.

CHAPTER FOURTEEN

Invalid Cooking

Cooking for invalids conjures up depressing memories of over-steamed fish, milk puddings and stewed fruit. All these things can, of course, be good in their way, but the people in charge who make the rules and carry out the results feel it is so good of them to make a special effort that the gastronomic result is often beside the point. Invalid food, in many people's minds, should be bland and tasteless – in return for being digestible. We believe that invalid food should taste delicious, nourish the eater and set him or her on the road to recovery. But it *is* a key point that the meal should be easy to digest.

If you are faced with cooking a meal for your family and friends *plus* an invalid, the first rule is not to cook two separate meals: it is curiously demoralizing to sit in front of a milk pudding or a steamed plaice while everybody else is tucking into roast lamb. It is perfectly possible to make a delicious meal that will suit everybody. The second rule is that whatever kind of invalid you are dealing with, a minimum of butter, cream, egg yolk or alcohol in the meal (and preferably none) is the kindest course. Alcohol and fats are hardest on the liver, and if you avoid them entirely, almost any invalid will benefit. Naturally, if you are faced with an invalid who announces beforehand that their doctor has told them to eat nothing but bananas, that is what you must provide – in which case you won't need to read this. Do, however, ask whether any particular food is taboo – apart from illness, there are such things as allergies.

The third rule is not ever to pile the invalid's plate: even if you feel that it would do them all the good in the world to eat more, you won't achieve it by this method. Give them a small helping, and after a decent interval, offer them a second. Invalids often start by thinking that they hardly want to eat, but usually, if sufficiently tempted, they can surprise themselves and you. Finally, we think a two-course meal is desirable: if you fill the invalid up with a starter, they may find it hard to keep going, and generally the main dish is what you want them to eat.

The following menus are almost without fat. The orange jelly contains a very little sherry, but provided your invalid is not recovering from hepatitis this should be allowable.

Supposing, however, that your invalid is not actually visiting but a resident, and entirely, or largely, in bed to boot? Many invalids have the tiresome habit of not wanting the meals you provide and then being overcome with hunger for a snack – a little something – an hour later. Hot and cold drinks are an essential part of an invalid diet. Almost all patients are better for as much liquid as you can get into them, and it is useful if some of the drinks are nourishing as well as enjoyable. For this reason, properly made beef tea is a first consideration. It seems expensive, and it takes time, but you can make a lot of it at once and if necessary, freeze some and then heat as required. We also think that fresh lemonade and barley water are a great boon, and so have included recipes for them. For a hot snack (or supper), poached soft roes on toast could be a winner as could a couple of steamed scallops. But all too often, the need for a snack comes at an awkward moment and a sandwich is what is wanted. So we have suggested a few sandwich fillings that are quick and easy to prepare. If sweet things are required, it is sensible to make a cake that will keep well, so a good cherry cake has been included.

Eggs as a hot snack have to be considered: if you can get a really fresh free-range egg, boiling or coddling it is unbeatable. (Samuel Butler used to range about the Home Counties telling farmers frightful lies about how he needed absolutely fresh eggs for an invalid friend. He then returned to London and triumphantly boiled them for himself.) If you can't buy an egg with real personality, then you will have to get good at omelettes, or scrambling.

Apart from the carrot and spinach soups in this chapter, soups that are nourishing and easy to make are watercress (*see* page 55), and celery (*see* page 227). Small salads are also acceptable. A tomato and Mozzarella could be one: cress, watercress and avocado would be another good combination.

Spinach Soup	Sandwich Fillings
Carrot Soup	Baked Apples
Œuf en Cocotte with Sautéed	Orange Jelly
Lettuce	Cherry Cake
Stuffed Fresh Haddock	Beef Tea
Poached Chicken	Lemonade
Soft Roes on Toast	Barley Water

Spinach Soup

Serves 4

1 large onion
2 lb/1 kg spinach
1 dessertspoon sunflower seed oil
2 cloves of garlic, chopped

1½ pints/1 litre chicken stock
salt, pepper and freshly grated
nutmeg

Chop the onion. Wash and roughly chop the spinach. Fry the onion in the oil until translucent. Add the garlic. Add the spinach and stir well so that it gets coated with oil and onion. Add the stock. Simmer for about 15 minutes, and then mouli or liquidize. Season (be sparing with nutmeg; taste the soup to see how much you like).

A handful of sorrel can be added to the spinach and gives the soup a light lemony sharpness.

Carrot Soup

Serves 4

1½ lb/750 g carrots
1 onion, peeled and chopped
1 dessertspoon sunflower seed oil

1½ pints/1 litre chicken stock
salt and pepper
sugar

Scrub and chop the carrots; if you have a food processor, you can grate them. Sauté the onion in the oil with a little salt to make it sweat. Add the carrots when the onion becomes transparent; stir until the carrots are well coated with oil and onion. Add the stock and simmer until the carrots are soft.

Liquidize everything or preferably use a French mouli which gives a far more interesting texture. Season with pepper and sugar if liked.

Œuf en Cocotte with Sautéed Lettuce

An egg baked in the oven is a comforting thing, reminiscent of being tucked up in bed. As we know from Peter Rabbit, lettuce is soporific so might help the invalid get to sleep.

Serves 1

knob of butter
3 or 4 leaves of lettuce cut into
  narrow strips

salt and pepper
1 free-range egg

Turn on the oven to 180°C/350°F, Gas 4. Boil a kettle of water. Using a piece of kitchen paper wipe the inside of a small cocotte (ramekin) with butter. Using some of the remaining butter gently sauté the lettuce until it is softened and some juices have run – a matter of a minute or two. Put the lettuce and its buttery juices into the small cocotte. Add a little salt and pepper. Break in the egg. Dab on the last of the butter. Place the egg in its cocotte in a larger heatproof dish and add hot water from the kettle to come two-thirds up the side of the cocotte. Place in the oven and check after 7 minutes.

The egg is cooked when an opaque film has covered the yolk but the yolk must not be allowed to get hard. Serve with thin toast. This is so good that unless your invalid is on a low-cholesterol diet, serve two *œufs*.

Stuffed Fresh Haddock

You may need two fish depending upon the size and how many people you are feeding: it is safe to say that a 4 lb/2 kg fish will do 6 people. Whether you buy fresh haddock, cod, or hake depends upon what looks best at your fishmonger that day. The stuffing calls for sorrel, but it can be quite difficult to buy. Sorrel is very easy to grow and we strongly recommend that anybody with room for one or two roots does so. It is invaluable for cooking and has a long picking season. However, if you cannot procure sorrel, use spinach.

Serves 6

4 lb/2 kg fish (see above)

FOR THE STUFFING:

12 oz/375 g fresh breadcrumbs   *grated rind of 2 lemons*
2 oz/60 g parsley, chopped   *salt and pepper*
2 oz/60 g sorrel, chopped   *4 oz/125 g butter*
a handful of chopped chives or 1   *1 egg yolk*
   small onion, chopped finely   *vegetable oil*

Put the first six stuffing ingredients in your food processor and add the butter straight from the fridge. When this is well-mixed, add the egg yolk.

Turn on the oven to 180°C/350°F, Gas 4. Stuff the fish. You can fasten the flaps with small wooden toothpicks, or you can sew the fish with a needle and fine twine. Paint the fish with oil and wrap in aluminium foil and bake in the oven. The cooking time will depend upon the size of the fish: test after 30 minutes by pricking the fish near its spine to see if the flesh is opaque.

Serve a purée of potato, and a steamed green vegetable, such as broccoli, spinach or french beans, with this dish.

Poached Chicken

Chicken is best poached in a previously prepared stock. If you go to a really good butcher who does a big trade, you may be able to get or buy a raw carcass of chicken as well as the one you are going to poach. In any case, you can use the giblets: be sure to cut off all the fat from the heart, etc.

Serves 4–6

3½-lb/1.75-kg roasting chicken
   (free-range if possible)

FOR THE STOCK:

3 large carrots, scrubbed and sliced   *herbs – including a sprig of rosemary*
1 onion, peeled and roughly   *3–4 cloves*
   chopped   *6 peppercorns*
2 stalks celery, chopped   *a little sea salt*

Simmer the vegetables and seasonings in 2 pints/1.1 litres cold water very slowly for 1½ hours and then strain.

Put the chicken into a deep pan, and pour over the strained stock. If the breast is above the stock, cover it with buttered paper. Simmer gently for half an hour and then add:

1 lb/500 g carrots, scrubbed and	*1 parsnip, peeled and sliced*
cut so that their size is uniform	*1 turnip, peeled and sliced*
1 lb/500 g onions, peeled and cut	*2 oz/60 g rice*
into quarters	

Simmer everything together until the chicken is cooked and the vegetables tender – this will take about an hour. This dish may be served with a parsley sauce, and it is also good with the vegetables mentioned in the previous recipe.

Soft Roes on Toast

Serves 1

½ teaspoon mustard powder	*4–6 oz/125–180 g soft roes*
salt	*1 slice wholemeal bread*
1 oz/30 g butter	

Put the mustard and a little salt into a bowl with the butter and work it all into a paste with a fork. Melt the paste in a double saucepan to avoid browning the butter, then put the roes into a non-stick pan and pour the melted butter over them. Cook gently for 8–10 minutes while you are toasting the bread. When the roes are cooked, arrange them on the toast.

Sandwich Fillings

Sandwiches can be very useful – not only as snacks for convalescent adults, but for children who are off their food. We have provided a small collection here: obviously you must choose what is suitable for the age and state of your patient. Do use the best wholemeal bread for your sandwiches, as this will provide much-needed fibre for your patient.

Honey and Oatmeal

Put a handful of oatmeal in a baking dish and bake it in a moderate oven until it is pale brown.

Butter thin slices of bread, and spread with honey. Do get good honey: read the label carefully. Also, it is easier and less messy for your recipient if you use the stiff honey rather than the kind that drips and oozes. Sprinkle toasted oatmeal on top of honey and add a second piece of buttered bread.

Egg and Watercress

Hard-boil 2 eggs. As most people hard-boil eggs until they are like cannon balls. it may be worth remarking that the best results are obtained by putting eggs into cold water, bringing them slowly to the boil and then boiling for exactly 5 minutes. Take out the eggs and plunge them into cold running water until cool. This way, the yolk will be a little soft, or at least yielding.

Mash up the eggs with a little top of the milk. Add salt and pepper to taste. Chop watercress (washed and dried, of course) fairly finely. Combine the mixtures.

Cheese and Sultana

Butter the bread. Grate mild Cheddar cheese coarsely, and put on the bread with a scattering of sultanas. These sandwiches, which became famous in the last war when they were served at the National Gallery in London at lunchtime concerts, are popular with children and very nourishing.

Cream Cheese and Tomato

Blanch and skin tomatoes – tomato skin is utterly indigestible. Put cream cheese – petit-suisse is good, or a double cream cheese bought from the delicatessen – on to unbuttered bread, then put thinly sliced tomato on top. The tomato may be garnished with chopped chives or finely chopped parsley but this is a matter of taste. A very light sprinkling of salt, and a touch of sugar will help the flavour of the tomatoes. Add a second slice of bread spread with cream cheese.

Cream Cheese and Blackcurrant Jam

Spread cream cheese as above. Use only home-made blackcurrant jam, or a superior brand such as Tiptree.

Banana and Brown Sugar

Slice bananas thinly and put them on buttered bread. Scatter with Demerara sugar and add a squeeze of lemon juice.

Baked Apples

Turn on the oven to 180°C/350°F, Gas 4.

Large Bramley apples are the best to use: one per person. Wipe the skin with a hot wet cloth and then, using an apple corer, be sure to remove all the core. This will make a slightly large hole in the middle of the apple, but you will need it for the stuffing.

Put the apples on a clean baking tray and stuff each cavity with butter, dark brown sugar and sultanas in that order until the hole is full; pour a little lemon juice into the top. Bake in the oven for about 45 minutes.

Baked apples are delicious with thick cream, but your invalid may also enjoy one without.

Orange Jelly

Most people think of jelly as being boring, but this is because it is made from packets. Home-made jellies are easy to make, and are refreshing and delicious.

Serves 6

4 oranges
2½ fl oz/75 ml sherry
⅔ packet of gelatine

4 oz/125 g white sugar
1 lemon

Wash the oranges and dry them. Buy good dessert oranges rather than oranges you would use for juice. Peel 2 of the oranges very thinly (a potato peeler is easiest) and steep the rind in sherry for 1 hour.

Soak the gelatine in 2½ fl/oz/75 ml water, stir over a gentle heat until dissolved, then strain on to the sugar and add another 2½ fl oz/75 ml hot water. When the sugar has melted, stir in the strained juice of the oranges and the lemon. Strain the sherry from the rind; add the sherry and discard the rind.

We put these jellies into small individual pots.

Cherry Cake

4 oz/125 g butter	*8 oz/250 g plain flour*
4 oz/125 g caster sugar	*1 teaspoon cream of tartar*
3 eggs, separated	*12 oz/375 g glacé cheeries*
4 fl oz/125 ml milk	*1 teaspoon bicarbonate of soda*

Beat the butter and sugar to a white cream. Add by degrees the yolks of the eggs, and then add the milk little by little – beating all the while.

Turn on the oven to 200°C/400°F, Gas 6.

Take the flour, add the cream of tartar to it, and use a little to coat the cherries. Add the flour to the creamed mixture, beating all the time. Fold in the cherries. Whisk the egg whites to a stiff froth and add bit by bit. Then add the bicarbonate of soda mixed in a little milk. Pour into a greased 7-in/17.5 cm tin and bake in the oven for 20 minutes until the cake has risen; then lower the temperature to 180°C/350°F, Gas 4.

The cake should take about an hour to cook, but you can test whether it is done by inserting a fine skewer or knitting needle. If the cake is done, the skewer will come out clean. Take out of the oven: leave to cool a little, and then turn out gently on to a cake rack.

Beef Tea

1 lb/500 g lean beef – shin is good	*1 small onion*
1 oz/30 g butter	*salt*
1 clove	

Cut the beef into small dice, and put into a saucepan with the butter, clove, onion and a little salt. Stir the meat over the heat until it produces a thin gravy: then add 1 quart/1.1 litres water and simmer for 1 hour, skimming off every particle of fat.

After cooking, strain the liquid through a sieve and keep cool until required.

As the beef tea is needed for the patient, heat it through in a double saucepan. These quantities make about 1 pint/625 ml of good beef tea and heating in a double saucepan means that you don't lose any of it by reduction.

Lemonade

Put 6 ice cubes, 1 whole lemon, 1 tablespoonful caster sugar and 1 pint/625 ml water into the liquidizer. Switch on to full for a slow count of 10. Strain. This makes excellent lemonade and is very little trouble to make.

Barley Water

2 oz/60 g pearl barley

Wash the barley in cold water, put it into a saucepan with 1 pint/ 625 ml cold water and when it has boiled for about 15 minutes, strain off the water and add 2 quarts/2.3 litres of freshly boiling water. Boil until the liquid is reduced to half, strain it and it is ready – if plain barley water is required. You can flavour it with a little lemon rind and sugar, or you can mix it with the lemonade described in the previous recipe. Barley water is very good for the kidneys.

CHAPTER FIFTEEN

Greedy People

The French make a distinction between those who insist upon very small quantities of delicious food (gourmet), and those who want everything to be frightfully good, but above all want a great deal of it (gourmand). Our experience in this country leads us to conclude that gourmands are thicker on the ground. The English do not, on the whole, pick at their food. In 1693, the Duke of Hamilton was spending over £1,000 a week on provisions: admittedly this covered the state banquets at Holyrood, but it did not include meat, butter and vegetables that were brought from his own estates – and £1,000 in the seventeenth century would be approximately £150,000 today. We must infer that apart from the excellence of the fare, people ate a very great deal of it. The habits of the Prince Regent were certainly gourmand, and Edward VII was no mean trencherman. One of many affectionate memories of James Robertson Justice is of his looking pensively at the carcass of a wild goose and remarking to his fellow diner, 'Tiresome bird: too much for one, and not enough for two.'

Greed is regarded as bad – is indeed famous for being sinful. We feel that as with so much else, it is a matter of degree. People who are utterly indifferent about what they eat are missing a basic, and often simple pleasure. On the other hand, people totally preoccupied with their bellies are dull – and usually unattractive to be with. We find it rewarding to cook for moderately greedy people, but we also recognize that, from time to time, the immoderates occur in life. Someone you are very fond of is married to one, for instance and marriage usually implies a social package deal.

The menu we suggest is comprised of dishes that any moderately greedy person might appreciate: for the immoderates, you simply double the quantities. In much the same way that heavy drinkers are disquieted by the absence of spare bottles of wine on the table, or at least in view, so heavy eaters will get nervy if they have to count the roast potatoes, or worse, won't count but will simply scoff an unfair share. They are also very keen on second helpings, however large the first one was. They expect a minimum of three courses; they don't like being fobbed off with cheese and fresh fruit instead of a pudding – although they will almost certainly want cheese as well. How much you pander to them is up to you.

Œuf Froid Câreme
Sizzling Prawns
Fried Sole with Iced Fennel Butter
Cold Poached Salmon
Cucumber Salad
Filet de Bœuf en Croûte
Saddle of Venison
Excellent Roast Potatoes

Mashed Potatoes with Olive Oil
and Cream
Potato Pie
Cornbread
Rich Cold Fruit Pudding
Îles Flottantes
Fromage à la Crème
Chocolate Profiteroles
Sticky Toffee Pudding

Œuf Froid Câreme

This is a Roux brothers' recipe that has always been, and still is, served at their 3-star Michelin restaurant, Le Gavroche in Brook Street, London. The recipe details are taken from *New Classic Cuisine*, the Roux brothers' first cookery book, packed with delights for greedy people.

Serves 4

4 globe artichokes, preferably
  Breton
juice of ½ lemon
6 tablespoons white wine vinegar
4 eggs
4 medium-sized slices of smoked
  salmon weighing altogether
  about 6 oz/180 g

1 small truffle, about 1 oz/30 g
mayonnaise made with 1 egg yolk and
  ½ pint/300 ml oil (see page 88)
1 tablespoon tomato ketchup
1 teaspoon Cognac
chervil (optional)
salt and pepper

Snap the stalks off the artichokes and, using a sharp knife, trim off the leaves until only the neatly shaped hearts are left. Squeeze a little lemon juice over them. Cook the artichoke hearts in a saucepan of boiling, salted water with 3 tablespoonfuls wine vinegar, or in a white *court bouillon* (1 tablespoonful flour, 3 tablespoonfuls wine vinegar and salted water). They will need 25–30 minutes, depending on their size. Use the point of a knife to test whether the artichoke hearts are done, then leave them to cool in their cooking liquid.

Next bring a shallow pan of water to the boil, add 3 tablespoonfuls vinegar and poach the eggs. Lift them out with a slotted spoon and place them in a bowl of very cold water; then remove to a tea towel and trim any ragged edges from the white.

Use a plain 3½-inch/9-cm pastry cutter to cut a neat circle from each slice of smoked salmon. Decorate prettily with some of the truffle and place in the refrigerator. Cut the smoked salmon trimmings into small dice and keep them in a bowl. Roughly chop the remaining truffle and add it to the diced salmon. Stir in the mayonnaise, add the ketchup and Cognac and season to taste with salt and pepper. Keep at room temperature.

To serve, remove the chokes from the artichoke hearts and pat dry with a cloth. Divide the mayonnaise mixture between the 4 artichoke bottoms. Place an egg on each one and top with a round of smoked salmon. You could add a sprig of chervil for colour (and in place of the truffle) if you wish.

Sizzling Prawns

Prawns – either the large ones you have to peel or the tiny brown ones (shrimps) that you can eat whole, whiskers and all – are delicious when fried in lots of oil spiked with garlic and chilli which provides a wonderful sauce for mopping with bread – an activity much enjoyed by the greedy.

Serves 4

2 pints/1.1 litres shrimps or 3
*   pints/1.75 litres larger prawns*
6 tablespoons olive oil or
*   vegetable oil, depending on*
*   preference*
3 cloves garlic, peeled and finely
*   sliced*

2 teaspoons cayenne pepper
1 teaspoon ground ginger or 2
*   teaspoons grated fresh root ginger*
1 teaspoon salt
French bread for mopping

In a sauté pan which you can bring to the table, heat the oil. Add the garlic, cayenne, ginger and salt. Sizzle for a moment but do not let the garlic brown. Add the prawns, turn up the heat and fry them fast and furiously, turning with a wooden fork or spoon until the shells are well coated with oil and seasonings. Take the pan to the table with the oil still bubbling.

Fried Sole with Iced Fennel Butter

Greedy people like a whole large sole each, no messing about. The crisp breadcrumb coating adds substance and deliciousness and the hot fish with cold butter is another appeal to the senses.

Serves 4

1 small head fennel
6 oz/180 g salted butter at room
   temperature
freshly ground black pepper
4 × 12-oz/375-g Dover soles

seasoned flour
2 eggs, beaten
6 oz/180 g dry white breadcrumbs
vegetable oil for frying

Trim the fennel, quarter it and steam until soft; then purée it in a food processor or liquidizer. Strain off the excess liquid, add the butter and whizz together. Season with pepper and whizz again. Pack into a small dish and freeze.

Skin and trim the soles, leaving the heads on, or ask the fishmonger to do this when you buy them. With a small sharp knife, make a cut, one side only, down the centre of the backbone. Raise the side fillets, loosening them with a knife, so that you can snip the bone just below the head and above the tail. Later you will remove the whole backbone, so work the fillets away from the bones, but leave them attached at each end and along the outer edge of the fish: you are working from the centre out. Rinse the fish and pat dry.

Dip each fish into seasoned flour, then into beaten egg and then press the fish into the breadcrumbs. Also egg and crumb the underside of the raised fillets. Heat the oil and fry the fish until golden brown, turning once. Drain on kitchen paper. Leave for a minute or two and then carefully pull out the backbone, taking care not to disturb too much of the breadcrumb coating.

Remove the fennel butter from the freezer, and cut into slices. Tuck the slices into the cavity of the soles. Serve with wedges of lemon.

Cold Poached Salmon

You should allow ½ lb/250 g salmon per person, with a bit over. Wild Scotch salmon is the best; it is also the most expensive. If you are buying a piece, try to get the middle cut of a large salmon, but you may find a smaller whole one that is the right weight for your party. For a whole salmon, you really need a fish kettle, otherwise you will have to cook it curved in a large pan: if you have no kettle, a piece may be the best answer.

salmon (see above)

COURT BOUILLON FOR POACHING:

½ bottle dry white wine
¼ pint/150 ml tarragon vinegar
1 lemon, cut in slices
2 onions, sliced
2 carrots, chopped

12 peppercorns
1 bay leaf
1 blade mace
2 sprigs fresh thyme or *1 heaped*
    teaspoon dried thyme
2 sprigs parsley

Put all the *court bouillon* ingredients into a pan with 3 quarts/3.5 litres water and simmer for 45 minutes. Allow to cool, then strain.

Put the *court bouillon* into a pan suitable for poaching the salmon, lay the fish in it and bring it very slowly to the boil. The moment that it reaches this point, turn down the heat, allow it to simmer for 1 minute and then turn off heat. Leave the salmon to cool in the liquid.

This method ensures that your salmon is not overcooked, but is juicy and *à point*. It should be served with a cucumber salad (*see* following recipe) and a mayonnaise; we suggest a *mayannaise verte* (*see* page 110).

Cucumber Salad

If possible, use rice vinegar rather than tarragon vinegar for the dressing. It is a sweeter vinegar and is particularly suitable for this salad. You can buy it at an oriental grocery shop.

Serves 4

1 large cucumber
1 tablespoon olive oil
1 tablespoon tarragon vinegar or
   rice vinegar

1 teaspoon sugar (if you are using
   tarragon vinegar)
½ teaspoon salt and black pepper
small bunch chives

Wipe the cucumber with a clean damp cloth. Leaving the skin on, slice it as finely as possible. Put it in a pudding basin and make a dressing of the oil, vinegar, sugar – if tarragon vinegar is being used – salt and pepper. Pour this over the cucumber and leave – turning it from time to time, so that all the slices get impregnated. Before serving, transfer it to a shallow dish and sprinkle with chopped chives.

Filet de Bœuf en Croûte

Serves 4–6

a piece of fillet steak weighing not
   less than 2 lb/1 kg
garlic
3 oz/90 g butter

8 oz/250 g button mushrooms, sliced
a wine glass of port or dark sherry
salt and freshly ground black pepper

FOR THE PASTRY:

12 oz/375 g plain flour

9 oz/275 g pure beef dripping

Rub the dripping into the flour (use dripping from the fridge so that it's not too soft), and mix with a little water until you have a soft dough. Put the pastry in the fridge to rest.

Turn on the oven to 190°C/375°F, Gas 5.

Spike the beef with a few slivers of garlic, rub it lightly with salt and freshly ground black pepper, then brown it lightly in a pan with the butter. Remove the beef and sauté the mushrooms in the pan with the meat juice and butter. Take mushrooms from the pan and add a wine glass of port or sherry. Let it bubble until thick.

Roll out the pastry to ¼-inch/0.6 cm thickness, put the beef on one side of the pastry with enough left to cover the top, put the mushrooms on top of the meat and then add the sauce from the pan. Fasten the pastry flap down firmly by using a little cold water and your fingers – so long as the pastry is properly closed along the front side and ends, no juice can escape. Bake in an oiled tin for 40–45 minutes.

We think this dish is best served with freshly made English mustard. It can be eaten hot or cold.

Saddle of Venison

A saddle of venison weighing at least 3½–4 lb/1.75–2 kg would be ideal for 6 greedy people.

2 cloves garlic	8 oz/250 g fat streaky bacon
1 oz/30 g bacon fat	1 tablespoon olive oil

FOR THE MARINADE:

½ pint/300 ml red wine	2 bay leaves
3 tablespoons olive oil	10 juniper berries, crushed
2 oz/60 g carrots, chopped small	8 peppercorns, crushed
2 oz/60 g onions, chopped small	½ teaspoon salt

FOR THE SAUCE:

2 tablespoons redcurrant jelly	1 dessertspoon arrowroot
1 port glass of port or dark sherry	salt

Put all the marinade ingredients into a pan, bring slowly to the boil, remove from the heat and leave to cool. When it is cold, pour it over the venison which you have laid in a narrow deep container – preferably one that will just hold it. Leave the venison in this marinade for 2 days in a cool place, turning it twice a day.

Turn on the oven to 200°C/400°F, Gas 6.

Take out the venison and wipe it dry with a cloth; retain the marinade for the sauce. With a sharp knife, remove the blue, muscley membrane from the top of the back. Do this gently, in layers if need be, but try to leave the flesh intact. Insert strips of garlic into the saddle's back. Melt the bacon fat in a frying pan large enough to hold the saddle, and when the fat is hot, brown the saddle. Put streaky bacon all over the top of the saddle, tucking it into the sides. Put the saddle into an ovenproof container – into which you have put 1 tablespoon olive oil; a baking tin will do, but we have got the best results from using a deeper earthenware dish. Cover the top with aluminium foil and roast for 1½ hours. Meanwhile, you can prepare the sauce.

Strain the vegetables etc. from the marinade, put the liquid in a saucepan, and boil briskly to reduce the mixture by about a half. Add the redcurrant jelly and the port or sherry. Slake the arrowroot in half a cupful of this liquid and add to the saucepan, stirring briskly until the mixture is smooth and thickens slightly. Taste the sauce, and correct the seasoning – it may want more salt, or jelly, or port according to your taste. You can then transfer the sauce to a double boiler where you can keep it hot until needed.

To test the venison, gently stick a sharp knife halfway between the backbone and side flaps. It should be tender without a lot of blood coming out. The time for cooking a saddle does depend upon the age of the deer, but greedy people will wait until it is ready. It will not take *less* than an hour and a half.

Excellent Roast Potatoes

As greedy people often like a lot of whatever they like, you should allow at least two medium-sized potatoes per person.

Serves 4

16 *potatoes*   8 *oz/250 g Trex* or *Cookeen*
salt

Turn on the oven to 200°C/400°F, Gas 6.

Peel the potatoes and then boil them in salted water for 15 minutes. Drain, and cut them in half horizontally. Lay them on a board and score the exposed part of the potato deeply with a fork, the ploughed field effect. Heat the lard in a large baking tin (two tins if you cannot get all the potatoes into one, in which case you may need more lard), and when it is very hot, put in the potatoes. Baste with a spoon and roast for 1 hour, basting twice. The potatoes should be covered with crispy ridges.

Mashed Potatoes with Olive Oil and Cream

This incredibly rich purée is based on a dish served by Fredy Girardet in his celebrated restaurant in Switzerland. So luxurious is it, that, even for the greedy, it is best served with meat or fish quite plainly cooked.

Serves 4

2 lb/1 kg potatoes
6 fl oz/180 ml double cream
6 fl oz/180 ml extra virgin olive
   oil

1 fat clove of garlic, peeled and crushed
   (optional but good)
salt, pinch of cayenne pepper

Scrub the potatoes and boil them in their skins until very well cooked. Drain and as soon as they can be handled, peel off the skins. You can now mash the potatoes with a potato masher but it is preferable to put them through a mouli or a potato ricer. In a small pan heat together the cream, oil and garlic, if you are using it, until they amalgamate. Over a low heat beat this mixture in a thin stream into the potatoes. Taste for seasoning and add salt and cayenne pepper. To keep the purée warm in a low oven, cover with a piece of oiled paper.

Potato Pie

Serves 6

1 lb/500 g new potatoes
1 lb/500 g puff pastry
2 good cloves garlic, finely
   chopped
2 oz/60 g butter

salt and black pepper
¼ teaspoon grated nutmeg
1 egg
2 tablespoons single cream

Turn on the oven to 220°C/425°F, Gas 7. Grease a round 10-inch/25-cm flan or tart tin.

Scrape the potatoes and cut them into thin slices. Put them in boiling salted water and cook until just tender – about 4–5 minutes. Drain them, rinse them under the cold tap, and drain again.

Divide the pastry into 2 pieces, one slightly larger than the other. Roll out the smaller half and line the tin. Arrange the potatoes on the pastry in layers, leaving a ½-inch/1.25-cm border round the edge. Dot each layer with the garlic and butter, and sprinkle with salt, pepper and nutmeg. Beat the egg with cream and brush the border. Roll out the second piece of pastry to about an 11-inch/27.5-cm circle and lay it over the potatoes; press the edges together to seal. Brush all over the top with the egg and cream mixture and bake for 25 minutes until golden brown. If it starts to get too brown too soon, put a piece of aluminium foil loosely over the top.

Just reading this, you can see that this pie will not improve the figure, but greedy people are so responsive to cream, butter and carbohydrates that they won't mind at all.

Cornbread

It is easy to make a greedy person out of anybody with freshly baked hot bread on to which butter so deliciously melts. The slightly sweet taste of cornbread makes it extra sinful and irresistible. Cornmeal is often sold under the name polenta or maize flour. Originally an American recipe, the quantities have been translated from their maddening addiction to cups. Because of that and because cornmeal comes in varying fineness and roughness, use your judgement over the consistency.

Serves 4–6

2½ oz/75 g plain flour	2 eggs, well beaten
7 oz/200 g cornmeal	8 fl oz/250 ml milk
1 teaspoon salt	2 fl oz/60 ml cream
1 teaspoon sugar	2½ tablespoons melted butter (approx.
2 teaspoons baking powder	1½ oz/45 g)

Turn on the oven to 200°C/400°F, Gas 6.

Sift the dry ingredients together into a mixing bowl. Add the eggs and milk and beat with a wooden spoon. Beat in the cream and lastly the melted butter. Pour into an 8½ × 11-inch/22 × 27.5-cm buttered cake tin. Cook for 15–20 minutes.

Cut the cornbread into squares while it is still hot and wrap in a cloth napkin.

Should, by some extraordinary chance, there be cornbread left over, it makes a splendid stuffing for a bird when it is mixed with sautéed onions, crumbled fried sausage meat, perhaps the bird's liver chopped and fried, and seasoning.

Rich Cold Fruit Pudding

Serves 4–6

8 oz/250 g dried apricots   1 lemon
1 jar or tin of Morello cherries   1 cupful of brown sugar
2 oranges

Turn on the oven to 150°C/300°F, Gas 2.

Soak the apricots in enough hot water to cover them. Retain the juice. Stone the cherries (unless you can find any already stoned). This can be done with the fingers; it does not matter if the cherries get broken up. Retain the cherry juice. Cut the apricots in half with a knife. Slice the oranges and lemon – including the rind – very thinly and cut the larger slices in half.

Put all the fruit into an earthenware oven dish, with lid, add juices and the sugar. Bake in the oven for about 3 hours, or until the rind of the citrus fruit is so soft it will cut with a spoon. It is a good idea to look at this after about 2 hours to see that it is not drying out, in which case, add the juice of another orange. The dish should be eaten when cold with plenty of whipped cream.

Îles Flottantes

We have known someone sink his face into the dish containing the custard for this pudding after everyone had been served, so blissful did he find it. The spun sugar is important for looks and also the contrast of texture.

Serves 4

6 egg yolks
7 oz/200 g caster sugar
salt
½ pint/300 ml single cream
6 fl oz/180 ml creamy (gold top)
  milk

1 vanilla pod
3 egg whites
1 pint/625 ml ordinary milk
4 oz/125 g sugar (for the caramel)

Combine the yolks, scant 4 oz/110 g sugar and a pinch of salt in the top of a double saucepan. Heat the cream, creamy milk and vanilla pod in the base saucepan of the double saucepan until it steams. Pour it slowly on to the yolks, whisking all the while. Rinse the base pan, fill with hot water and set on the stove with the yolk mixture above. Cook over simmering water, stirring constantly, until the mixture coats the back of a metal spoon (it thickens also upon cooling). Strain the custard through a sieve or *chinois* into a shallow dish in which you will serve the floating islands. Set in the fridge.

Near the time of dinner, whisk the 3 egg whites with a pinch of salt to soft peaks. Add the remaining 3 oz/90 g sugar a tablespoonful at a time, whisking until the peaks are stiff and glistening. Heat the ordinary milk and enough water to fill a grill pan to the depth of ½ inch/1.25 cm. When it is near boiling, pour it into the grill pan. Float spoonfuls of the meringue on the milk and grill under a low to medium heat until they are set and just tinged with brown – a matter of minutes. Lift them out with a slotted spoon and keep them on a large plate, tilted, or in a large colander – they tend to exude liquid.

When it comes to dessert time, pile the meringues prettily on to the custard. Put the 4 oz/125 g sugar for the caramel into a small heavy-bottomed saucepan. Add enough water to wet it thoroughly. Bring it slowly to the boil and, when the sugar is dissolved, boil quickly until the syrup begins to look golden and will spin a thread if dripped from the tines of a fork. Test that you have reached the right point by letting a drop of syrup fall into a cup of cold water. It should set hard. Turn off the heat. Working quickly and using two forks, weave threads of the caramel and drop splodges of it on to the îles flottantes. Try to spin a shining nest on top but don't worry if all you get is brittle droplets – they will give the requisite crunch. Take to the table. You cannot do the sugar work much before dessert time as it quickly softens and loses the point.

Fromage à la Crème

This is a dish designed to eat with fresh fruit – raspberries are the best, but any of the berries are good with it. It is marvellously greedy with the rich cold fruit pudding.

Serves 8

1 lb/500 g fresh double cream   *5 egg whites*
* cheese*   *½ pint/300 ml double cream*
4 tablespoons caster sugar

Beat the cream cheese in a large bowl until it is perfectly smooth – a hand whisk is best for this – and then add the sugar. Whisk the egg whites until they are stiff and then mix them in thoroughly with the cheese. Put the cheese mixture into a piece of muslin or a large old handkerchief (the old-fashioned nappy called a Harrington Square is ideal), and then you can either place the muslin in a colander, or more simply tie the corners of the muslin together and hang it over a basin to drip in a cool place. It should be left for at least 4 hours.

Turn the cheese out of the muslin. Whip the double cream very slightly and pour over the cheese; this can be done just before you serve the dish.

Chocolate Profiteroles

Choux pastry is not difficult to make provided you obey the rules.
The following quantities will make enough profiteroles for eight.

3 oz/90 g unsalted butter   *3¾ oz/120 g plain flour*
6 fl oz/180 ml water   *3 eggs*

Bring the butter and water to the boil. While this is heating, sieve the flour on to a piece of paper so that when the butter and water are boiling, you can shoot all the flour straight into the mixture. You take the pan off the heat to do that and you beat until the paste is smooth and will come away from the sides of the pan. This will happen quickly, and the moment it does, stop beating, or you will have a heavy paste. Set aside to cool in a basin of water.

Turn on the oven to 220°C/425°F, Gas 7. Beat the eggs, and when the paste is cool add by degrees, beating thoroughly. If the eggs are very large keep back the last spoonful until you are sure you need it. The paste should not be too wet, but should be smooth and shiny.

Grease two baking sheets with butter and put loaded tea-spoonfuls of paste in rows on the tin, leaving a good inch between each blob. Bake in the oven until light brown and firm to the touch. Do not take out of the oven until you are sure of this or your profiteroles will sink as they cool. The baking should take about 25 minutes, but you need to watch its progress. Cool the profiteroles on a wire rack, and shortly before you want them, split them and fill them either with whipped sweetened cream or ice cream if you prefer. If you are eating them for dinner, you should bake them any time after five in the afternoon: they need to be very fresh.

CHOCOLATE SAUCE

6 oz/180 g plain dark chocolate,   2 tablespoons butter
  broken up   1 tablespoon single cream
4 fl oz/125 ml water

Put the chocolate and water in a double saucepan and when the chocolate is melted, whisk in the butter and cream. Serve hot.

Sticky Toffee Pudding

This is a pudding we have both lapped up at the estimable restaurant the Fox & Goose at Fressingfield. Owner Ruth Watson does not claim authorship. It is John Tovey's recipe filtered through Delia Smith and then her own kitchen; she has cut down on the dates and substituted brown sugar for white.

5 oz/150 g dark brown   ¾ teaspoon bicarbonate of soda
  Muscovado sugar   2 teaspoons Camp coffee liquid
3 oz/90 g unsalted butter   ½ teaspoon real vanilla essence
4 oz/125 g stoned dates   6 oz/180 g sieved self-raising flour
6 fl oz/180 ml nearly boiling   2 large eggs, well beaten
  water

SAUCE:

4 oz/125 g unsalted butter   *6 fl oz/180 ml double cream*
6 oz/180 g dark brown sugar   *a handful of pecan nuts*

Turn on the oven to 200°C/400°F, Gas 6.

Cream together the sugar and butter in a mixer or food processor until quite pale and very soft. Soak the dates in the hot water. Drain when soft, keeping the liquid, and chop them roughly into quarters. Mix into the date liquid the bicarbonate of soda, Camp coffee and vanilla essence. You will get a slight frothing. First add about one-quarter of the flour to the sugar and butter mixture and beat in well, then add one-quarter of the egg and beat in gently. Continue alternating until it has all been incorporated. This prevents curdling, which makes the pudding lighter. Now add the dates to the liquid mixture. The end result will be very sloppy and you won't believe it will work. Don't panic. Lightly butter a cake tin or 8 small metal pudding moulds (more attractive) and fill with the mixture, leaving at least a ¾-inch/2-cm space for rising. Place in the hot oven. To prevent sticking the pudding must rise in the first 10 minutes or so. If the oven is too slow, it will cook all right but will tend to stick. It takes between 20 and 25 minutes to cook. Test by pressing the top, which should be a dark golden brown and should bounce back from the pressure.

Leave for 10 minutes and then turn out on to a wire tray. When cool it can be clingfilmed – it freezes perfectly and can be revived with about 1½ minutes in the microwave.

For the sauce, heat together the butter, sugar and cream until combined, then boil for about 30 seconds. Sprinkle some pecan nuts on the pudding(s) and coat with the sauce.

CHAPTER SIXTEEN

New Year's Eve

The good thing about New Year's Eve – is that you don't *have* to ask people because you are sorry for them or because they are related to you or even because you are sorry that they are related to you; you can ask your friends, people you love and like and want to entertain. It is important to ask them early, however, or you'll find that they are going somewhere else. It is an occasion for careful planning of food, since everybody will have been sated with straightforward Christmas fare and you should aim to avoid things like being clever with the remains of turkey, or of bombarding people with yet more mince pies.

Some New Year's Eve parties have no food at all; others fall back on quiches like savoury underfelt, plus bowls of nuts and seaweed biscuits. We think all good parties should include food: hosts should say that they are going to and then do it. Ideally, people should be able to sit to eat: we are not herbivores and few people are much good at dealing with a plateful of food and a glass (and a handbag if they carry one) while standing – which, if you are occidental, entails being bumped into – *and* carrying on a conversation with someone in like plight which is no fun for either of you. This could be known as the bad method of entertaining. So, don't have more people than you can seat – even if you can't provide tables for all of them.

The following menu provides ample food for 24 people: quantities could be adjusted either way depending upon the room and geography of your home. This menu will do equally well for a sitting-at-table dinner or a buffet where guests help themselves. It is a simple meal to prepare, but none the worse for that. It is important when you are cooking for this quantity to clear your fridge of all inessentials to make room for party dishes.

If you prepare a shopping list carefully and make sure that you have everything, you should be able to cook the whole thing if you start after lunch. We always make puddings first in order that there will be no danger of onion or any other obtrusive tastes. We would do the fish terrines next and put the potatoes in the oven as soon as they are done. Meanwhile, lentils can be cooked, the other salad can be made and dressings and sauces prepared.

Finally, don't start the party too early. It is the one party that is going to go on until well after midnight, which means food around 9.30 and most people seem to need feeding after about an hour of drink.

Fish Terrines	Baked Potatoes
Cooked Ham	Lentil Salad
Avocado Sauce	Apple, Beetroot and Celery Salad
Walnut and Horseradish Sauce	Cold Lemon Soufflé
Cold Rolled Stuffed Veal	Port Wine Jelly

Fish Terrines

You will need two of these, and as most food processors will only cope with one at a time, we are giving quantities for one. You simply make it twice. Fresh haddock is the best white fish to use; the contrasting fish is to add to the flavour and also to make the terrine look pretty when you cut it; smoked haddock, smoked salmon pieces, fresh shrimps or prawns are all good.

1 lb/500 g white fish (see *above*)
2 egg whites
½ pint/300 ml whipping cream
juice of 1 lemon

salt and pepper
12 oz/375 g contrasting fish (see *above*)

Turn on the oven to 180°C/350°F, Gas 4. Chill all ingredients including the food processor bowl. The actual making should be done fast while everything is still as cold as possible.

Dice the white fish and put into the food processor with the egg whites. Whizz until the mixture is smooth and add the cream. Season, and add lemon juice – taste to see whether you need the juice of the whole lemon or not.

Butter the terrine dish and add the white fish mixture in layers with strips of contrasting fish. Cover with aluminium foil and put the terrine into a baking dish half-filled with boiling water. Put in the oven. Test after 25 minutes with a skewer which will come out clean when the terrine is cooked. Leave it to cool in the baking dish and then put it in the fridge.

Remove the terrine from the fridge about half an hour before you eat it, and turn it out. It can then be garnished with shrimps, parsley, pieces of lemon, etc.

Cooked Ham

Two things are important about a cooked ham. You need to know that your supplier does produce good hams. Go to your local delicatessen or grocer and buy 4 oz/125 g of whatever ham he recommends that will also be available in the piece. If you don't like it, try again. The second point is that the ham should be properly carved. This means a really sharp ham knife – i.e. a long, slender knife that is flexible or whippy. If you are no good at carving, find a friend who is coming to the party who is. People who are good at it (like anything else) enjoy carving and it makes all the difference.

The two sauces which follow are delicious with ham.

Avocado Sauce

Scoop out the flesh from two avocados. Put it in the food processor with some black pepper, salt and lemon juice. When puréed, turn it into a small bowl and cover with a damp cloth to prevent it going brown and put it in the fridge. This should be made as late as you can manage.

Walnut and Horseradish Sauce

6 fl oz/180 ml natural yoghurt
1 tablespoon horseradish sauce
salt
sugar
2 oz/60 g walnuts

Mix in a pudding basin the yoghurt with the horseradish sauce. Add a pinch of salt and a little sugar. Put the walnuts into a liquidizer and mix for 3 seconds; you can chop them finely if you prefer a more gritty texture. Add these to the horseradish mixture. Taste it, and see whether you have enough of the two main ingredients for your liking.

Cold Rolled Stuffed Veal

This roll stuffed with what is basically a flat omelette looks very pretty when carved, with a thread of yellow, green and pink running through, and makes a change from the more usual cold meats offered. As butchers get more and more conservative about what they sell on a day to day basis, make sure you order the boned breast or shoulder of veal well beforehand. If you happen to live near an Italian butcher's, they will understand what you are after. If the butcher is boning the veal for you, ask for the bones for stock.

2–3 eggs	*3 lb/1.5 kg boned shoulder or breast of*
3 slices of pancetta or mortadella	*veal*
1 oz/30 g grated Parmesan	*2 tablespoons olive oil*
2 tablespoons finely chopped	*1 onion, peeled and chopped*
parsley	*1 cup milk*
2 oz/60 g butter	

Beat the eggs with a dessertspoon of water. Chop the pancetta or mortadella and add to the egg mixture with the Parmesan and parsley. Melt half the butter in a frying pan and make a flat omelette, cooking until the eggs are set on the underneath side. Flatten the veal as best you can, beating it out with a heavy implement. Cover it with the omelette, trimming the omelette if necessary to get a fit. Roll up the meat and tie in several places with string. In a pot that will hold the meat, sauté the onion in the mixture of oil and butter. Brown the meat all over. Meanwhile heat (but do not boil) the milk. Pour it over the meat. Cover the pot and simmer very gently on top of the stove for 2 hours, checking from time to time that the milk has not boiled away. Remove the meat, wrap in greaseproof paper and place it under a board with a weight such as a couple of tins of soup (nothing too heavy). Leave to cool. Slice thinly when serving. The mustardy preserved fruits called mostarda di Cremona would go well.

Baked Potatoes

*18 potatoes will be enough for 24
  people*

These are only acceptable if they are prepared beforehand. Nobody enjoys opening them, scalding their fingers and trundling butter into them with a fork. Bake them during the afternoon of the party. When cooked, cut them in half and scoop out the insides. Mix the potato in a big bowl with a fork, adding melted butter, milk, pepper and salt. When you have got the mixture right (by which we mean *you* like the taste of it), put it back into the skins and set the potato halves on baking trays ready to be warmed up in the oven. In our experience *everybody* eats them if they are presented in this way – particularly if you paint the skins with oil before the first baking to get them crisp, and score the mash with a fork.

Lentil Salad

1½ lb/750 g brown lentils
4 tablespoons olive oil
2 tablespoons wine vinegar

salt and pepper
2 sweet onions, finely chopped
4 tablespoons coarsely chopped parsley

Soak the lentils for about an hour. Cook in boiling water with some salt until they are just cooked, 45 minutes to an hour, *al dente* as the Italians say, before they go into a mush. Drain, and while they are still warm, add a mixture of the olive oil, the wine vinegar and a little salt and pepper. Mix thoroughly. When cool, add finely chopped onion and coarsely chopped parsley.

Apple, Beetroot and Celery Salad

3 lb/1.5 kg cooked beetroot
3 lb/1.5 kg Cox's apples

2 large heads of celery

FOR THE DRESSING:

6 tablespoons olive oil
2 tablespoons vinegar
2 teaspoons mustard powder

4 teaspoons sugar
2 teaspoons salt
black pepper – a generous screwing

Peel and dice the beetroot and set aside. Peel, core and dice the apples and mix with the beetroot in the bottom of a salad bowl. Wash and chop the celery and add to the bowl. (It is best to put this bowl in a cool place covered by a damp cloth.) Make the dressing by mixing the ingredients thoroughly; leave it in the kitchen, not in the fridge.

Dress and mix the salad just before you eat.

Cold Lemon Soufflé

These ingredients make enough for about 10 people. If you want to have enough for 24, you should make it twice as processor bowls and liquidizers will not cope with a greater quantity than this. However, if you are also making port wine jelly, you will probably find that this quantity of soufflé seems enough.

6 lemons
6 eggs
6 tablespoons caster sugar

½ oz/15 g gelatine
½ pint/300 ml double cream

Grate the rind from three of the lemons and squeeze all six. Separate the yolks from the whites of the eggs. Put the egg yolks, lemon juice and sugar in a double saucepan, whisk over hot water until the sugar is dissolved and the mixture thickens, and pour into a basin. Thoroughly dissolve the gelatine in 2 tablespoons of hot water in a small bowl over a saucepan of hot water, and add to the lemon mixture. Add the grated lemon rind and stir in well. Put the bowl in a basin of cold water to help it cool. Meanwhile, whip the cream lightly. It should be thick, but without peaking. When the lemon mixture is almost cold and near setting, whisk the egg whites stiffly – so that the bowl will turn upside-down without the mixture falling out. Add the cream to the lemon mixture and then add the egg whites, folding them in lightly but thoroughly.

Put the combined mixture into a 3-pint/1.75-litre soufflé dish, or individual pots if you have them. This should be done as quickly as possible so that the whites don't start to dissolve. Put the pudding into the fridge.

Port Wine Jelly

This is best made in small pots or glasses. It is quite rich and the quantity given here will fill 10 of the small white pots in which the French put chocolate mousse or cold creams or soufflés, but custard glasses or any small and pretty containers would do.

1 pint/625 ml port
¾ pint/475 ml water
½ oz/15 g (or ¾ packet) gelatine
4 oz/125 g lump sugar

1-inch/2.5-cm cinnamon stick
grated rind of 1 lemon
a good pinch of freshly grated nutmeg

Put all the ingredients, except half the port, into a double saucepan and heat until it is well blended. Strain through muslin. Add the rest of the port. Pour into pots or glasses and chill.

CHAPTER SEVENTEEN

House-Moving Supper

Nowadays, everybody moves house far more often in their lives than they used to do. The combination of people being moved because of their work and the terrifying inflation of house prices has meant that everybody has had to start by buying any place, anywhere, that they could afford, but luck, age, affluence and attachments – not to mention progeny – make further moves inevitable. However, excluding the professionals, like Foreign Office staff or Service families, most people don't move often enough to get really good at it.

This means that after a day of seemingly endless excitement and fatigue they may find themselves at eight in the evening feverishly unpacking tea chests full of kitchen equipment in a vain attempt to find their tin opener, the electric kettle and the bread knife. Of course, it isn't always as awful as that, but you may have done quite a lot of planning and made a nourishing stew only to find that the previous owners decided to take the cooker after all, or the Gas Board has declined to connect yours as arranged – and when it comes to eating cold stew, your family won't feel that it was the thought that counted.

Even if you know perfectly how to organize and make the first meal in your new house, the nesting instinct (very noticeable – particularly in women – when confronting new territory) dictates that you should be arranging saucepans on shelves rather than cooking in them, and hanging up your clothes or making at least one room feel like your home before you fall into bed. If only a meal would simply *appear* – a picnic or a feast, preferably a bit of both, anything, or almost anything that you have not had to think about! This is where real friends come in, and where *you* could come in for your friends.

The following recipes are all designed to be easy to transport and not too complicated to serve: we do suggest, however, that you should assume that the china and cutlery won't have been unpacked, so take the bare necessities. The soup can be transported in Thermos flasks and drunk or spooned out of mugs; all the other dishes can be eaten with a fork or with the fingers. This might be an occasion for paper plates although, personally, we don't care for them. In addition to a mug, glass, fork and plate for each person, you should take serving spoons, drink, sugar, salt and pepper and a couple of tea towels – and don't forget the corkscrew. If the recipients have a telephone, you can ask them if they have a kettle for tea or coffee. If you want to be really munificent, add a loaf of bread, ½ lb/250 g of butter, a jar of marmalade – preferably made by you – and two pints of milk for breakfast.

Spring Minestrone   Lasagne with Meat Sauce
Spinach Pâté   Mixed Meat Salad
Stuffed Anchovy Eggs   Lemon Meringue Tarts
Tomato and Mustard Quiche   Brownies
Pissaladière   Walnut Cake

Spring Minestrone

The important thing about this soup is to keep the vegetables in the same colour range and avoid the Dolly Mixture look of commercial minestrone. A plus about this recipe is that it actually improves on being served lukewarm, as the flavour of the vegetables comes through more positively – a fact understood in Mediterranean countries. The better the olive oil you use, the better the soup will be.

Serves 4–6

1½ lb/750 g fresh broad beans in
   their pods
1 lb/500 g fresh peas in their pods
1 oz/30 g butter
4 tablespoons virgin olive oil
8 oz/250 g asparagus
8 oz/250 g broccoli
¼ cauliflower

1 bunch spring onions, trimmed and
   peeled
2 cloves garlic, peeled and chopped
8 oz/250 g French green beans
salt and freshly ground black pepper
3 oz/90 g Parmesan cheese, freshly
   grated

Prepare the vegetables, shelling the broad beans and peas, cleaning and chopping the rest quite small. Heat the butter and 2 tablespoonfuls

of the olive oil in a large heavy-bottomed sauté pan. Add the asparagus stalks (saving the tips for later), the broccoli, cauliflower, spring
onions, garlic and green beans. Toss them in the fat until they are
glistening and beginning to soften. Add the peas and beans. Add just
enough water to cover and season with salt and pepper. When the
vegetables are tender, but still crunchy, turn off the heat. Remove
half the vegetables and whizz in a food processor or liquidizer until
you have a none too smooth purée.

Pour the mixture into a clean pan and bring to a simmer, adding
more water if you want a thinner consistency. Add the remaining
vegetables plus the asparagus tips. Stir and heat through. Taste for
seasoning and for texture.

If you are serving this soup in the context of a picnic, take some
olive oil along separately and trickle a little into each plate or cup and
also hand round some grated Parmesan cheese.

Spinach Pâté

Serves 6

1 small onion, chopped	2 hard-boiled eggs
½ lb/250 g butter	tarragon
½ lb/250 g cooked spinach	salt and pepper
1 tin anchovy fillets	1 fl oz/30 ml cream

Soften the onion in ¼ lb/125 g butter. Put all the ingredients into a
liquidizer and blend. Pour the mixture into an oblong dish and chill.
Serve sliced with toast or crusty bread. This will keep in the fridge
for 2–3 days.

Stuffed Anchovy Eggs

Serves 4–6

6 anchovy fillets	2 tablespoons single cream
6 eggs	salt and black pepper (optional)
2 tablespoons mayonnaise	paprika or parsley to garnish

Hard-boil the eggs, cool and peel. Cut the eggs in half, scoop out the yolks and put them into a small bowl. Trim the bottoms of the whites so that each half is stable. Chop the anchovy fillets as finely as possible and add the yolks with the mayonnaise.

Mix and mash the contents very thoroughly with a fork, adding cream by degrees until the consistency is creamy, but not sloppy. Test for seasoning. Pile the mixture into the egg whites and garnish with a pinch of paprika and/or parsley.

Note: you could transport these in egg boxes quite safely.

Tomato and Mustard Quiche

The sort of quiche to avoid is the sort that the owners of the new house might feel would come in handy for lagging the attic. In this recipe, the tomatoes add a nice moistness. Blandness is side-stepped by the unexpected sting of mustard.

Serves 4–6

1 shortcrust pastry case, baked
   blind for 10 minutes (see page
   204)
2 tablespoons Dijon mustard (or
   whatever mustard you favour)
1 lb/500 g ripe tomatoes

4 eggs
½ pint/300 ml double cream
1 tablespoon finely chopped parsley
sea salt and freshly ground black
   pepper
3 oz/90 g Gruyère cheese, grated

Turn on the oven to 170°C/325°F, Gas 3.

Spread the mustard on the base of the partially cooked pastry case. Skin the tomatoes by plunging them briefly into boiling water. De-seed them and chop roughly. In a large pudding basin, beat the eggs and add the cream, parsley, salt and pepper. Stir in the tomatoes and two-thirds of the cheese. Pour into the pastry case and sprinkle the remaining cheese over the top. Bake for 35–40 minutes until golden and endeavour to transport and consume the quiche while it is warm.

Pissaladière

This Niçoise version of a pizza should be made with a bread base but we think it works just as well with pastry which, if crisp, provides a nice contrast to the softness of the onions. If you are truly in a hurry, you could use thick slices of bread cut lengthways from a loaf and then fried on one side in olive oil. However, the key to the success of this dish is long, slow cooking of the onions – allow at least 40 minutes for the process – so during that time you might just as well knock up some shortcrust pastry.

Serves 4–6

¼ pint/150 ml olive oil
2½ lb/1.25 kg onions, peeled and
    quite thinly sliced

2 cloves garlic, peeled and crushed or
    chopped
8 anchovy fillets
8 black olives

FOR THE PASTRY:

6 oz/180 g plain flour
2 generous teaspoons mustard
    powder
2 oz/60 g butter

1 oz/30 g lard
pinch of salt
cold water

Make up the shortcrust pastry using the quantities, or your own recipe, but taking on board the inclusion of mustard which goes well with the onions. Roll out thinly and line a large pie dish. Bake for 15 minutes in an oven set at 190°C/375°F, Gas 5 with foil over the base of the pastry and some dried beans dotted about on top: 'baking blind' gives a crisper result.

In 4 fl oz/125 ml oil, cook the sliced onions gently, stirring occasionally. After about 20 minutes, add the garlic. At the end of the cooking time, the onions should almost be a purée.

Spread the onion mixture on the pastry. Arrange the anchovy fillets in a lattice pattern and place olives in some of the diamond-shaped spaces. Dribble on the remaining oil and bake in the oven (temperature as before), for 30 minutes. This is at its best neither hot nor cold, but lukewarm.

Lasagne with Meat Sauce

This recipe for meat sauce comes from Marcella Hazan's *Classic Italian Cookbook* because it is quite simply the best we know. When we make the sauce, we always make treble quantities and freeze some. It is an invaluable standby for a quick and delicious meal.

Serves 6

FOR THE SAUCE:

2 tablespoons chopped Spanish
   onion
3 tablespoons olive oil
1½ oz/45 g butter
2 tablespoons chopped celery
2 tablespoons chopped carrots
12 oz/375 g best beef mince

salt
8 fl oz/250 ml dry white whine
4 fl oz/125 ml milk
⅛ teaspoon freshly grated nutmeg
14-oz/425-g can of Italian tomatoes,
   roughly chopped, with their juice

An earthenware pot should be your first choice for making the *ragù*. If you don't have one available, use a heavy, enamelled cast-iron casserole, the deepest one you have (to keep the *ragù* from reducing too quickly). Put in the chopped onion with all the oil and butter, and sauté briefly over a medium heat until just translucent. Add the celery and carrots and cook gently for 2 minutes.

Add the mince, crumbling it in the pot with a fork. Add 1 teaspoon salt, stir and cook only until the meat has lost its raw, red colour. Add the wine, turn the heat up to medium-high and cook, stirring occasionally, until all the wine has evaporated.

Turn the heat down to medium, add the milk and the nutmeg, and cook until the milk has evaporated. Stir frequently. When the milk has evaporated, add the tomatoes and stir thoroughly. When the mixture has started to bubble, turn the heat down until the sauce cooks at the laziest simmer, just an occasional bubble. Cook uncovered, for a minimum of 3½–4 hours, stirring occasionally. Taste and correct for salt. (If you cannot watch the sauce for such a long stretch, you can turn off the heat and resume cooking later. But do finish cooking in one day.)

This sounds a trouble to make, but it works very well if you are cooking other things, and if you treble the quantities, you won't find you have wasted your time: it is delicious.

You can now buy fresh lasagne in many delicatessens or super-markets. Don't buy the dried lasagne; it is far too thick and is stodgy.

1 lb/500 g fresh lasagne
1½ pints/900 ml béchamel sauce
(the consistency of cream)

6 oz/180 g Parmesan cheese
2 oz/60 g butter

Turn on the oven to 190°C/375°F, Gas 5.

This dish is better put together after the *ragù* has cooked. Use a 14-inch/35-cm dish deep enough to contain 6 layers of meat and pasta. Smear the bottom of the dish with the fat that will have risen to the top of the meat sauce, and then place a single layer of pasta in the dish, overlapping strips but no more than ¼ inch/0.6 cm. Spread a thin layer of meat sauce, then a thin layer of béchamel over the sauce. Sprinkle with cheese. Then add another layer of pasta, and so on. Finish with a pasta layer, cover that with béchamel, sprinkle with cheese and dot with butter.

Bake at the top of the oven for 10–15 minutes until a light golden crust forms on top. If after 10 minutes, the crust is not forming, turn up the oven for the last 5 minutes. Do not cook longer, or it will become dry.

Mixed Meat Salad

This salad can be made with various selections of meat: we are suggesting beef, tongue and chicken. It is an excellent way of using up the remains of a roast chicken or a tongue that you have served hot. We suggest that you cook a piece of beef and use the other meats if they are easily available: the salad is very good simply with beef.

Serves 8–10

TO COOK THE BEEF:

4 large carrots
2 large onions
1 stalk celery with leaves
4 leeks
1 turnip
3 lb/1.5 kg (approx.) beef –
topside or *silverside*

3 sprigs parsley
2 sprigs thyme or *1 teaspoon dried*
thyme
3 bay leaves
1 dessertspoon sea salt

Chop all the vegetables and put them, the beef and the other ingredients into a pan that will just accommodate the beef, and cover with cold water. Bring very slowly to simmering point. Skim off the scum that accumulates during the next 15 minutes and then allow to simmer for about 2½ hours, or until the beef feels tender with a sharp knife. Turn off the heat and allow the beef to cool in its liquid.

FOR THE SALAD:

2 lb/1 kg potatoes
1 bunch spring onions or ½ lb/
  250 g shallots
1 bunch radishes

2 hard-boiled eggs
4 large dill cucumbers
2 oz/60 g capers
2 oz/60 g fresh parsley

FOR THE DRESSING:

1 tablespoon tarragon vinegar
3 tablespoons olive oil
1 teaspoon made mustard

1 teaspoon sugar
1 teaspoon salt
generous screws of black pepper

New potatoes are infinitely preferable, but the salad can be made with old ones. Boil the potatoes gently until they are cooked. When cool, slice them. Chop the spring onions or shallots finely.

Slice the cold beef thinly and arrange in layers with the potatoes, soaking each layer with the prepared dressing. If you need a larger quantity of dressing, be sure to stay with the proportions above.

Garnish with radishes and hard-boiled eggs, sliced cucumbers, capers, chopped spring onions and parsley.

Lemon Meringue Tarts

Serves 6

FOR THE PASTRY:

8 oz/250 g self-raising flour
2 oz/60 g butter

2 oz/60 g Trex
juice of ½ lemon

Rub the fats into the flour until you have fine crumbs. Make a hole in the centre of the mixture, and pour in a little of the lemon juice which has been diluted with an equal quantity of cold water, and mix with a wooden spoon. Add just enough of the lemon water to make the pastry into a soft dough so that the sides of the bowl are clean. Put the pastry in the fridge while you make the curd.

FOR THE LEMON CURD:

4 eggs	*6 oz/180 g caster sugar*
2 lemons	*3½ oz/100 g caster sugar (for*
2 oz/60 g butter	*meringue)*

Separate the egg yolks from the whites (the whites will be used for the meringue). Grate the rind of both lemons and then squeeze the juice. Put the butter, sugar and lemon juice into a double saucepan and stir until everything has dissolved. Then add the beaten egg yolks in a thin stream, stirring vigorously all the time. Continue stirring the mixture until it thickens slightly; it will stiffen more when cold. Add the grated lemon rind and put the mixture in a bowl to cool.

Turn on the oven to 180°C/350°F, Gas 4.

Roll out the pastry as thinly as you can, and cut out rounds for tartlet tins. We use non-stick pans but if you don't have them, you must of course butter the pan. If you haven't got a pastry cutter, you can use a cup or a glass, but it must be of a size that allows the pastry to reach the top of the sides of the tart tin hollows. Put the tins in the oven and bake until they are a pale biscuit colour. Allow to cool.

Whip the egg whites stiffly, and then fold in the caster sugar. Put a rounded teaspoonful of lemon curd in each tartlet and cover with a generous helping of meringue. Bake in a very cool oven (70°C/150°F, Gas ¼), until the meringue is the colour of milky coffee.

These tarts should be eaten the same day, or the meringue may become sticky. If you don't have tart pans, you can make a pie, but the tarts can be eaten with the fingers which is useful for a possibly crockery-free new household.

Brownies

Serves 6

2 oz/60 g bitter chocolate	*½ teaspoon baking powder*
4 oz/125 g butter	*2 oz/60 g plain flour*
8 oz/250 g brown sugar	*8 oz/250 g walnuts, coarsely chopped*
2 eggs	*1 teaspoon vanilla essence*
½ teaspoon salt	

Turn on the oven to 180°C/350°F, Gas 4.

Melt the chocolate and let it cool slightly. Cream the butter and sugar, add the eggs and then the cooled chocolate, and mix well. Add the salt and baking powder to the flour, mix, and then add to the chocolate mixture. Beat well, and then add the chopped nuts and vanilla essence.

Put the mixture into a shallow buttered baking tin (8 inches/20 cm square is about right), and bake for 30–35 minutes, until the testing skewer comes out clean. Allow to cool for 10 minutes before cutting it into small squares.

Walnut Cake

6 oz/180 g caster sugar
6 oz/180 g margarine
3 eggs
1½ level teaspoons baking powder

8 oz/250 g plain flour
3 oz/90 g chopped walnuts
2 tablespoons milk

Turn on the oven to 160°C/325°F, Gas 3. Cream the sugar and margarine and add the beaten eggs. Mix the baking powder with the flour before adding it to the mixture, then add the walnuts and milk. Bake in a buttered tin until cooked. Use a skewer: when it is plunged into the cake, it should (if it is cooked) come out clean.

ICING:

3 oz/90 g butter
3 dessertspoons milk
1 dessertspoon water

1 dessertspoon Camp coffee (or
    instant; but the old Camp in a
    bottle is far the best for a good coffee
    flavour)
12 oz/375 g icing sugar
walnuts

Warm the butter and milk, water and coffee. Beat in the icing sugar. Cover the cake and use a fork to make an interesting texture. Decorate with walnuts.

CHAPTER EIGHTEEN

Picnics

Our earliest memories of picnics turned out to be identical: sitting on a beach, in a gale, aubergine coloured from a short battle with the sea, crunching our way through sandwiches that for years one of us thought were called that because of the high proportion of beach they contained. Some people don't mind this sort of thing, they expect conditions to be rough: if not a gale, then being bitten by gnats or stung by wasps, or drenched to the skin. They seem to feel that a picnic is a sort of organized *emergency* – that dry sandwiches and half a cup of fairly warm tea with that mercifully unique taste associated with an ill-kept Thermos flask is what to expect or provide.

There are those who have so little faith in the weather or their enjoyment that they like to picnic on the doubtful verge of some highway, comfortingly near their own car and with any suggestions of rural solitude enlivened by the traffic. But some people think of picnics as a *fête champêtre* – an outdoor feast with elaborate and elegant food that happens not to be consumed in the dining-room. We agree with this, with the proviso that as much food as possible should be able to be eaten with the fingers or, failing that, in some cases with either a spoon *or* a fork. Cutting things up with a knife and fork is no fun with a plate on your lap.

We have divided our suggestions into those best suited to summer and those desirable in winter, although in some cases the food is suitable for any time of the year. The first thing to take into account when catering for a picnic is that everybody is mysteriously hungrier out of doors. This would not be surprising if it were a shooting picnic, or one where the participants were engaged in a lot of healthy exercise, but it is equally true of people going to Glyndebourne, for instance, or simply driving somewhere in order to eat. So although we don't suggest that you make everything on either the summer or winter menus, we do advise your making more of whatever you choose than you would for an indoor meal.

Then there is the question of picnic equipment. The elderly find sitting on the ground difficult and uncomfortable, and a surprising number of men behave like frightfully old deck chairs whose hinges will not adjust to outdoor sitting conditions. If you are catering for either of these categories, a couple of those small and very light folding canvas and metal chairs would be popular. You should also provide a large American cloth or plastic sheet on which to lay out the food: a large plate apiece, a glass and a cup, spoons, forks, and bowls if you are serving fruit salad, and an extra cup apiece if you are serving soup. Paper plates – and cups – can save a lot of trouble. China is also heavy to carry, and if you are not a verge picnicker, you should take this into consideration. You also need ladles for soup and fruit salad, large sharp knives for cutting up pie or cake and plenty of paper napkins, a corkscrew for wine, and containers of salt, sugar and pepper, and finally, of course, Thermos flasks of soup, coffee or tea (bring milk separately and the tea will taste better) and whatever refrigerating bags are needed to keep cold drinks cold.

Finally, we are assuming yours will be a lunch or supper picnic: if you are doing a tea, some of the things on these menus will be suitable and there are other cakes and sandwiches elsewhere in this book that could be used.

Summer

Scotch Quails' Eggs	Brown Bread, Walnut and Crème
Kuku	d'Isigny Sandwiches
Greek Loaf	Individual Summer Puddings
Cold Lamb Cutlets	Geranium Cream
Lettuce-wrapped Duck	Peaches in Orange and Lemon
Tomato and Cucumber Salad	Juice

Winter

Giblet Soup	Home-made Sausage Roll
Cold Rabbit and Gammon Pie	Mary's Fruit Cake
Pheasant Croquettes	Coffee Eclairs

SUMMER

Scotch Quails' Eggs

Bought Scotch eggs can be a dire thing and if you make them at home using hen's eggs and sausage meat they can be too much of a mouthful even for the great outdoors. Quails' eggs give a more delicate result and there is something rather sweet about them, particularly if they are arranged in a nest of lettuce leaves. Take along a jar of good chutney or some home-made tomato sauce as an accompaniment. Do not emulate the supermarket by using those bright orange packet breadcrumbs. For the sausage meat, use high quality sausages and remove the meat from the skins by cutting a slit in the skin and holding the sausage under the cold tap.

Serves 4

8 quails' eggs
1 lb/500 g sausage meat
flour seasoned with salt and
   freshly ground black pepper

2 small eggs, lightly beaten
4 oz/125 g fine breadcrumbs
vegetable oil for frying

Boil the quails' eggs for 3 minutes, immerse in cold water and shell carefully. Divide the sausage meat into 8 balls and pat each one out thin and flat. Roll the eggs in seasoned flour, then in the sausage meat; roll each in the beaten egg and finally in the crumbs. It is less messy if you perform the first two processes with all the eggs before applying the crumbs which will stick to your eggy fingers.

Heat enough oil to come halfway up the eggs. Cook, turning in two stages; once at a medium-hot heat to cook the sausage meat, the second time at a higher heat to crisp and brown the crumbs. Drain on kitchen paper.

Kuku

This Iranian omelette – the idea comes from Claudia Roden's *A Book of Middle Eastern Food* – is ideal picnic food, easy to slice, faintly exotic and not heavy on the stomach. Take along a spot of natural yoghurt, preferably the creamy Greek variety, as an accompaniment.

Serves 4–6

1 large onion, peeled and finely chopped
2 tablespoons vegetable oil
1 large leek, peeled, washed and finely sliced or *4 spring onions, cleaned and chopped*

1 lb/500 g minced beef
4 oz/125 g chopped spinach (frozen will suffice)
salt and freshly ground black pepper
1 teaspoon ground cinnamon
6 eggs

Fry the onion in half the vegetable oil with the leek or spring onions until they are soft. Add the minced beef and cook it until it has changed colour and completely lost its rawness. Add the spinach, salt, pepper and cinnamon and cook gently.

In a large mixing bowl, beat the eggs lightly. Add the meat mixture, which shouldn't be too hot or it will start to cook the eggs. Clean the frying pan. Heat up the other tablespoonful of vegetable oil and pour in the mixture. Cook over a gentle heat for about 15 minutes, until the eggs have set on the bottom and, indeed, most of the way through.

Turn on the grill, slip the pan under and cook until the top of the omelette is golden. Serve lukewarm or cool. If you have used a heavy-bottomed frying pan, the kuku should be easy to cut into wedges for it will have shrunk slightly from the sides in the cooking and cooling process.

Greek Loaf

This recipe was devised by artist Dickie Chopping on a holiday in Greece when each day he saw a more elaborate picnic being prepared to be taken by boat to a remote and primitive beach. The contents were dictated by what was available in a relatively small village but the principle can successfully be applied to more sophisticated fillings.

Serves 8

1 large rectangular loaf: the one
   used in the original was white
   but brown would work
5 tablespoons (approx.) olive oil
2 large onions, peeled and sliced

2 large green peppers, cored,
   de-seeded, trimmed of membranes
   and sliced
6 rashers streaky bacon, crisply fried
4–5 eggs
a handful of stoned black olives

FOR THE TOMATO SAUCE:

1½–2 lb/750 g–1 kg fresh
   tomatoes, peeled and sliced or 1
   14-oz/425-g tin peeled
   tomatoes
1 heaped tablespoon tomato purée

2 cloves garlic, peeled and chopped
1 small glass red wine
salt and freshly ground black pepper
a good pinch of sugar
2 teaspoons oregano or chopped basil

Turn on the oven to 180°C/350°F, Gas 4.

With a small sharp knife, cut around the loaf about ¼ inch/0.6 cm in from the edge and without hitting the bottom. The idea is to create a container and a lid. Carefully ease the knife under one of the short ends of the 'lid' and cut off. Pull out the crumbs from the loaf and from the lid until you have a box with a base and walls about ¼-inch/0.6 cm thick, and a thin lid. Do not make the container too thin or it will collapse in the carrying. Using about 3 tablespoonfuls olive oil (or you may need more), paint the inside of the box and lid and set in the oven to crisp – 15–20 minutes.

Meanwhile, in 2 tablespoonfuls olive oil, sauté the onions and peppers until they are softened and just beginning to brown. Take them from the pan and set aside.

Make the tomato sauce by simmering together the tomatoes, tomato purée, the garlic and wine. Season with salt, pepper, sugar, oregano or basil. Cook for about 20–30 minutes, or until the sauce has thickened. Taste for seasoning and adjust.

In the bottom of the loaf, spread the onions and peppers, well drained of any oil that has accumulated. Lay on the bacon slices. Pour on the tomato sauce, which shouldn't be too liquid or it will sog the loaf. Break the eggs along the surface of the sauce. Dot with black olives. Return the loaf to the oven and bake until the eggs are set – about 10 minutes. Place the lid on the loaf and slice at the picnic site.

Cold Lamb Cutlets

This is a very simple dish, but how good it is depends on obtaining first-class lamb and a butcher who understands what a cutlet is, i.e. not a chop, and not a cutlet off the best end of some middle-aged lamb or sheep. It should be from the best end of young lamb, and the butcher should trim the fat from the cutlet for you.

Heat the grill very hot, paint the cutlets with sunflower seed oil and a sprinkle of salt and grill them for about 5 minutes on the first side, and about 3 minutes on the reverse. Cool them on a rack, so that any excess fat may drip away. They should be just pink inside when done. They look pretty with white paper cutlet frills round their stems.

Lettuce-wrapped Duck

This method for cooking the duck is similar to that employed for Peking Duck, but with the option of speeding the process by using a hairdryer trained on the bird rather than letting it hang in an airy place overnight. If you have the time, however, the latter process can give a crisper result.

Serves 6

1 large fresh duck
1 large Cos lettuce or *Webb's Wonder* (or *similarly crisp variety*)
2 tablespoons honey

plum sauce or *Hoisin sauce (available in supermarkets)*
½ cucumber
1 bunch spring onions

Wash the duck and place it in a large sieve or colander. Bring a kettle full of water to the boil and, when boiling, pour it over the duck, turning the bird once or twice so that it is well and truly scalded. Pat dry and place in a large bowl.

Melt the honey in a jug with ½ pint/300 ml hot water. Pour it over the duck, then drain it off back into the jug and repeat. Turn the duck over and repeat again. Contrive some way of hanging up the duck (e.g. with a butcher's hook or sturdy wire coat hanger) and train a warm (not hot) hairdryer on it until it is dry. You can, of course, just leave it in an airy place overnight.

Heat the oven to 200°C/400°F, Gas 6. Without any fat, roast the duck on a wire grid, breast side up, for 20 minutes. Turn over (being careful not to puncture the skin) and roast for a further 25 minutes. Turn over again and roast for 20 minutes more. The skin should be golden and crisp. Remove from the oven, let cool and then carve, prising every morsel of flesh from the bones.

The lettuce leaves should be separated, and washed and dried if necessary; the cucumber should be cut into matchsticks, but leave on the skin; and the spring onions should be trimmed, cleaned and sliced lengthways. Bite-sized pieces of skin and meat are taken to the picnic in one container, with the prepared lettuce, cucumber and spring onions packed in another. The Hoisin or Chinese plum sauce can be carried in its jar.

A teaspoonful or so of sauce is spread on to the lettuce leaf, meat and crispy skin is added, then strips of cucumber and spring onion, and the whole made into a delectable parcel.

Tomato and Cucumber Salad

This is a very simple salad, but it is crunchy and refreshing and can be easily eaten with just a fork.

Serves 6–8

2 lb/1 kg tomatoes
2 medium-sized cucumbers
¼ pint/150 ml natural yoghurt

1 clove garlic
salt and pepper and sugar to taste

Cut the tomatoes into quarters, then in half. Cut the cucumber into ½-inch/1.25 cm cubes. Put both in a container. Mix the yoghurt, crushed garlic, salt, pepper and sugar and return the dressing to the yoghurt carton. Dress the salad just before serving for the picnic.

Brown Bread, Walnut and Crème d'Isigny Sandwiches

4 Crème d'Isigny cheeses or   3 oz/90 g walnuts, finely chopped
    4 oz/125 g double cream cheese   1 small brown wholemeal loaf

Mix the cheese and the chopped walnuts well together and spread on thin slices of unbuttered bread. Be generous with the filling and cover with a second slice of bread. Cut off the crusts.

Individual Summer Puddings

Serves 6

6 × 4-inch/10-cm diameter   3 oz/90 g caster sugar
    pudding basins   1 stale white loaf
1½ lb/750 g raspberries   arrowroot
12 oz/375 g redcurrants   ½ pint/300 ml double cream

Note: Other soft fruit is good for this pudding: blackberries (with a small amount of apple), loganberries, black and white currants, mulberries and stoned black cherries when in season.

Put the fruit and sugar into a stainless steel pan with ½ pint/300 ml water and cook very gently to draw the juice from the fruit. Cut the bread very thinly and line the bottoms and the sides of the basins. Strain the fruit from its juice: at this point, taste it to see if there is enough sugar for your liking. Measure the juice in a pint/.5 litre jug – it will vary with the fruit that you use. To each ½ pint/300 ml of juice, use one heaped teaspoonful of arrowroot, which you should slake in a little of the juice in a separate bowl. Return the juice to the pan and pour in the slaked arrowroot mixture. Bring to the boil and cook until it has the consistency of thin cream. Leave to cool.

Now add the fruit to the pudding basins until they are half full. Pour in a little of the juice. Then add a layer of bread; then the rest of the fruit. Cover the fruit with a final layer of bread and pour over the rest of the juice. Put a coffee saucer on top of each pudding basin and use paperweights or kitchen weights wrapped completely in aluminium foil to weight down the saucers. Leave overnight. There should be no trace of white bread in these puddings.

They can be transported to the picnic in their basins and turned out on to soup plates. Serve with slightly whipped double cream.

Geranium Cream

This recipe comes from Elizabeth David's *Summer Cooking*.

Serves 6

½ pint/300 ml double cream
3 tablespoons caster sugar
6 sweet scented geranium leaves

6 small fresh cream cheeses – Crème
d'Isigny or Chambourcy

Put the cream in a double saucepan, and add the sugar and geranium leaves. Heat gently to let the mixture get thoroughly hot without boiling. Leave it to cool with the leaves still in the cream. When cool, gently beat in the cream cheeses with a spoon – a fork will break up the geranium leaves, which you take out before serving.

We put this cream into little pots and garnish them with geranium petals. It should be served very cold.

Peaches in Orange and Lemon Juice

Resist the temptation to add alcohol to this mixture – it is in the clarity of the flavours where lies the appeal. You could always carry a flask of peach brandy in the basket. A swig is champion should the weather get nippy.

Serves 6

6 ripe peaches
juice of 2 oranges

juice of 2 lemons
caster sugar – optional

Put the peaches in a large bowl and pour on boiling water to cover. Strain them immediately into a sieve or colander. This brief immersion should make the skins slide off with ease. Slice the peaches into segments about ½ inch/1.25 cm thick. If the fruit is ripe, the flesh should pull away easily from the stone. Place the peaches in a bowl. Pour on the orange and lemon juice, then leave in the fridge for a few hours. Taste and only add sugar if you feel it is really necessary.

Transport the peaches in a chilled wide-mouthed Thermos.

WINTER

Giblet Soup

The subtle stroke of this soup is the use of cucumbers, fresh and pickled. Although it is the same vegetable, it is almost like two different ingredients. If you want to emphasize the difference, take the fresh cucumber strips to the picnic separately and add them at the moment of serving the hot soup.

Serves 6

carcass of a turkey or game birds,
   the feet, neck and giblets of the
   same
1 onion
1 large carrot
1 stalk celery
1 tablespoon vegetable oil
2 oz/60 g bacon or salt pork or
   ham in a piece (optional)
1 clove garlic
1 teaspoon peppercorns

2 dried mushrooms, if you have some
5 juniper berries (optional)
1 pickled cucumber, cut into
   matchsticks
1 tablespoon port or a heaped
   teaspoon redcurrant jelly
a squeeze of lemon juice
salt
½ small fresh cucumber, cut into
   matchsticks

Chop up the carcass, leaving on any meat, raw or cooked, that is attached. Separate the liver from the giblets, cut away any greenish parts and set aside. Cut along the outside wall of the gizzard where there is a natural seam and peel it away from the inner bag of grit; throw away the grit and wash the gizzard. Peel the onion and scrape the carrot clean; cut them and the washed celery stalk into large dice.

Heat the oil in a large pan. Dice the bacon, salt pork or ham and heat it in the oil until the fat begins to run. Add the vegetables and the carcasses and cook carefully until the vegetables begin to brown and the meat on the bones begins to darken. Don't let them char or burn, but the browning is an important step that guarantees an appetizing colour of soup. Add about 4 pints/2.5 litres water, the feet and neck (if you have them), the heart, the gizzard and kidney. Add the peeled clove of garlic, the peppercorns, and the dried mushrooms and juniper berries if you have them. Simmer over a low heat until the stock is considerably reduced and of a flavour.

Strain the stock into a clean pan and then pick out the kidneys, heart and gizzard, bacon and any meat; chop into small cubes. Sauté the liver in a little butter in a small pan and chop. Return the giblets, meat and bacon to the stock, add the liver, the pickled cucumber and the port or redcurrant jelly. Simmer for a few minutes. Taste and see if you think a little lemon juice would be good; sometimes the tart taste of pickled cucumber is enough. Taste again for salt and add it if necessary.

Pour the soup into a Thermos jar which you have rinsed out with extremely hot water. Serve in fairly small quantities garnished with the fresh cucumber.

Cold Rabbit and Gammon Pie

Serves 6

1 large rabbit or 2 small ones	3 carrots, scrubbed and sliced
1 lb/500 g lean gammon	lengthways
2 pig's trotters	2 stalks celery
1 large glass white wine	8 peppercorns
½ lemon, sliced	1 blade mace
1 bay leaf	1 sprig thyme or flat teaspoon dried
1 onion, peeled and sliced	thyme
	6 coriander seeds, crushed

FOR THE CRUST:

1 lb/500 g plain flour mixed with	4 oz/125 g lard
a good pinch of salt	

Put the rabbit and gammon together with all the other ingredients into a large pot. Cover with water and bring gently to the boil. Lower the heat and simmer until the gammon feels tender and the rabbit comes away from the bones when you probe it: this will take approximately 1½ hours, but depends upon the age of the rabbit. Remove the rabbit and gammon from the pot, but continue simmering the rest. Bone the rabbit carefully and cut it into largish chunks. Cut the gammon into cubes.

Turn on oven to 180°C/350°F, Gas 4.

Now make the crust as follows. If you don't have a pie mould, you will need a round cake tin 7 inches/17.5 cm in diameter.

Put the seasoned flour into a large bowl. Bring the lard and 7½ fl oz/ 235 ml water to boiling point; pour immediately onto the flour. Mix to a dough. You must do this very quickly because the paste must be moulded into shape before the lard has time to set; done too slowly and the paste would become brittle. Use your hands to mould the paste.

Put one-third of the paste in a cloth and keep warm (the linen cupboard is a good place); put the rest of the paste into the cake tin and press it down over the bottom and then up the sides with your fingers. Now take the rabbit and gammon and fill the tin but don't press the meat down. Take the remaining third of pastry and press it lightly with the palm of your hand into a round for the lid. Place this on top of the pie and pinch it round the edges to seal. You can use the left-over trimmings to decorate the pie with diamond-shaped pieces, etc. Make a hole in the centre of the pie with your little finger. Bake in the oven for about 1½ hours. The pastry should be golden brown.

Meanwhile, remove the stock from the heat and strain.

When the pie is cold and the stock has become a jelly, take some of it (about ½–¾ pint/300–450 ml) and warm it in a pan until it is just dissolved. Pour this liquid gently through the centre hole of the pie. Do this in little spurts; you will find that if you wait a moment between each pouring, the pie will absorb a surprising amount of liquid. Leave pie to set. There will be stock left in the pan, but you can freeze this for future use.

Pheasant Croquettes

These patties would not be appetizing stone cold, so although you can, and should, prepare them well ahead of time, fry them just before setting out and insulate them well to keep them warm and the coating crunchy. Green peppercorns can be bought in tins or jars and can be used whole. They are included to contribute a bit of zest, but if you cannot obtain them, add instead a splash of Worcestershire sauce or some other savoury condiment.

Serves 4

1½ oz/45 g butter
1 onion, peeled and finely
   chopped
2 tablespoons flour
1 teaspoon mustard powder
12 fl oz/375 ml milk
8 oz/250 g cold cooked pheasant,
   chopped

2 oz/60 g Prosciutto or San Daniele
   ham, chopped
1 level dessertspoon green peppercorns
1 tablespoon chopped parsley
salt and pepper
seasoned flour
1 egg, beaten
fresh breadcrumbs for the coating
vegetable oil for frying

Ideally start the recipe the day before the picnic. Melt the butter in a heavy-bottomed pan and gently cook the onion until softened; don't let the butter burn. Stir in the flour and mustard powder and cook for a minute or two. Add the milk in stages and cook as for a thick béchamel sauce. Stir in the pheasant, ham, peppercorns, parsley and salt and pepper to taste. Tip into a shallow dish and chill overnight. If you cannot start the recipe this far ahead, chill the mixture in the freezer.

When it is solid enough to handle, form the mixture into small patties. Dust them with seasoned flour, coat with beaten egg and then the breadcrumbs. Fry in hot oil in two batches, turning them a few times to make sure the mixture is well heated through and the coating crisp. Pack surrounded by kitchen paper to absorb any excess oil.

A spicy tomato sauce or some chutney goes well with these.

Home-Made Sausage Roll

Serves 8

1 tablespoon vegetable oil
1 large onion, peeled and finely
   chopped
2 lb/1 kg belly of pork, rind
   removed
1 egg
4 oz/125 g fresh breadcrumbs,
   white or wholemeal
grainy French mustard

soya sauce
thyme
sea salt
black pepper
1 lb/500 g puff pastry (frozen bought
   puff pastry, defrosted, is fine)
1 egg + 1 tablespoon milk for pastry
   wash

Turn on the oven to 180°C/350°F, Gas 4.

In the vegetable oil, sauté the chopped onion until softened. Mince the belly of pork or chop it in a food processor; turn it into a large bowl. Add the egg, the cooked onion, the breadcrumbs and the seasonings. Seasoning should be a matter of taste but a guideline is 2 teaspoons mustard, 1 tablespoon soya sauce, 1 level teaspoon dried thyme, a hefty pinch of salt and 12 screws of black pepper. Form the mixture into a large sausage shape and bake for 15 minutes.

Turn up the oven to 200°C/425°F, Gas 7.

Roll out the pastry into a rectangle about ½ inch/1.25 cm thick. Place the sausage down one long side, leaving an inch (2.5 cm) clear at the edge. Bring the pastry flap over the sausage and seal at the three ends using cold water and your fingers. Beat together the egg and milk and brush over the pastry. Bake in the oven for 25–30 minutes until the pastry is puffed and golden. This is good eaten cold.

Mary's Fruit Cake

This cake, made from a recipe of Mary Coventry, mother of one of the authors, was taken on many a chilly seaside picnic at Westward Ho! in Devon. Its richness is just what is needed to uncurl fingers and toes numb from Atlantic waves. If you happen to have a cake tin with a central funnel, i.e. an angel cake tin, this helps to bake the cake evenly by providing a heat source in the centre. Otherwise, use a 10-inch/25-cm cake tin.

8 oz/250 g glacé cherries	*3 tablespoons brandy*
8 oz/250 g currants	*12 oz/375 g butter*
8 oz/250 g sultanas	*12 oz/375 g caster sugar*
6 oz/180 g raisins	*4 eggs*
2 oz/60 g muscatel raisins	*12 oz/375 g plain flour*
(optional)	*1 teaspoon baking powder*
4 oz/125 g mixed peel	*1 teaspoon ground cinnamon*

Pre-heat the oven to 140°C/275°F, Gas 1.

Cut half the glacé cherries in two, keeping the others whole for decoration. Mix together the halved cherries with the rest of the dried fruit, pour on the brandy and leave to steep a while.

Cream the butter and sugar, then beat the eggs. Add alternately, and in stages, the flour, sifted with the baking powder and cinnamon, the fruit and the eggs.

Line the cake tin with greaseproof paper. Pour in the mixture and smooth the surface, and dot with the whole cherries. Wrap brown paper around the outside of the tin and tie with string. Bake the cake for 3 hours at the given temperature, then at 130°C/250°F, Gas ½ for a further half-hour. Cool the cake on a rack, then store in a tin with a tight-fitting lid.

Coffee Eclairs

These should be made the day they are eaten.

Serves 4

3¾ oz/110 g plain flour	*3 eggs*
3 oz/90 g butter	*½ pint/300 ml double cream*

FOR THE ICING:

8 oz/250 g icing sugar, sieved	*1 tablespoonful incredibly strong*
2 egg whites	*instant coffee*

Turn on the oven to 220°C/425°F, Gas 7. Have ready the non-stick baking sheets, or greased sheets if you don't have non-stick.

Sift the flour and put it onto a piece of paper so that you can shoot it into the boiling liquid all at once. Put the butter and 7½ fl oz/235 ml water into a pan and boil together. When bubbling, draw the pan aside and shoot in the flour. Beat the mixture until it is smooth, and at the moment that the paste will leave the sides of the pan, set it aside to cool. Do not overbeat the mixture or it will become heavy and won't rise properly.

Whisk the eggs lightly, and then add to the cooled mixture by degrees. At this point, you should beat the mixture very thoroughly, and if your eggs are large, you may not need all of them. When finished, the paste should be smooth and shiny.

Put spoonfuls of paste on the baking sheet – round or long, whichever shape you prefer for éclairs – and bake until the paste is quite firm to the touch, 20–25 minutes. If you take the pastry out too soon, it will sink when taken from the oven. Put the éclairs onto a cake rack to cool.

Whip the cream stiffly, split the éclairs when cool and fill.

Next make the icing: add the sugar by degrees to the egg whites, beating all the time. Add the coffee. The proportions of sugar to egg white will vary depending upon the size of the egg. The icing should be fairly stiff to prevent it running down the sides of the éclairs. The longer you beat, the shinier your icing will be. Smooth the icing on to the tops of the éclairs with a knife dipped in hot water.

CHAPTER NINETEEN

Funeral Tea

Most of us, at some time or another, are presented with this sad, and often difficult occasion. Even if you are not the person most intimately bereaved, it may fall to your lot to be the organizer of what is to happen after the funeral. Why tea, you may ask? Well, if it is a country funeral, it usually happens early in the afternoon, in order to give people time to make the journey to wherever it may be. But, in fact, the following menu could as well be a lunch if that is what is required.

You may think that people coming away from a funeral, whatever their feelings, will not want to eat very much – or anything at all. This is not so. The North Country wakes were encrusted with food: it was a sign of respect to the departed to provide a heavy, rich and varied repast and this, in turn, was because no serious friends or relatives would contemplate leaving the widow, say, immediately after the funeral to go home alone. The ritual of mourning – too much neglected until very recently when it is beginning to be recognized as a psychological necessity to those most affected – is all about accepting that death is an occasion. It needs marking and serious acknowledgement, and is no small matter; it is, after all, the last great adventure for the person concerned and therefore a send off; a farewell party is due to them.

Another aspect of funerals is that, apart from relations who may not ordinarily keep in touch with one another, they invariably contain a disparate collection of friends of the bereaved, who have nothing but the occasion in common. Food helps to break down some of the awkwardness that can arise.

The party, or tea, or gathering after the funeral is also often of some comfort to those who most feel their loss. If you know someone in this situation who is feeling too stunned to cope with the domestic side of the funeral, it can be a kindness to offer to do that part of it for them.

When planning the food, it is well to remember that funeral gatherings may have people of all ages, and that many of them may not have had time or opportunity for much lunch, on top of which they may have a long journey home. Simple, but substantial food is the best solution, but also food that people can eat standing, or which they can have as little or as much of as they please. Also, if you are making the food for someone else, it is necessary to have food that you can largely prepare at home and transport fairly easily. Finally, we cannot give quantities here, as the number may vary from a dozen to sixty or seventy. Ask how many people are expected and then cater for ten more to be on the safe side. Be responsible for any extra china, glass or cutlery that may be needed.

Suggested beverages to go with this menu – apart from strong Indian and weak China tea – are hot chocolate (very popular with children), lemonade (*see* page 177), sloe gin (if you have been provident enough to make any) and, if the weather is icy, a mulled wine.

Celery Soup   Lemon Curd Sponge Cake
Chicken Sandwiches   Gingerbread
Ham Sandwiches   Flapjacks
Cucumber Sandwiches   Mulled Wine
Mona's Fruit Cake   Summer Punch

Celery Soup

If this meal is not to be a tea, but a midday affair, we suggest that you make a soup. The following is good and can be drunk from a cup which is easier than having to deal with a spoon and bowl for those who are standing.

Serves 8

1 large head of celery   salt and pepper
1 oz/30 g butter   2 pints/1.1 litres chicken stock
1 dessertspoon sunflower seed oil   single cream (optional)
1 large onion, chopped

Clean and chop the celery into pieces about ¼ inch/0.6 cm wide. Melt the butter and oil in a pan and sauté the onion until transparent. Add the celery, and a level teaspoonful of salt and a good grinding of pepper. Cook gently, stirring, until the celery is well coated in the onion mixture. Add the stock and simmer until the celery is completely soft. Liquidize, or pass through a mouli. You can add a tablespoonful of single cream to this soup when you are heating it up, but it is not necessary.

Chicken Sandwiches

1 chicken	*1 wholemeal loaf (rectangular, rather*
1 small onion	*than oval or round)*
8 oz/250 g butter	*½ pint/300 ml mayonnaise*
	salt and pepper

Roast the chicken: for sandwiches, cooking chicken in a chicken-brick is the best way as the chicken remains moist and you won't be using the skin. (If you don't have a chicken-brick, cook it as you normally do.) Peel the onion and put it inside the bird with a knob of butter. Rub a little more butter over the breast and cook. If using a chicken-brick, put it into a cold oven and turn the oven to 180°C/ 350°F, Gas 4, for about 1¾ hours, but test it after 1 hour 20 minutes. Set aside to cool.

People are divided about whether or not they like crusts on sandwiches. We like them, but if you don't, they are your sandwiches. To make nice thin slices of buttered bread, you need an extremely sharp knife and soft butter which you spread thinly on each slice before you cut it. (You may feel that these remarks are kids' stuff, but we have been on the receiving end of so many badly made sandwiches that it seems worth going through the process.)

When the chicken is cool, joint and bone it, removing all the skin. Chop the chicken meat on a board and then put it into a large bowl. Now add the mayonnaise, bit by bit: you only want to bind the chicken meat a little, not produce chicken in a cold sauce. Season with salt and pepper. Spread the chicken fairly thickly on one piece of bread, cover with a second and press gently together. If the sandwiches are going to be crustless, this is the moment to remove the crusts. In any case, the rounds must be divided – either into two triangles, or into four.

Unless you are going to store them in plastic boxes with a lid, they should be covered with a damp cloth until wanted.

Ham Sandwiches

2 lb/1 kg sweet cured ham
1 wholemeal loaf

8 oz/250 g butter
English mustard

The only difference between making these and making the chicken sandwiches is that the bread should be buttered more thickly, and that one slice should be thinly spread with mustard, and the other covered with the ham (which should be preferably cut off the bone, but certainly not be slippery slices from a polythene packet).

Cucumber Sandwiches

2 cucumbers
1 wholemeal loaf

½ lb/250 g double cream cheese (Crème
d'Isigny is very good)
curry powder

Peel the cucumbers and then slice them as thinly as possible. Spread cream cheese on the unbuttered bread and sprinkle one piece with a very little curry powder. Lay cucumber on alternate slices and put together.

Mona's Fruit Cake

7 oz/210 g caster sugar
6 oz/180 g margarine
2 tablespoons milk
3 eggs, beaten
2 oz/60 g glacé cherries

8 oz/250 g plain flour
½ teaspoon baking powder
½ teaspoon salt
½ teaspoon mixed spice
18 oz/550 g mixed dried fruit

Turn on the oven to 180°C/350°F, Gas 4.

Cream the sugar and margarine and add the milk and beaten eggs. Chop the cherries in half and roll them in some of the flour. Sift the baking powder into the rest of the flour and add to the creamed mixture with the salt and mixed spice. Finally add the dried fruit and cherries.

Line the bottom and sides of an 8-in/20-cm round or the equivalent square cake tin with greased greaseproof paper and fill it with the mixture; bake in the oven for about 2¼ hours. Test after 2 hours with a skewer; if it comes out clean, the cake is cooked. Allow it to cool in its tin before turning it on to a cake rack.

Lemon Curd Sponge Cake

butter	*3 eggs*
4 oz/125 g self-raising flour	*grated rind of 1 lemon*
4½ oz/140 g caster sugar	*1 oz/30 g icing sugar for top of cake*

FOR THE LEMON CURD:

1 oz/30 g butter	*juice and grated rind of 1 lemon*
3 oz/90 g granulated sugar	*2 egg yolks, beaten*

Turn on the oven to 180°C/350°F, Gas 4.

Butter a 7-inch/17.5-cm cake tin and dust it with a mixture of 1 teaspoonful flour and 1 teaspoonful sugar. Break the eggs into a basin, add the rest of the sugar and beat over a saucepan of hot water until warm; then remove from the heat and whisk until quite cold and thick. Sieve the flour, add the rind, and stir lightly into the beaten eggs. Put the mixture into the cake tin and bake for 1 hour.

While the cake is baking, make the lemon curd. Put the butter, sugar, lemon rind and juice into a double saucepan, and when the sugar has dissolved, gradually add the thoroughly beaten egg yolks. Stir until the mixture thickens. (If you want to do this fast, take the top half of the saucepan and put it on a direct flame, but you must stir continuously to prevent the eggs scrambling.) The mixture thickens more as it cools.

When the cake is cool, cut it in half carefully, spread with lemon curd and put it back together. Dust the top with icing sugar.

Gingerbread

A certain stickiness is essential in gingerbread and this will be found if the gingerbread is wrapped in greaseproof paper and stored in a tin for a few days before being eaten.

4 oz/125 g butter
3 tablespoons Golden Syrup
3 tablespoons black treacle
4 oz/125 g dark brown sugar
¼ pint/150 ml milk
1 teaspoon bicarbonate of soda
8 oz/250 g plain flour

3 teaspoons ground ginger
1 teaspoon ground cinnamon
1 egg, beaten
handful of sultanas or chopped dates
   or best of all chopped crystallized
   or preserved ginger (optional)

Turn on the oven to 150°C/300°F, Gas 2. Gently melt the butter, syrup, treacle, sugar and milk in a medium to large saucepan. Let the mixture cool and then stir in the bicarbonate of soda. Sift in the flour, ginger and cinnamon and then add the egg. Mix well. Add the sultanas, dates or ginger if using them and stir thoroughly. Transfer the mixture to a deep-sided square baking tin. Bake in the centre of the pre-heated oven for 1½–2 hours. When the gingerbread is cool, remove from the tin, wrap and store.

Flapjacks

1 lb/500 g dark brown sugar
1 lb/500 g margarine

2 tablespoons Golden Syrup (see page
   97 for measuring)
1½ lb/750 g rolled oats

Turn on the oven to 180°C/350°F, Gas 4.

Melt the sugar and margarine in a saucepan and add the Golden Syrup. Then add the oats, and stir well. Press this mixture down into a greased and floured baking tin – 10 × 12 inches/25 × 30 cm – and cook in the oven for 35 minutes.

Mulled Wine

Serves 8

1 bottle decent red wine
1 tablespoon sugar
½ sherry glass curaçao or 1 sherry
   glass port

1 cinnamon stick
a little grated nutmeg

Don't make the mistake of thinking that really awful plonk, heated, will stop being really awful plonk.

Heat the wine with the rest of the ingredients, but do not boil. A good way to keep it hot is to strain it back into wine bottles and stand them in buckets of hot water.

Summer Punch

Mix 1 bottle of white wine with an equal quantity of soda water. Add a good dash of brandy and sweeten to taste.

The best way to do this is to make a sugar syrup by boiling water and sugar together (10 oz/275 g granulated sugar to 1 pint/625 ml water). When it is cool, you can add cut up peaches, nectarines, strawberries, greengages, cherries (score them down their crease first), orange and lemon slices, or any other fruit in season that you like. This is not very alcoholic, but people do tend to drink quite a lot of it. The base of 1 bottle of wine should do 8 people.

CHAPTER TWENTY

Holiday Cooking

From the moment of starting a family, women have very little prospect of a grown-up holiday, which in many ways means that for her the holiday isn't one at all: a change, but hardly a rest. Added to this is the incontrovertible fact that self-catering holidays cost less than staying in a hotel or boarding house and for most people with young families, finances dictate the holiday. But there are advantages. Trying to keep a four-year-old sitting through an hotel meal can be quite as tiring as making him or her something you know he will eat, with premises other than an hotel dining-room to riot in after he has been charged up by the meal. But if you don't want to be a domestic slave while everybody else bathes, basks and generally enjoy themselves, it is as well to make some plans and devise a routine that gives you some spare time.

One main cooked meal a day is enough and, depending upon the age of your family, you can make it lunch or dinner. Breakfast can be continental: rolls, croissants, bread, toast, etc. with butter and jam; cereals, if insisted upon, hot drinks and fresh fruit. The secondary meal – picnic lunch or snack supper – can be food bought from delicatessens; cheeses, salamis, ham, quiche, pâté, crusty bread and whatever fruit is abundantly available and consequently cheap. The main meal should have one substantial course with a large salad or a cooked green vegetable. In France and Italy, there are cake or pastry shops even in quite small villages where treats can easily be bought.

As most family holidays take place in August and as many families now go abroad, we are assuming that it will be hot, and if that is a fact about your holiday, it will be well worth taking a cold bag or two with you. The fridges in rented accommodation are seldom large enough: you can save on your shopping expeditions if you can shop for two days and for this you need ample cool storage space.

We also suggest that you take your own sharp knife or knives with you; we have neither of us ever encountered a rented kitchen where there was a knife that would cut anything sturdier than butter with ease. If you are contemplating regular picnics, then containers for transporting food and a Thermos or two are also desirable and, of course, the cold bags come in here as well.

Unless you really hate getting up in the mornings, early shopping is a good idea: it is not so hot or so crowded and the whole process will be quicker and easier. Make the family do their share of clearing up and organize the working part of your day so that you will have one long, clear period when you are not expected to do anything. If you are cooking lunch, then it should be from three o'clock until the children's supper time. If you are cooking dinner, it should be from eleven in the morning – by which time you will have shopped and put a picnic lunch together – until six in the evening. Of course, all this does depend upon the age or ages of your family, but in principle it is a good rough schedule.

Finally, the menu for this section is also only a guideline: if your family are keen on pasta, there are several other sauces that you could make for it in this book. If your holiday is by the sea and fish is easily obtainable, there are a number of other fish dishes – and so on. Holiday cooking is to some extent dictated by where you are; not so much because you wouldn't be able to get the ingredients of the dishes we suggest, as that there may be specialities of the region or a seasonal glut of some fruit or vegetable it would be sensible to use.

<table>
<tr><td>Egg in a Bun</td><td>Coq au Vin</td></tr>
<tr><td>Swiss Eggs and Ham</td><td>A Simple Cassoulet</td></tr>
<tr><td>Cold Omelettes</td><td>Meat Loaf</td></tr>
<tr><td>Pan Bagna</td><td>Bollito Misto</td></tr>
<tr><td>Hot Pasta with Cold Tomato Sauce</td><td>Fried Aubergines with Skordalia</td></tr>
<tr><td>Baked Fish with Anchovy Sauce</td><td>Fruit Fools</td></tr>
<tr><td>Paella</td><td>German Fritters</td></tr>
</table>

Egg in a Bun

Serves 4

4 round bread rolls (the soft kind are the best)	1 oz/30 g grated cheese
2 oz/60 g butter	4 eggs, separated
	salt and pepper

Turn on the oven to 180°C/350°F, Gas 4.

Cut the tops of the buns, scoop out the soft part, butter the inside and put them in the oven for about 5 minutes to make them crisp. Then put half the grated cheese inside each bun. Put one egg yolk in each bun. Season the eggs. Turn up the oven to 200°C/400°F, Gas 6.

Whisk the egg whites stiffly, add the rest of the grated cheese to the whites and put the mixture on top of the yolks. Bake the buns in the oven until the whites are set.

Note: This recipe comes from Fortune Stanley's book, *English Country House Cooking*, as does the recipe for Swiss eggs and ham which follows.

Swiss Eggs and Ham

Serves 4

4 tablespoons double cream	*4 eggs*
8 oz/250 g cooked ham, chopped	*salt and pepper*
2 oz/60 g grated cheese	

Turn on the oven to 200°C/400°F, Gas 6.

Into an ovenproof dish, pour 3 tablespoonfuls cream, the chopped ham and half the cheese. Stir and bake in the oven for 5 minutes. Turn the oven down to 180°C/350°F, Gas 4.

Break the eggs into the dish, season, add 1 tablespoonful cream and sprinkle with the rest of the cheese. Bake in the oven 5–10 minutes, until the whites are set.

Cold Omelettes

Middle Eastern and Iberian cold omelettes tend to be solid affairs ideal for picnics or served in wedges with salad for lunch. French omelettes, altogether more delicate affairs, are also good served cold, wrapped round a bland creamy cheese, fresh vegetable purée, or shellfish, such as crab, in mayonnaise. A completely plain flat omelette can be cut into strips when cold and used as a garnish or a salad ingredient. An example of each kind of recipe is given below but holidays are the time for improvisation and imagination, so use them also as starting points.

Vegetable Omelette

Serves 4–6

3 tablespoons vegetable oil
1 large onion, peeled and chopped
2 cloves garlic, peeled and crushed
2 leeks, washed and cut into rings
   or a handful of fresh spinach,
   roughly chopped
4 oz/125 g broad beans or peas,
   podded
2 tomatoes, skinned, de-seeded
   and chopped

1 green chilli, de-seeded and cut into
   threads (optional, but surprisingly
   nice)
salt and pepper
grated nutmeg
2 oz/60 g fresh parsley, finely
   chopped
6 eggs
1½ oz/45 g butter

Heat the oil and sauté the vegetables until soft, adding a little water if they are sticking. Season with salt, pepper and a little nutmeg. Stir in the parsley.

Beat the eggs in a large bowl. Add the cooked vegetables (make sure they are not so hot that they cook the eggs). Melt the butter in a large frying pan about 10 inches/25 cm in diameter. Pour in the egg mixture and cook gently until the bottom is set. Slide under a heated grill to brown the top. If you have no grill, cook the omelette in a suitable pan in a moderate oven until just set. Serve cold in wedges.

Tortilla

The simplicity of this makes it perhaps the nicest of all omelettes – wonderful for picnics.

Serves 4–6

4 fl oz/125 ml olive oil
3 onions, peeled and chopped
3 large potatoes, peeled and diced

salt and pepper
6 eggs

Heat the oil in a large heavy-bottomed pan and cook the onions and potatoes, stirring intermittently for about 20 minutes or until they are tender. Season with salt and pepper. Beat the eggs in a bowl. Lift out the vegetables and stir into the eggs. Pour off remaining oil into a cup. Clean the pan. Return the oil, adding more if you think you need it for frying the omelette.

Heat the oil, then pour in the egg mixture. Press down gently and cook until the egg is set. Slide under the grill and cook the top. If you have no grill, you can turn the omelette and slip it back into the pan top-side down or alternatively cook the omelette in a suitable dish in a moderate oven until the eggs are set through.

This is good hot, warm, or cool, but perhaps best of all warm.

French Omelettes

FOR EACH OMELETTE:

1 large egg

½ oz/15 g butter

salt and pepper

POSSIBLE FILLINGS:

1 tablespoon fromage blanc or other soft cheese, mixed with fresh herbs and a small clove of garlic, crushed

1 tomato, skinned, de-seeded and chopped, mixed with chopped basil, salt, pepper and a small pinch of sugar

a few prawns mixed with a little mayonnaise and some cayenne pepper

crabmeat – treated the same as above

chopped bacon crisply cooked, mixed with shredded lettuce and dressed with a light vinaigrette

some sliced mushrooms sautéed in butter to which you add a spoonful of cream

left-over vegetables such as peas or broad beans, puréed

Beat the egg with a teaspoon of water. Season with salt and pepper. Melt the butter in a 6-inch/15-cm diameter omelette pan. Pour in the egg and cook until set. Spoon your choice of filling on one side of the omelette – being quite restrained with the filling. Turn the omelette out on to a serving dish. Repeat as many times as you have guests. Serve with salad and good bread, and perhaps some slices of salami.

Cold Omelette as Garnish

2 eggs

salt

tiny pinch sugar

1 dessertspoon vegetable oil

Beat the eggs so that they are well amalgamated, but not frothy. Season with salt and sugar. Heat the oil in a pan and pour in the egg mixture.

Turn the heat to low, cover (using foil if necessary), and cook gently for about 5 minutes, until the egg is set. Turn the omelette over to seal the other side. Take out the omelette and cool.

Cut into strips and use either in a salad, as a garnish for soup (in which case make the omelette thin), as a garnish for rice dishes or dressed with a vinaigrette or a light mayonnaise and mixed with spring onions and parsley to make a version of egg salad.

Pan Bagna

For this sustaining pressed sandwich, use either a French loaf or round flat soft bread cut horizontally which is, in fact, the sort of container that would be used in Provence.

Serves 4

1 loaf (see above)
¼ pint/150 ml virgin olive oil
2–3 tablespoons wine vinegar
salt and pepper
1 clove garlic, peeled and crushed
2 large 'Mediterranean' tomatoes, sliced

1 large Spanish onion
1 green or red pepper, de-seeded and thinly sliced
1 small tin anchovy fillets
2 oz/60 g black olives, stoned

Slice the loaf in half horizontally. Make up a vinaigrette with the oil, wine vinegar to taste, salt, pepper and garlic. Sprinkle the cut sides of the bread liberally with the vinaigrette.

Arrange the sliced tomatoes, onion and pepper on the bottom half of the bread. Garnish with the anchovy fillets and olives. Place the top half of the bread on the sandwich, wrap it tightly in aluminium foil and leave for 1–2 hours with weights on top; this helps the flavours to meld and the sandwich to form a solid mass easy to slice and serve.

Pan Bagna is traditionally eaten while playing *boules*.

Hot Pasta with Cold Tomato Sauce

This is one of the best of all summer dishes using that herb that encapsulates the scent of summer – basil. The sauce should be mixed with the pasta at the moment of serving, and the dish served quickly before the sauce warms or the pasta cools.

Serves 4–6

*4 tomatoes, skinned and chopped
or 2 'beef' tomatoes, skinned
and chopped
6 spring onions, cleaned and
finely chopped
1 tablespoon finely chopped
parsley*

*10–12 fresh basil leaves, roughly
chopped
3 tablespoons virgin olive oil
1 tablespoon red wine vinegar
salt and freshly ground black pepper*

Mix the above ingredients together, if possible letting them sit awhile for the flavours to meld. Cook 1 lb/500 g fresh pasta until it is *al dente*. Drain, pile into a hot dish and add the sauce at the table.

Baked Fish with Anchovy Sauce

Since it is even possible nowadays to buy fresh fish in English seaside resorts, it is useful to know about this anchovy sauce, which has an interesting, positive relationship of result for the effort entailed. Most whole white fish, such as cod, haddock, grey mullet, or, if you are lucky enough to find it, sea bass, stand up well to being roasted in the oven.

Serves 4

*1 whole fish weighing about 2–3
lb/1–1.5 kg
herbs (fennel, dill or parsley)
1 bay leaf
a slice of lemon*

*sea salt and freshly ground black
pepper
olive oil
1 small tin anchovy fillets
2 oz/60 g butter
½ pint/300 ml double cream*

Ask the fishmonger to clean the fish, leaving on the head and tail.

Turn on the oven to 220°C/425°F, Gas 7.

Using a small sharp knife, make three diagonal slashes on each side of the fish, cutting practically down to the bone. Tuck herbs and the bay leaf plus a slice of lemon, into the body cavity. Rub sea salt and freshly ground black pepper into the surfaces of the fish, making sure that some topples into the slashes. Trickle olive oil over the fish and place in a roasting pan; then put it into the pre-heated oven. An average-size fish should be cooked in approximately 25–30 minutes. The cuts in the sides will enable you to see if the flesh is opaque to the bone.

To make the sauce, open the tin of anchovies and rinse about 5 fillets in warm water to remove excess salt. Melt the butter in a frying pan or sauté pan. Add the anchovies and stir round until they break up and more or less disintegrate. Add the cream, bring to the boil and stir.

Add some freshly ground black pepper and taste to see if the sauce could stand the addition of another anchovy. The flavour should be robust. Carefully lift the fish (whose skin should be brown and crisp) onto a serving dish and serve the sauce separately.

Plain boiled potatoes are the best accompaniment.

Paella

There are many versions of paella and no doubt much Spanish argy-bargy about which are authentic. The right sort of rice (from Valencia) is an important factor. It is a round, stubby variety, in shape like pudding rice but nothing like it in texture. Italian arborio risotto rice is a good substitute if you cannot get Spanish rice. Paella should be cooked in quantity so as to accommodate a variety of ingredients, and therefore a large pan is essential. Paella is often cooked outside on an open fire, which of course contributes to the flavour, and if your pan is large, it is a good heat source. If the pan overlaps a gas or electric ring by a long way, keep gently turning the rice sides to middle to ensure even cooking.

The ingredients below are a guideline. Feel free to add or subtract, within reason. If your funds do not run to saffron, then substitute 1 teaspoon ground turmeric as a sunny yellow colour is essential.

Serves 6

*1 small roasting chicken, chopped
  into small pieces*
*1 pint/625 ml mussels, scrubbed
  and checked for duds*
2 tablespoons white wine
1 lb/500 g small squid (optional)
6 tablespoons olive oil
*1 large Spanish onion, peeled and
  chopped*
3 cloves garlic, peeled and crushed
*6 oz/180 g bacon in a piece or salt
  pork*

*8 oz/250 g tomatoes, skinned and
  chopped*
*4 oz/125 g French beans or shelled
  peas*
*1 green or red pepper, grilled, peeled
  and cut into strips*
1 lb/500 g Valencia rice (see above)
1 pint/625 ml unshelled prawns
*1 teaspoon saffron strands or turmeric
pimentón/paprika
salt and pepper*

Use the chicken carcass plus giblets (if any) to make 2 pints/1.1 litres of good stock, adding in if you have them to hand, a carrot, stalk of celery and a bouquet garni.

Open the mussels by heating them with the white wine (or water) in a heavy pan with the lid on. Remove and strain the accumulated liquid and save it. Clean the squid if you are using it and cut the bodies into rings and separate the tentacles.

Heat the oil and sauté the onion. Add the chicken pieces and garlic. Cook slowly, turning and moving until golden, then remove the chicken. Cut the bacon or salt pork into small cubes and sauté them until lightly browned. Return the chicken pieces; add the squid and cook for 5 minutes. Next add the tomatoes, beans or peas and the pepper. Add 6 fl oz/180 ml chicken stock and simmer for 10 minutes. Combine the rest of the chicken stock with the mussel liquid and measure out 1¾ pints/1 litre.

Add the rice to the pan and stir. Add the prawns (peeled or unpeeled, depending on preference), the opened mussels still in their shells and salt and pepper. Start adding the stock as you would for risotto, i.e. letting some be absorbed before adding more. After the first addition of stock, scatter in the saffron or turmeric. Cook until the rice absorbs no more stock and is tender.

Sprinkle a little paprika or pimentón (the same thing really) on top and let the paella sit for a few minutes in a warm place before serving. It should not be boiling hot.

Coq au Vin

Should you happen to be holidaying where wine is cheap, it is the moment to steer a bottle in the direction of a *coq au vin*. Of course a red Burgundy is the correct ingredient but you can fudge a little as long as you use a fairly decent bottle; plonk will just spoil a good chicken. If you are making this dish in Burgundy, use a few tablespoons of Marc de Bourgogne in addition; otherwise see if you have some duty-free cognac left.

There are many recipes for *coq au vin*, most of them requiring too many processes for relaxed cooking, so we have adapted a gracefully simple method given by Elizabeth David in *French Country Cooking*. To assuage holiday appetites, make sure there are plenty of triangles of fried bread as an accompaniment.

Serves 6

1 plump chicken	15–20 button onions or small shallots
salt and pepper	butter for frying vegetables
lemon juice	sugar
2 fl oz/60 ml vegetable oil	12 oz/375 g button mushrooms
2 oz/60g butter	BEURRE MANIÉ made from 1 level
4 oz/125 g piece bacon or salt	tablespoon flour worked into
pork, cut into cubes	1 oz/30 g softened butter
1 small glass brandy	slices of white country bread
1 bottle red wine (see above)	oil for frying
the giblets of the bird, excluding	fresh parsley, chopped
the liver	

Season the bird inside and out with salt, pepper and lemon juice. In a deep, thick-bottomed pan, melt the oil and butter. Fry the cubes of bacon, remove, and then carefully brown the bird on all sides. Pour on the brandy. When it is warm, set it alight and then let the flames die down.

Return the bacon to the pan, stir round and add the bottle of wine. Add the giblets of the bird, excluding the liver, cover the pan and simmer very gently for about 1 hour. Near the end of the cooking time, peel the onions and sauté in a little butter. Sprinkle on some sugar and let it caramelize and add a splash of red wine. In a clean pan, sauté the mushrooms (wiped clean, if necessary) in some more butter.

Remove the giblets from the chicken pan and discard; remove the chicken to a serving dish and keep warm. Add the glazed onions and cooked mushrooms to the pan, then reduce the liquid by boiling. If it needs additional thickening, add the *beurre manié* piece by piece and simmer until you have a glossy sauce. Pour it over the chicken and serve with triangles of bread fried in hot oil, the corners of them dipped into finely chopped parsley.

A Simple Cassoulet

Cassoulet is another fine way of feeding numbers and numerous people with keen appetites is usually a feature of holiday catering. A true cassoulet worthy of the appellation Castelnaudary or Carcassonne takes time and attention. This is a pared-down approach, but none the less good. In France it is easy to buy *confit* of duck or goose, but if you happen not to be in France, never mind. Aim for something that gives unctuousness, even if it is only a good quality sausage. Any left-over haricot beans are a splendid basis for a soup, e.g. minestrone. Or should your rented accommodation run to a liquidizer, they can be whizzed into a cream and spiked with garlic.

Serves 6–8

2 lb/1 kg dried white haricot beans
½ lb/250 g gammon or bacon
1 tablespoon vegetable oil
3 onions, peeled and sliced
2 tomatoes, peeled and chopped
1 heaped teaspoon honey or syrup
   or treacle
5 cloves garlic, peeled and slivered
1 bay leaf
a generous pinch of thyme or
   oregano or rosemary

stock – either homemade, or from a
   cube
1 duck or 1 chicken
1 lb/500 g good sausages, e.g.
   Toulouse sausage or any
   interesting boiling sausage
1 leg confit of duck or goose, if
   available
fresh breadcrumbs

Soak the beans overnight or, alternatively, bring them to the boil, boil for 5 minutes and leave for 1 hour to swell. Then cook them in fresh water for 1 hour until they are three-quarters cooked. Turn on the oven to 180°C/350°F, Gas 4.

Cut the bacon or gammon into cubes. Using 1 tablespoon of oil if it is gammon, sauté the cubes and then add the onions and let them soften. Add the tomatoes, honey, garlic and herbs. Pour on the stock just to cover and simmer. Meanwhile roast the chicken or duck until nearly done.

Towards the end of the cooking time of the chicken or duck, add the sausages to brown in the roasting pan. When they are done, turn down the oven to 140°C/275°F, Gas 1. Rub a large earthenware pot with garlic. If you have some *confit*, place it, with some of the fat adhering, in the bottom of the pot. Slice the browned sausage into chunks, then add the chicken or duck, carved into 8–10 pieces, and sausage chunks to the pot. Cover with the beans and give the pot a good shake to make them settle. Pour on the stock which should be at simmering point.

Place in the cooled oven; after half an hour, strew breadcrumbs over the top of the dish and cook for 1 hour more. A crust should form on the top. If necessary, raise the heat at the end to brown the crust. A good deal of wine goes well with this dish.

Meat Loaf

The best meat loaf is made with a mixture of meats, i.e. beef, lamb and pork. It can be made with beef alone, but it then tends to lack unctuousness. Many supermarkets now sell minced lamb and pork, or a winning smile at the butcher should persuade him to mince these meats for you. Whilst meat loaf should never be a receptacle for left-overs, it can accommodate a variety of vegetables and also grains such as kasha, cous-cous or even corn flakes.

The recipe below contains our suggestions, but if you have other ideas – for example, chopped green pepper or cracked wheat in place of bread crumbs – you should feel free to experiment. Meat loaf is good either hot with a spicy tomato sauce as an accompaniment, or cold with chutney or Cumberland sauce.

Serves 6–8

1 lb/500 g minced beef ⎱ (or 2	2 oz/60 g mushrooms, cleaned and
½ lb/250 g minced lamb ⎰ lb/1 kg	chopped
½ lb/250 g minced pork ⎰ beef	2 onions, peeled and finely chopped
alone)	2 cloves garlic, peeled and chopped
2 eggs	½ aubergine, cut into small cubes
6 oz/180 g fresh breadcrumbs,	(optional)
brown or white	a dash of soya sauce or Tabasco
2 carrots, peeled and grated	salt and freshly ground black pepper

Turn on the oven to 180°C/350°F, Gas 4. If you are using aubergine, which actually adds a nice texture, salt the cubes and let them sweat out their bitterness. Pat dry.

Mix all the ingredients – use your hands for the best results – and then press the mixture into a loaf tin or a casserole of suitable size. Give the top a slightly rounded shape. Bake in the oven for 1–1½ hours. Pour off any accumulated fat and serve. If you prefer to serve it cold, wrap it in foil, and weight it with a couple of tins until quite cool. Refrigerate.

An alternative method is to sauté the vegetables until soft before you mix them with the meats; drain off any fat first. If you are using aubergine, it is a good idea.

Bollito Misto

A *bollito misto*, properly made and served from a trolley in an Italian restaurant, is a grand thing indeed. For the purposes of holiday cooking, it is an easy way of feeding numbers, requiring unsophisticated equipment and bequeathing you with ideal leftovers of cold meat from which to make salads or sandwiches. A classic *bollito misto* contains beef or veal, chicken, tongue and a *zampone*, a superior sausage with a casing made from a pig's trotter. On holiday, use what is to hand, but aim for a contrast of white meat, dark meat and something spicy and interesting such as a high meat-content sausage. The sauces are what make this dish special.

Serves 8–10

2 carrots, peeled
1 onion, peeled
2 tomatoes
1 bay leaf
parsley
salt and pepper
2 lb/1 kg beef for boiling, e.g.,
    brisket or chuck steak in a piece

1 small salted tongue (optional)
2 pig's trotters or 1 calf's foot
    (optional)
1 chicken
1 large country sausage or several
    smaller ones

Bring enough water to cover the meats (excluding the sausage) to the boil with the vegetables, herbs and seasonings. Add the beef and the tongue, and trotters if you are using them. Let them all simmer and skim off any scum. After 2 hours, remove the tongue and peel away the skin; trim off any fat and gristle and return to the pan. Add the chicken, and top up with more water if necessary. Simmer for 45 minutes to 1 hour, then turn off the heat. Next poach the sausage in a separate pan. To serve, slice the meat, arrange it prettily on a dish and hand round with the sauces below. Plain boiled potatoes are a good accompaniment.

Note: Slice only as much meat as you want for one serving and return the rest to keep it moist and flavoursome in the broth. The broth will give you wonderful stock for soups.

Salsa Verde

2½ tablespoons finely chopped
    parsley
2 tablespoons finely chopped
    capers
6 anchovy fillets, mashed

1 clove garlic, peeled and crushed
1 teaspoon Dijon mustard
1 teaspoon red wine vinegar
8 tablespoons olive oil

Put the first five ingredients into a bowl and mix thoroughly. Stir in the vinegar. Slowly add the oil, beating all the while. Taste and check if you want to add salt or more vinegar. You can, of course, add other fresh herbs according to your supplies.

Salsa Rossa

3 onions, peeled and thinly sliced
4 tablespoons vegetable oil
2 green peppers
1 lb/500 g ripe tomatoes, peeled
   and chopped or 1 14-oz/425-g
   tin Italian tomatoes

a drop of chilli sauce or 1 small green
   or red chilli, de-seeded and finely
   sliced
a pinch of sugar
salt and pepper

Cook the onion in the oil until soft. Remove the seeds and core from
the peppers; chop them finely and add to the onions. Cook until
softened. Add the tomatoes, chilli, a pinch of sugar and salt and
pepper. Cook gently for 30 minutes. Serve warm.

Fried Aubergines with Skordalia

This Greek mode of serving aubergines is perfect holiday food. The
sooner you eat the aubergines after they are fried, the better. They do
not hang around gracefully. You could, if you wish, substitute
mashed potato for the breadcrumbs in the recipe. Many Greek
women would, but we like the rough texture donated by the
crumbs.

Serves 4 as a substantial first course

1 large or 2 medium aubergines
4 plump cloves garlic
1 fat slice stale white bread
3 oz/90 g ground almonds
olive oil

salt and pepper
lemon juice
seasoned flour
more olive oil or vegetable oil

Aubergine slices must be salted and left to bead with perspiration to
remove bitterness and stop them mopping up quantities of oil. So
wipe the aubergine, trim off the calyx and cut into ¼-inch/0.6-cm
slices. Lay in a colander and sprinkle with salt.

   The sauce can be made with a pestle and mortar, but a liquidizer
or food processor speeds it up immeasurably. Peel and crush the
garlic cloves. Trim the bread of its crusts, soak it in water and
squeeze tightly in your hand. Put the garlic and bread into the
machine for a brief whizz. Add the almonds and blend.

Slowly add the olive oil as if for mayonnaise until you have a homogeneous thick sauce. Season with salt, pepper, and lemon juice to taste. If it looks a bit porridgey, the texture and colour can be improved with a little milk or thin cream. Pile into a pretty bowl.

Wipe the aubergines with kitchen paper, then shake them in a bag with seasoned flour. Heat the oil to a depth of about ¼ inch/0.6 cm in a frying pan; vegetable oil can be used for economy. Fry the aubergine slices, turning them once, until golden. Drain on kitchen paper. You will have to do this in batches, keeping them warm the while.

Serve immediately with the skordalia sauce.

Fruit Fools

Since the main holiday is a time when there is a good variety of fruit available, and all children love puddings even when they don't much like raw fruit, fools make an easy and popular dessert.

Most soft fruit is good for a fool, but some are used puréed raw and some need to be cooked. Strawberries, raspberries and black-berries should not be cooked, but apples, apricots, gooseberries, blackcurrants and red or white currants should be stewed first, until just soft.

Stew the fruit gently in a very little water (e.g., 3 tablespoonfuls water to 1 lb/500 g apricots or gooseberries or any currants). To this water, you should add sugar. As taste about sweetness varies so much, as well as the varying tartness of the fruit you may choose, it is impossible to give an exact quantity of sugar. We would suggest 2 tablespoonfuls sugar for 1 lb/500 g apricots and probably 3 table-spoonfuls for gooseberries. Use what you think fit, and then taste the syrup when the fruit has stewed. If there isn't enough sugar, add more. If too much, pour off a little of the syrup and add the juice of a lemon. If the fruit has made a great deal of juice in the cooking, pour off most of the syrup before you purée the fruit.

When the fruit is cold, add lightly whipped cream. The propor-tions should be ½ pint/300 ml to 1 pint/625 ml fruit purée. If you like, you can add half whipped cream and half creamy yoghurt to the mixture. If you are somewhere where cream is difficult or impossible to obtain, you can do the whole thing with yoghurt. Put the fool in the fridge for at least 1 hour before serving. This will make enough fool for 6–8 people.

German Fritters

Serves 6

1 egg + 2 egg yolks
2 tablespoons top of the milk
2 oz/60 g butter
3 tablespoons sunflower seed oil

12 slices white bread, with the crusts
    cut off
raspberry jam
caster sugar

Mix the eggs and beat them with the milk. Heat the butter and oil in a pan. When very hot, dip slices of bread in the egg mixture, drain for a second and fry quickly, until light brown and crisp. Put on kitchen paper to drain, and then spread raspberry jam on half the slices, put the other slices on top and dust each sandwich with caster sugar.

Index